Egon Harings • German(ic) History, Volume 1

Egon Harings

German(ic) History

Volume 1

The great time of the Germanic tribes

FOUQUÉ PUBLISHERS NEW YORK

Copyright ©2012 by Fouqué Publishers New York
Originally published as *German(ic) History, Volume 1*
by August von Goethe Literaturverlag

First American Edition
Printed on acid-free paper

Library of Congress Cataloging-in-Publication Data
Author (Harings, Egon)
[German(ic) History, Volume 1]

ISBN
978-0-578-11502-3

The Teutones, root of the German nation

Rome began to expand starting around 200 BC. The Second Punic War against Hannibal, the great Carthaginian, was over. Rome was the victor and had dictated the conditions of peace, including that Carthage had to relinquish all possessions outside of Africa. The Etruscan Empire on the Apennine Peninsula had long ceased to exist, and following the suppression of a rebellion in Gaul, the province of Gallia Cisalpina had been established. Hispania on the Iberian Peninsula would soon follow. Rome's might approached its zenith. No one expected that dark clouds would form years later in the skies above northern Europe. A heretofore unknown group stepped suddenly into the light of history, composed of culturally interconnected clans whose territories encompassed southern Scandinavia, Denmark, and northern Germany. Probably due to the pressure of overpopulation, but perhaps also influenced by climatic influences, these Germanic tribes had spread to the borders of the Celtic settlements. There was no sign initially that any Germanic tribe could ever pose a threat to Rome. Years later, it would be a different story entirely.

In the year 113 BC mysterious rumours reached the city of Rome. Travelling merchants who had pushed through to the deep wild forests between the Oder and the Elbe, brought them. Legionaries who had guarded the northern borders of the Empire, spread them. In the Forum, in the Circus Maximus, in the teeming apartment block of the city and the atria of the villas on the Via Appia, people whispered among each other, with worried expressions, contemptuous laughter, and grim prophecy.

Up in the North, on the other side of the Alpine passes, a people was on the march, a number so gigantic that no one had ever seen its like. A million vagabonding people, crowded into oxdrawn carts, with their children and dogs, women and livestock, were said to be stripping the land bare as locusts. Three hundred thousand strong was the horde of their warriors, fearsome in appearance, true Huns, six feet tall most of them, blond and blue-eyed all of them, the children with white-blond hair like the very old. Old women, clad in raw linen, led them barefoot, prophesying from the splashed blood of the prisoners offered to their god as sacrifices. There were thousands of prisoners, for no one who dared to stand against them had a chance, so awesome were they in combat. And brave, without fear of death. Only death on the battlefield was viewed as honourable, not a 'death of straw', a pitiful wasting away in bed.

Long swords and throwing spears were their weapons, along with iron shields. Some, the highbred, wore helmets made of animal heads ripped open at the mouth. Only a few wore any sort of mail; they preferred to show the enemy their bare chests. They had come down from the North Sea, there where the sea met the heavens. After they had tried, with barbaric simplicity, to fight the floods threatening their land with their swords, they had left their homelands. They were said to belong to the folk of the Celts, or perhaps to the Scythians, but they called themselves Cimbri.

With the dramatic march of the Cimbri, which derives from the name of an area in Jutland/Denmark (Himmerland/Cimbriland = home of the Cimbri), the Germans entered the light of history. This has nothing to do with the fact that the Romans took them for Celtic or Scythians. It was Caesar who first recognized that there was a fundamental difference between Celts (Gauls) and Germans. The people of the North weren't known as Germans until later; the Romans initially called them barbarians.

The Cimbri had been on the march for a decade before they first came upon a Roman legion under the leadership of Papirius Carbo. This was near Noreia, the land of the Taurisci who were allies of Rome. The first battle between Germans and Romans was decided in favour of the Germans (i.e. the Cimbri). The Romans now expected an invasion of the Cimbri. However, they did not turn southward to defenceless Italy. Instead, they wandered northwest to the Celtic Helvetii, who had settled from the Alps to the river Main. The Helvetii were a peaceful folk, and they took the Cimbri in and allowed them to settle among them, in order to avoid a battle with unknown result. They felt their cleverness had been confirmed, as they saw how tame the wild men from the North could be, as long as they gave them the one thing they coveted above all else – land that they could cultivate for grazing and crops.

The Teutones, named after their last great leader Teutobod and re-lated to the Cimbri, left Jutland like the Cimbri in desperation. No one knows exactly when the Cimbri and the Teutones encountered each other the first time (Cimbri Teutonique). It is believed to have happened even before the Battle of Noreia (in the foothills of the Alps, in today's Steiermark region of Austria/Styria), or perhaps lat-er among the Helvetii. The name "Teutones" was first mentioned by the Greek explorer Pytheas, around 345 BC. Pytheas undertook an adventurous trip to the northern sea: "Across from a coastline... lies the island of Abalus (Helgoland)... In the spring the waves wash up amber on the shores of this island, which is a product of the frozen seas. The inhabitants use it as fuel instead of wood...and also sell it to the Teutones who live nearest to them on the mainland." Thus we learn that the Teutones were the neighbours of the Cimbri.

In any case, the Teutones and the Cimbri had joined together by the time they reached the Helvetii. However, after a time the majority of the Teutones and Cimbri left the land of the Helvetii and moved further. They were driven by a sense of discontent over what they had achieved. Once again a giant horde set itself in motion; women and children in the wagons, the old men on foot, riders to the right and left driving the livestock; troops of warriors guarding the flanks; the highbred made up the vanguard and rearguard.

They crossed the Rhine on rafts they made themselves, and trekked through the Belfort Gap via modern day Besançon into the Rhône Valley. Their reputation as "Roman killers" ensured them freedom of passage. The Celtic Sequani did not oppose them; instead, they settled transit contracts with them, though with gritted teeth. This transit was in fact more pillaging and plundering. Soon the Cimbri and the Teutones reached another area of Roman influence, this time the territory of the Celtic Allobroges. If their territory were to fall into enemy hand, the western route to Italy would be open. Ju-nius Silanus was the Consul who met the "Cimbri Teutonique" with his army. Instead of fighting, he first attempted to reach his goals through diplomatic means, but he saw himself confronted with a delegation of gigantic figures, who with the help of translators attempted to explain to him that they had not undertaken their journey to conquer others, but rather to find a new home. Their only wish was to be able to settle peacefully somewhere. But for that they needed land, and whoever gave it to them would not regret it, for they were prepared to offer their services as soldiers in exchange. This proposal exceeded the Consul's brief. He recommended that the delegation bring their request before the Senate in Rome. The Cimbri and Teutones agreed, and sent a group of representatives of their highest nobility to Rome.

Once in Rome, the Cimbri and Teutones were astonished by the standard of living they saw; by the gladiator competitions, and by the haggling in the market halls of the butchers, bakers, and shoemakers. They were amazed by the way the Romans amused themselves in the baths and bordellos, or in the countless pubs where they went for their drinking bouts. Here there were theatres and places with beautiful paintings, bathrooms with bathtubs and well-tended courtyards. Their wonder knew no end, coming as they did from lowly villages whose houses were made of wood, mud and wattle. The only towns they had seen where the simple walled settlements of the Celts.

For the inhabitants of Rome, the Germans were a definite sensation. The monsters from the north, about whom they had heard so many awful things since the Battle of Noreia, could be observed for the first time away from the natural habitat. They weren't quite as gigantic as they had imagined them to be, but in any case taller than the tallest Roman. Their hair was more red than blond, and seemed such a flattering colour, that it wasn't long before traders were importing large quantities of red and blond hair from Germania, in order to supply fashionable ladies with wigs.

Rome offered the representatives no land; they returned to their people with the laconic advice to try elsewhere, perhaps in the Hispanic province (Spain). They made their report, and turned again to Consul Junius Silanus, asking what to do next. His answer was to attack the Cimbri and Teutones with all the troops at his disposal, although he did not have the permission of the Senate. The result was a repetition of Noreia, but this time much worse: four legions, comprising over 24,000 legionaries, were annihilated.

The Cimbri and Teutones began to move restlessly throughout southern France, offering their services as mercenaries to the Gallic tribes against their enemies, in the hope of receiving land in return. They plundered, stole, and hunted the farmers off the land and into the towns, where soon the famines were so bad that the imprisoned inhabitants were forced to resort to cannibalism. This aimless, pointless migration lasted for years. The Cimbri and Teutones had separated for a time and committed their atrocities alone, but they reunited and started on the way to Italy together. The Romans had used the four years to place a strong army along the Rhône. On the west bank of the Rhône, the legions of the Proconsul Sevilius Caepio were stationed; on the east bank, those of the Consul Mallius Maximus. The legions of Consul Aurelius Scaurus formed the furthest advance guard in the area of present-day Vienna.

Aurelius Scaurus met the first onslaught of the Germanic tribes (i.e., Cimbri and Teutones). No Roman commander had ever been defeated more quickly or more thoroughly than he. Before the sun had set, his legions had fallen, were taken prisoner, or fled. His pleas to his fellow commanders to send help were ignored. The rivalry among them was too great: they each wanted to preserve their troops for the decisive battle in order to return in triumph in Rome. Aurelius Scaurus was captured and stabbed to death by an impetuous youth named Boiorix in the enemy camp after he had warned the Germans not to cross the Alps into Italy as the Romans were invincible.

Scaurus was dead, his legions dispersed, and the remaining armies themselves were confronted with a deadly threat. But if the legionaries thought that their commanding officers would now bury their differences, they were sadly mistaken. Each still begrudged the other the victory. Maximus told Caepio to bring his legions across the Rhône immediately, in the correct assumption that the legions needed to be united in order to withstand the expected onslaught of the enemy. This was an order, since Maximus was a Consul and therefore one of the highest officials in the Roman Republic; Caepio was merely Proconsul, the governor of a province, and thus lower in rank. Caepio answered the request with the following words: "I am guarding my territory; you guard your own." It was only after lengthy hesitation and at the insistence of his officers that he finally agreed to cross the river.

A tragedy resulted. In front of the entire troop, Caepio accused his commander-in-chief of cowardice. He refused to occupy the same fortified camp, and was not even willing to cooperate in preparing a plan of operation. Some of the officers were brave enough to force the two commanders to meet together, but both merely insulted each other at the negotiating table. They parted in hate and discord. In the meantime, representatives from the Senate had arrived with the order to achieve a unified command. This came to nothing, however; neither Caepio nor Maximus so much as listened to what they had to say.

The Cimbri and Teutones appeared to be unaware of the disputes in the enemy camp when they sent a delegation to the Romans. They had followed protocol and announced themselves to the Consul; he was, after all, the commander-in-chief of the Roman troops. The Proconsul was so enraged by this that he threatened to kill the delegation if they did not leave immediately. The ambassadors returned to their barricade. As soon as they reported their dishonourable treatment, the die was cast. Nothing could have offended them more than an insult to their honour. They resolved to attack, and in the event of a victory, swore to sacrifice their spoils and prisoners to the gods.

The battle that ensued took place on the plains between the town of Arausio (Orange) and the Rhône. It was October 6, 105 BC. Caepio, still under the delusion that Maximus wanted to steal his laurels, attacked in haste in the first light of dawn. He was in difficulty immediately. When Maximus finally decided to come to his aid at midday, it was too late. The Roman legions were annihilated.

The Cimbri and Teutones are said to have killed or taken prisoner over 100,000 of the enemy. They had taken immense spoils as they stormed the Roman camp. Now they destroyed it all, as they had vowed to do. Gold and silver were thrown into the river; the horses of the enemy were drowned in the current; the Roman prisoners were hanged from the trees. These prisoners were dedicated to the god Wotan. Wotan (Odin) was the father of all Germanic gods and people, god of war and god of the dead.

As the first tidings of the slaughter reached Rome, panic ensued. They were used to losing a single battle here and there, but they had always won the last battle, and thus the war. Rome was not only eternal, she was invincible. Now, however, their position seemed as hopeless as in the day when the cries of "Hannibal ante portas" rang out. Arausio was a horrible catastrophe because there was no longer a large allocation of troops, and the passes of the Alps were open to the enemy. Italy was defenceless.

Rome resorted to hard measures and searched for a scapegoat. No able-bodied man was allowed to leave the land. Whoever tried and was caught paid with his life. Caepio, who had been able to escape the massacre, now faced the people's wrath. He was stripped of his offices and his fortune was confiscated. He was thrown in prison. An influential friend rescued him although he sacrificed his own existence as a citizen in the attempt. Maximus, who had also managed to escape the battlefield unscathed, was similarly punished.

It was much more difficult to find someone who was competent to save the land from a final catastrophe than it was to punish the incompetent. Surprisingly, Rome could take her time in the search. The "odd Northmen" once again wasted their chance; they turned their backs on the gates to Italy that lay open before them, and weakened their own forces by cutting them in half: The Cimbri left for Spain, the Teutones for northern Gaul (Gallia). The Romans considered this to be a "miracle", for they would surely have fallen had the barbaric Germans attacked.

The end of the Cimbri and Teutones

Rome was searching for a strong man, one who could defeat the Cimbri and Teutones. The Roman Senate finally found such a man in Gaius Marius, who was made commander-in-chief with the mission to rescue the Fatherland from the northern barbarians. Marius was the son of a state-tenant farmer from a village in central Italy (Casamare), and thus not a member of the nobility. He had distinguished himself in the African theatre through unusual bravery and a cool head. Much to the annoyance of the patricians, he had been chosen as a Consul, and eventually, as the "Commander-in-Chief of Africa", brought the rebellious king of the Numidians, Jugurtha, in a triumph to Rome to be executed.

Marius put together a new army. He pulled people from the slums of Rome, from the grim quarters of the seaports, from the workshops and latifundia. Slaves, antisocial elements, adventurers, failed existences, proletarians – these are the men he made into legionaries. The heart of his army, the first-ever mercenary army Rome had ever had, were the veterans of the African campaign, in addition to the remainder of the soldiers who had been wiped out by the barbarians. With this host, Gaius Marius travelled to the Rhône in 104 BC.

When they arrived, there was no sign of the Cimbri and Teutones. Marius could take his time to turn his mismatched crowd into legionaries. He achieved his goal through relentless drilling, day in and day out, to the point of exhaustion. Long marches alternated with trench work. The commander did not spare himself, either. The year 104 passed, as did part of 103. The legions were restless, but Marius remained in command of the situation. He made his soldiers dig a canal with picks and shovels, connecting the Rhône with the nearby sea, enabling ships to bypass the silted delta. Thus he both kept the soldiers occupied and made significant improvements to the supply line from Rome.

A year later the scouts announced that the Cimbri and Teutones were approaching from northern Gaul. Marius awaited their arrival calmly; his troops were well-prepared. They watched for the enemy from the safety of a strongly fortified camp that lay in the between the Isère and the Rhône, thus blocking the way over the Alps at the Little St. Bernard Pass as well as at Col de Montgenèvre. The Roman fort known as castra proved its worth. More than just a place of refuge, it gave the legionaries a feeling of home, an important factor in maintaining morale.

The Teutones had spent the previous years moving through northern Gaul (France), involved in countless minor wars and tribal disputes. Eventually the reunited in Normandy with the Cimbri who had been in Spain. Both groups had amassed great spoils in their travels, but neither had achieved their original goal -- land. Now they decided to attempt the ultimate risk, an attack on Italy and the storming of Rome itself. In order to remain mobile, they left most of their baggage behind in Belgium, guarded by 6,000 warriors. This was the origin of the tribe of the Aduatuci. Since it would have been impossible to provide for such a large army while it was marching, they divided up again. The Cimbri crossed the Rhine and headed for the eastern Alps while the Teutones followed the Rhône downstream, with the intention of invading Italy via the western Alps. Thus the Romans were threatened from two sides simultaneously.

The Teutones met their enemy first, and attempted to settle the issue immediately. They organized their train into several circles, with the oxdrawn carts building triple concentric rings, and sent their speakers to the gates of Marius' camp, challenging him to battle. When they received no answer, they attacked. For three days they flung themselves against the trenches but were beaten back bloodily by the Romans who were superior in the defence of fortification. On the morning of the fourth day, something occurred that filled the legionaries with both horror and admiration. The Teutones broke camp and passed the Roman castrum with all their belongings. For the first time the Romans could see how great the number of barbarians must be, based on the duration and length of the procession; it took them six full days of uninterruped marching to pass the Roman camp.

Marius did not allow himself to be provoked by this attack, although it seemed an opportune time to stage an attack; a wagon train is cumbersome, and can be manoeuvred only with difficulty. His soldiers' appetite for blood had been whetted, but he remained sensible and took pains to appease them.

When the Teutones had passed, Marius followed them with utmost caution. Every night when they made camp, he made his troops fortify it so strongly that it could withstand a week-long siege. Despite all his care, he was faster than his opponent, since he was more familiar with the territory. He passed them on their flank, and as he reached the area around Aquae Sextiae (today's Aix-en-Provence in the south of France), he met up with the enemy's advance guard. This consisted of the Ambrones, a tribe allied to the Teutones, who had fought with particular fearsomeness in the Battle of Arauso. The Ambrones now experienced the Romans' revenge.

The legionaries, who were up on the slopes sweating to dig themselves in yet again, couldn't believe their eyes: down in the valley, on the right bank of a small river where there were some hot springs, the barbarians were splashing with abandon. They sprayed each other, cheered, yelled, and in general behaved themselves like bathers on holiday, not at all like warriors being pursued by a couple of heavily armed legions.

By the time the Romans had finished digging their trenches, they were thirsty, but there was no source of water on the mountain. They hadn't taken that into consideration when choosing the campsite. Marius now made a virtue of necessity. He pointed his thirsty legionaries to the valley and said: "Down there you'll find plenty of water to buy – in exchange for blood." The time had come to risk a battle.

The first fighting occurred between Ambrones and the Roman camp followers who had gone to the river to draw water. At first there were only scraps, then skirmishes. The main body crossed the river (Arc) to come to the aid of their countrymen, whilst the Roman elite troops from Liguria in turn descended the mountain.

Soon a battle raged in full force that had not been planned by either side, and that was conducted with no tactical or strategic leadership. Soon the blood of countless fallen soldiers coloured the river red. The Ambrones were driven across the river. The Ligurians, whose homeland was being threatened, fought bravely and would have taken their wagon train if an opponent had not appeared, with whom no legionary could possibly have reckoned: women. The Germanic women struck with axes and clubs, tore away their shields with their bare hands, and did not even spare their own men; in their eyes, whoever fled had forfeited his life. As evening fell, most of the Ambrone warriors had been killed. The Teutones had not come to their aid.

The Teutones, who comprised the main body of the forces, attacked neither the next day nor the day after. They buried the dead of their brothers and held elaborate funeral ceremonies. This led them to overlook a clever move by the Romans, which would prove to be decisive. Three thousand select legionaries, under the leadership of the Legate Claudius Marcellus, had stolen to a hidden valley behind their lines. There they waited for the command to attack. The Germanic tribes made their second mistake the next day, when they allowed themselves to be provoked by the Roman cavalry to such an extent that they stormed the Roman fortification in blind rage – uphill. They were met by a hail of javelins that brought their attack to a standstill. Marius had given the command to wait until the last minute to throw them, and then to engage the Teutones in hand-to-hand fighting with their swords.

The Romans had the advantage, since it was easier to fight downhill than uphill. Because of this territorial disadvantage, the Teutones' thrust was weaker, and their shield walls offered little opposition as their bodies twisted and turned on the uneven ground. Gaius Marius showed his legionaries how to fight on such rough ground by leaping into the fray personally. Whilst fighting, he demonstrated how to turn their difficult surroundings to their advantage.

The Teutones were pushed back down the mountainside. Once on level ground, their ranks dissolved, but they soon reformed, and stood like a formidable wall. Just as they slowly regained the upper hand, they were attacked from the rear by Marcellus' legionaries. Pressed from both sides, the first Teutones began to give way. Complete companies fled. Panic ensued, and the battle dissolved into scattered skirmishes that lasted late into the night. The fighting continued all the next day, but it was no longer a battle; it was a slaughter.

The Teutones had been annihilated. The scene of the battlefield afterwards was terrible. One hundred thousand Teutones had been killed or taken prisoner. It is said that the inhabitants of southern France used their bones to enclose their vineyards. The earth was so well fertilized by the decaying corpses that an especially good harvest resulted.

Teutobod, the chief of the Teutones, was able to escape the massacre and set off northward with his followers to the Sequani, a Celtic tribe that he hoped would offer him asylum. But the Sequani valued their good relations with the Romans, and besides, they had not forgotten the plundering and looting that the Cimbri and Teutones had conducted in their territory. They laid Teutobod in chains and handed him over to the Romans. The Romans treated him well; they wanted him to arrive unharmed in Rome, where he was to appear in a triumphal procession and subsequently be sacrificed to the Roman gods.

Meanwihle, the Cimbri were still marching southwards. They knew nothing of the catastrophic defeat of their brothers. They had crossed the Brenner Pass and attacked the Romans. The Roman commander there, Catulus, had fled immediately. He himself called it a "tactical retreat", but subsequently also abandoned his defensive position on the banks of the Adige (Etsch) below Trento without a struggle after his soldiers panicked. He had also abandoned a castell; but the garrison was promised free passage, a promise the Cimbri kept. Now the whole of northern Italy was in the hands of the Germanic invaders, placing Rome in grave danger.

The thing that saved Rome was the phenomenon of "la dolce vita". The Cimbri, who were exhausted from their eternal wandering, arrived in the fertile lands along the Po (a river in northern Italy) and devoted themselves to all the pleasures they had dreamed of for so long. Instead of millet mush and oat porridge, they now found meat and bread, fresh every day; instead of milk, heavy sweet wine; instead of washing in icy cold water, lovely warm baths; and instead of their virtuous but unerotic women, wanton, experienced girls. The awaking from this rose-coloured dream came in the summer of the next year: Gaius Marius approached with troops steeled in the battlefield of Aquae Sextiae.

The Cimbri were not inclined to give up the good life and return to war. They had reached the land of their dreams. They sent a legation to Marius and demanded the sanctioning of their de facto acquisition of the land. They were also trying to buy some time whilst they awaited the arrival of the Teutones – they truly had heard nothing of the downfall of their brothers.

As the Cimbri spoke of their allies, Gaius Marius answered: "As far as your brothers are concerned, have no fear. We have given them land that they may possess forever." The Cimbri bridled against this mockery, and assured Marius that the Teutones would challenge him as soon as they arrived. "Arrival? But they are already here. It would be very impolite of you to simply ignore them without greeting them", answered Marius. Then he had the leaders of the Teutones, including Teutobod, brought before them in chains. The legation of the Cimbri left the Roman camp in outrage.

The following day saw Boiorix, who had been such an impetuous youth but was now chief of the Cimbri, ride to the Romans with the challenge to name the date and place for a battle, since there was nothing left to do but to fight. To the wily Marius, hero of the African campaigns, conqueror of the cunning Jugurtha, who knew all the tricks of war and politics, this challenge was incomprehensible. This barbarian leader was challenging a Roman army of 55,000 men as though it were an athletic competition. No one was sure whether to feel admiration or merely surprise. Marius sent a legation

17

The big trek of the Cimbri and Teutones

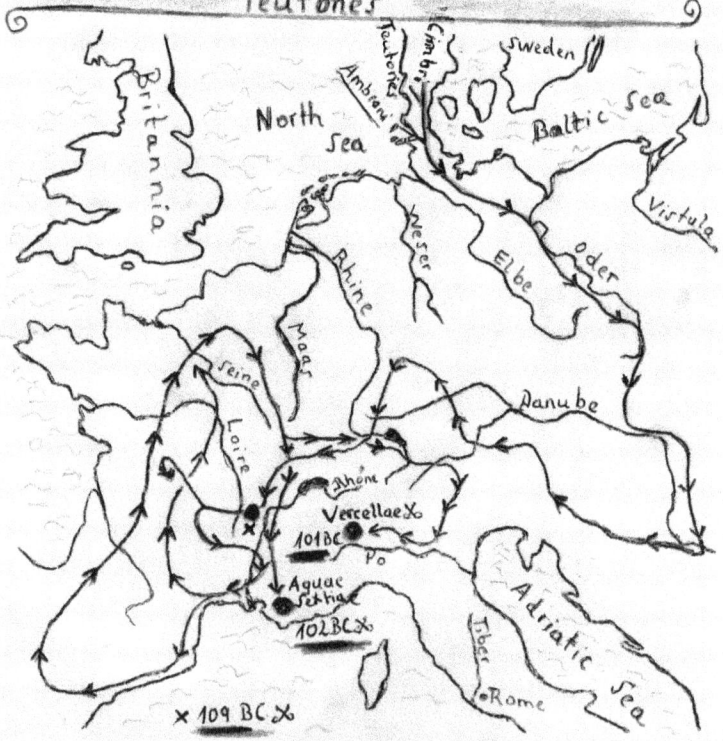

Britannia

North Sea

Sweden

Baltic Sea

Ambrons

Teutones

Cimbri

Vistula

Weser

Elbe

Oder

Rhine

Maas

Seine

Loire

Danube

Rhône

Vercellae X
101 BC

Po

Aquae Sextiae
102 BC X

Adriatic Sea

Tiber

Rome

X 109 BC X

to the Cimbrian camp and let them know that the Romans would never have asked an enemy about when they would prefer to engage in battle. In this case, however, he would allow an exception, and suggested that the battle be held in three days' time on the Raudine Plain near Vercellae (present-day Vercelli, capital of the Italian province Vercelli, Piedmont).

Bioirix accepted innocently, not suspecting that he had just been tricked. On the appointed day it turned out that his warriors had to fight looking directly into the blazing sun, with the dust blowing into their eyes. Marius was familiar with the local winds, and knew that they blew strongly at certain times, forming gigantic dust clouds. Furthermore, the flat plain offered optimal conditions for the superior Roman cavalry.

The Cimbri had plundered excellent weapons, and so were better armed than the Teutones had been. Their riders wore chain mail and helmets. They carried double-pointed lances and long swords, armour that was prohibitively expensive for the average Germanic soldier. And yet it was precisely these riders who were thrown back by the numerically stronger Roman cavalry, colliding with the infantry troops now making their way into the battle.

The Cimbri were forced to draw up their troops anew. They met with the middle of the Roman army and swinging to the right, forced their way into the seam between the centre and the left flank. The Romans interpreted their movements as flight, and took off in pursuit, but they met with no opposition. Chaos resulted, filled with biting dust, scorching sun, and clashing weapons, accompanied by the dull roar from the pack trains, where the Cimbrian women beat on cattle skins that had been stretched over the oxcarts.

This day, 30 July 101 BC, was long and bloody. The end was in sight as soon as the Romans managed to surround the Cimbri. Again, as at Aquae Sextiae, panic overtook the Germanic tribes, resulting in a horrible massacre. Boiorix died in battle, but other Cimbrian leaders killed each other when they realized how hopeless their situation was. The legionaries waded through blood, climbed over dead barbarians who had tied themselves together so as not to give ground, and finally reached the enemy's baggage train. This was defended by the women, as had been the case two years before on the Rhône. Only three hundred survived the following clash. In the other wars that their men had fought in Gaul and Spain, they had seen that women were prized as spoils. Blond women went for unusually high prices on the slaves markets – if they even reached a market, since they were fair game for soldiers of all nationalities.

The women, who were only loot to the soldiers, asked Marius for protection. They requested that he let them go to the Vestal Virgins where they could devote themselves to the gods and protect their chastity. Marius rejected their request. In return, the women turned the swords they had used to fight against themselves and their own families. Some struck each other down; others tied ropes around their horses after first placing a noose around their own neck, then drove the horses with whips. They were dragged by the horses and crushed to death. Still others hanged themselves on the shafts of the carts which they had fixed in an upright position.

Thus the Cimbri were also annihilated and the Romans could again breathe easier. They celebrated their victory by dancing in the streets, and feasting and drinking for weeks. The high point of the festivities was the triumph accorded Gaius Marius. He rode on a chariot drawn by four horses from the Field of Mars through the porta triumphis to the Circus Flaminius, clad in the purple toga of a vir triumphalis, with a laurel branch in his right hand and an ivory scepter in his left, his face dyed red with minium. A slave stood at his side holding the golden crown of Jupiter over his (Marius') head and calling loudly to drown out the noise of the crowd, "remember, you are but a man." Before his chariot went the chained enemy army commanders, amongst them Teutobod, the last remaining chief of the Teutones. It was his fate, along with the others, to be killed immediately after the procession.

"Teutone" became a byword in Italy. Even today Germans are called Teutones by many, in many other nations as well. From the name Teuton(e) the term Teutsch(land) developed – later Deutschland.

Caesar and Ariovist

Around 2000 BC Indo-Germanic groups that had not yet formed nations began moving into northern Europe. The intruders intermarried with the native population in the following centuries and extended their settlements throughout the whole of Europe. By around 1400 BC national groups had formed. The first Germanic tribes settled in the north. Around 1000 BC the Germanic people had reached the lower Weser and had even advanced as far as the Harz Mountains, the Havel River, and the central Elbe region. Several Germanic groups had also arrived at the area around the lower Rhine.

Worsening climatic conditions set the Germanic tribes on the move around 750 BC, and they pressed into Celtic territory. The Celts were an autonomous group, and had been in central and western Europe since about 1200 BC. The Germanic tribes were unable to proceed quickly through central Germany, as they met with fierce resistance from the local Celtic population. It should be noted that several Germanic tribal groups were already living in northern and northwestern Germany at the time of the Cimbri and Teutones: The Ambrones, Frisians, Chauci, Harudes, Batavians and Chatti. Other tribes, such as the Suebi, would soon follow. All these tribes either displaced the Celts or intermarried with them. Around the time of the birth of Christ the Germanic tribes had settled the whole of central Europe, all the way to the Alps.

A large number of the Suebi had moved to the area of southern Germany which had been abandoned following the Helvetian wars. Amongst them were warriors of the tribes of the Marcomanni, a tribe related to the Suebi, but which had separated themselves from them on the way towards south. The Marcomanni settled later in Bohemia. We will hear more about this folk presently – the forefathers of the Bavarii, who became today's Bavarians.

The Suebi (forefathers of the present-day Swabians) at this time had a leader who possessed virtues that distinguished him from his predecessors. In place of the rash impetuousness that had characterized

Boiorix and Teutobod he was level-headed and considered courageous; the contempt for death of the berserker was replaced by discipline; the tendency to blindly storm forth, by strategic calculation;
and petty-bourgeois mentality by statesmanlike thinking. This man,
who dared to attack Gaul and challenge Caesar, was Ariovist(us).

It is not known where Ariovist was born. At some point he emerged
as the head of the Suebi, who had begun moving around the beginning of the first century BC, and who had reached the upper
Rhine in their unstoppable forward push. The times were uneasy,
torn apart by feuds, plundering, petty wars, and campaigns, an ideal
breeding-ground for a warrior who thrived on war.

Ariovist's reputation as a commander reached far beyond his own
tribe, the Suebian Tribocci. More and more Suebian groups sub-
jected themselves voluntarily to his leadership, in the hope of as-
sociating with a successful commander who promised plenty of loot.

Ariovist had a good chance to expand his power in 71 BC, when he
was approached by the Sequani seeking his help. The Sequani were
Celts and lived between present-day Besançon and the Jura region in
Switzerland, an area belonging to Gaul (Gallia). They were engaged
in a bitter conflict with their archenemies, the Haedui, concerning
the tolls along the Saône. This river was an important trade route,
carrying amongst other things ore from the British Isles to Marseilles,
and manufactured goods from Rome to the upper Rhine regions.

However, the customs revenues were not the true reason for the
dispute. The cause lay deeper: The Haedui were friends of Rome,
and they used this alliance however they could, to the disadvantage
of the Sequani.

Ariovist crossed the Rhine with 15,000 warriors and obtained justice for the Sequani – at least, as they saw it. This resulted in a year-
long series of petty wars in which each side alternated victory and
defeat, and which led at last to a final, decisive battle. This battle
took place in 61 BC at Admagetobriga, sometimes also called Magetobriga. No one knows exactly where this is; some believe it lies in

Burgundy, others in the province of Franche-Comté. Here, for the first time, Ariovist demonstrated his strategic genius, and above all his ability to wait coolly for the perfect moment of strike.

This is something that the Germanic tribes had found very difficult until now. Their honour and their rage had always been so easily provoked that they tended to storm senselessly into battle, allowing their opponents to determine the place and time, as had happened to the Cimbri in the Battle of Vercellae. Such behaviour was destined to end in catastrophe, as not only the Cimbri but also the Teutones at Aquae Sextiae were forced to realize.

Ariovist built himself a fortified camp in the manner of the Romans, and nothing could move him to agree to a battle, because he knew how badly he was outnumbered by the Haedui. He didn't emerge for weeks from his den in the midst of swamps, until he finally heard that his besiegers were beginning to break the camp. Conducting war at that time was principally a matter of organizing supplies. Whoever was able to keep a large number of troops supplied over a long period of time was already halfway to victory. The Cimbri and Teutones hadn't been able to support such a large army, which was why they had had to separate before entering Italy.

Ariovist abruptly emerged from his camp and swooped down on the enemy in a surprise attack. Their various contingents were already in the process of retreating to their homes. The Haedui were so thoroughly beaten that they were forced to accept all the terms of the peace treaty – which was actually a dictate – unconditionally. They vowed never to ask the Romans for assistance again, to recognize the supremacy of the Sequani, and to pay tribute. Ariovist knew that such agreements were regularly broken as soon as the losers regained their strength, so he took the children of the most noble families hostage. Their lives guaranteed that the conditions of the treaty would be adhered to.

The Sequani had rid themselves of their worst enemies, and soon forgot who had helped them to achieve this. They would have preferred to see the Germanic tribes go back over the Rhine to where they had come from. But Ariovist had taken a liking to Alsace, that fertile stretch of land on the western banks of the upper Rhine. Besides which, he still expected remuneration for his services; "there's no such thing as a free lunch", especially not when it involves such a weighty matter as delivery from a mortal enemy. He refused gold as payment. According to the old Germanic custom, he sought land and property.

Ariovist demanded – and received – a third of the lands of the Sequani, to be a settlement for his own tribe. This was the region around Strasbourg, Speyer and Worms. Soon his appetite became even more voracious, as more and more Germanic bands crossed the Rhine. Some of them had come at his bidding, providing necessary reinforcements, some had come independently, hoping to have a part of the spoils. Within a short time over 120,000 more Germanic people had crossed the Rhine, with no end in sight. Ariovist was compelled to demand even more land.

His power and influence continued to grow. Soon he controlled the majority of eastern Gaul. His goal was to establish a Germanic principality under Suebian leadership on Gallic (French) soil. He reinforced his army with troops from the Harudes, a tribe of Germanic elite warriors he summoned from Jutland. He also organized his private life to serve his grand goal: he married the sister of the king of Noricum, a Celtic federation with lands encompassing most of Austria and a part of Slovenia. He already had a Germanic wife, but political considerations led him to take the Celtic bride as well – Noricum was famous for its iron deposits, and made a good alliance.

Ariovist avoided the Roman sphere of influence in Gaul, even though his chances of success looked favourable in light of Rome's civil conflict (for example the uprising of the slaves under Spartacus). He was clever enough not to pick a quarrel with Rome just yet. He even tried to establish good relations with them. Surprisingly, Rome agreed, although they had every reason to hold a grudge against him after Magetobriga, where a Roman ally had after all been defeated. The Senate even awarded him the titles of "rex" and "amicus populi Romani", and added him to the list of rulers who were friends of Rome. The man so honoured reciprocated with a special gift: two Eskimos, who had been washed ashore in Schleswig-Holstein. Slaves were amongst the most desirable tokens that sovereigns exchanged.

Reciprocal visits from delegations and influential persons became the order of the day, although Ariovist was astonished at his guests, who besieged him with the strangest wishes – nay, demands! As an official ally of Rome, it was his duty to kill… a Roman, a certain "Caesar"! The enemies of the governor in Gaul did not rest.

Gaius Julius Caesar had been named by the Senate as the governor of the new Roman province of Gallia (Gaul), and had just finished driving back the restless horde of the Helvetii to their place of origin on Lake Geneva. They had threatened his sovereign territory, an affront which he was not prepared to accept from anyone, including Ariovist, about whom he had heard many impressive things, but whom he had never met.

The province Gallia (Gaul) was something of an exercise ground for Gaius Julius Caesar which allowed him to build up a later position of supremacy in Rome. From the very beginning he set as his goal the annexation of the whole of Gaul (France), not just the southern part that they already held, in order to render service to the people of Rome and to place the Senate in his debt. It came naturally to him to disguise his aims, portraying himself as victim rather than aggressor. He was not only a military commander, but also a statesman.

Ariovist was obviously the most dangerous opponent on his long march to Rome and to power, and it was necessary to destroy him. This did not appear to be simple. This Germanic man was not only distinguished, he also had been blessed with good fortune, not to mention the impressive size of his well-trained troops. He was additionally an official ally of Rome. He couldn't be treated as some minor satrap (provincial governor), and simply ordered to make an appearance. In fact, Ceasar did just that, with the intention of provoking him. He decided to send an envoy to Ariovist, demanding that he choose a location somewhere near the half-way point between them for a talk. He wanted to discuss issues of state and other questions of greatest importance to them both. Ariovist gave the envoy the following reply: "When I want something from Caesar, I'll come to him; if Caesar wants something from me, he will have to come to me… Furthermore, I ask myself in astonishment, what business Caesar, or any Roman whatsoever for that matter, has in my Gaul, that I conquered in battle." These were the proud words of a sovereign who was supremely self-confident, and so conscious of the importance of his own position that he failed to be impressed even by a superpower.

Following Ariovist's gruff refusal, Caesar made demands that took the form of an ultimatum: He must agree to allow no further troops to cross the Rhine into Gallia (Gaul), he must free the Haeduian hostages immediately, and refrain any hostile activity. Otherwise he would be compelled to bring his legions to the assistance of the Gauls (Gallians).

Ariovist let him know that he allowed no one to give him orders, and furthermore, no one had ever attempted to fight against him without losing: "If it pleases Caesar to do battle, then he will see for himself what invincible heroes the Germanic men are – men who have been trained in the use of weapons from their youth, and who haven't slept indoors for fourteen years."

Separated from house and home for fourteen years, these men lived as mercenaries, a life that often left them blunted and brutalized, sometimes desperate, spurred by the spark of hope that they would someday own their own land.

Caesar, the great victor over the Suebi

Caesar received the answer from Ariovist that he had hoped for and expected. But this alone was not sufficient for a declaration of war. He arranged it so that the hastily-convened Gallic (Gallian) council would request his help, by depicting the Germanic danger as a dreadful portent and Ariovist as 'Public Enemy #1'. "If Caesar and the Romans don't help us, all the Gauls (Gallians) must emigrate and try and find a new home far from the Germans" was the tenor of the council.

As Caesar received the news that further Germanic reinforcements were on their way to the eastern side of the upper Rhine, the die was cast. He gathered his legions and set out for non-Roman territory. His goal was Vesontio (Besançon), the capital city of the Sequani. Vesontio was easy to defend, thanks to its position between river and mountains, and due to its good cache of provisions, it was also an excellent source of reinforcements. Whoever controlled this town would have a decisive influence on the course of the war. Caesar realized this, as did his opponent. Thus it was imperative that he should forestall Ariovist. The forced marches that Caesar ordered caused as many losses as the subsequent storming of the walls of Vosentio.

The town was conquered. But then a strange phenomenon occurred. The Romans fell into a panic. They were told that the Germanic warriors they now had to fight against were men of tremendous size, unbelievably courageous and skilled with weapons. Whoever had fought against them had been unable to withstand the mere sight of their faces and their penetrating glance.

Caesar expended a great deal of energy in order to motivate his troops to fight further. He achieved a stroke of rhetorical genius, transforming their fear into the necessary resolution and courage. The troops were brought into fighting form again. Marching by day and by night, Caesar brought them as far as the plains of Alsatia

(Alsace/Elsass), when a scout informed him that the enemy was within a mere 36 km.

It should be noted that Caesar must have covered a phenomenal stretch. The normal daily marching distance of a Roman legionary was about 22 km, although of course the prevailing conditions along the route played a central role. The famous march from Corfinium to Brundisium (Brindisi in the south of Italy) involved covering 465 km in only 17 days. During forced marches, normal legionaries had to carry quite a lot. Their weapons alone – short sword, throwing spear, dagger, iron helmet, armour, shield – weighed over 15 kg. Additionally, their packs comprised cooking pots, a hatchet, saw, shovel, rope, trench baskets, provisions for three days, and when necessary three or four trench poles. Although some of this was packed on mules (one mule for ten men), more than 20 kg remained for each soldier. They did not carry the entire load in a knapsack, however, the luggage was attached to a pole carried over the left shoulder which could be laid aside in case of sudden attack. Their rations consisted almost entirely of grains, about 1 kg per person per day. The kernels were freshly ground with a handmill before each meal, and cooked into a sort of porridge, similar to polenta. Wine was provided only immediately after a battle when the enemy had been plundered.

Once in Alsatia (Alsace), Caesar commanded that a camp should be set up. This camp measured 660 m on each side. It was marked out by lances and surrounded by a trench that was 1 m deep and 1.5 m wide. The earth obtained in digging this trench was used to build a defensive rampart which was additionally lined with stakes. Within the camp, tents were erected according to a strict plan. Construction of this camp required only four hours.

The camp was barely completed when a group of riders on small shaggy ponies appeared. They were representatives from Ariovist, who was encamped near present-day Colmar. Ariovist announced that he was now ready for the personal discussion that Caesar had requested earlier. The meeting point for these talks was to be a nearby hill. Each side would be accompanied by a cavalry escort which would halt 200 paces before the hill. Only ten riders would be allowed to accompany the two leaders and be present at the talks.

Ariovist had carefully considered when he made the condition about the cavalry escort. He knew that the Roman cavalry, which entirely consisted of Gallic (Gallian) mercenaries, was notorious for their unreliability. There would be little to fear from them in the case of an incident. And 'incidents' were always a possibility, be it an attempt by Caesar to overpower him, or a sudden chance to kidnap the Roman.

It didn't take a man of Caesar's ability to recognize what his enemy was thinking. He ordered the Gallic (Gallian) riders to dismount and replaced them with soldiers from the tried and true Tenth Legion. As members of the infantry, they didn't exactly feel at home in the saddle, but in critical situations, Caesar knew that he could depend on them. Now one of his men joked: "First you make us your bodyguards, Caesar, and now you raise us to knighthood!"

The summit conference between Caesar and Ariovist is one of the most moving moments of the Roman-Germanic relationship. On this hill, in sight of everyone, the old civilization of Rome met the youthful barbarism of the Germans; Rome's dark-eyed sons met the Germans' pale, clever, wild men.

Caesar began the talks on the hill by listing the advantages which Ariovist had already enjoyed thanks to the Romans: the titles 'rex' and 'amicus', the the many gifts – all honours which were not bestowed lightly by the Senate. Referring to the Aedui (Haedui, a Celtic tribe, they lived between Loire and Saône/France), he then reiterated that Rome had never abandoned an ally, and repeated his demands for the release of hostages, cessation of aggression, and termination of the Germanic invasion.

Ariovist proved to be equal to his opponent in the exchange of words. He argued with disarming logic and polemic sharpness: "The friendship of the Roman people must be a source of honour and security for me, not a hazard, and it was with this expectation that I applied for your alliance… If I bring Germans into Gaul (Gallia), I am doing it only for my own safety, not to fight the Gauls (Gallians). This is confirmed by the fact that I have only come at their request, and so have only led a defensive war, not an offensive one. I arrived in Gaul before the Romans. Never before have Roman troops gone beyond the border of the Roman part of Gaul. What led you to do this, Caesar? What are you trying to accomplish in a territory that owes allegiance only to me? This part of Gaul is my province, as other parts of Gaul are yours. Just as no one would forgive me for invading your territory, so is it also unfair of you to interfere with my rights."

This discussion was held with the help of translators. Ariovist spoke a Celtic dialect, but it would never have occurred to Caesar to attempt to learn a provincial language. In this, he was completely Roman, a representative of an occupying power.

Ariovist continued in such a way that it was clear that he had thoroughly understood Caesar's motives: "After all that has happened, I suspect that your so-called friendship with the Aedui (Haedui) is merely an excuse to attack me. If you do not pull back with your troops, I will no longer treat you as a friend, but as an enemy... But if you leave this land without hindering my ownership in any way, I will reward you richly and fight for you, and you will not have to face any hardships or dangers of war yourself."

Caesar did not accept this naive offer, and the talks came to an end quickly. One of the tribunes arrived and announced that the Germanic cavalry escort had started throwing their spears at the Romans.

Ariovist returned to his camp and continued to send negotiators to try and arrange new talks. Ariovist, however, was only interested in trying to win more time. Reinforcements were nearing from every direction – a large force from the North had already reached the confluence of the Main River. Ariovist planned to enjoin battle only after this large group of warriors had joined them. Until then, he attempted to keep his troops inside the barricade of wagons. This movable fortress served the Germans as their camp during their migrations, and in war it was both deployment basis and fortress. The utility of a Germanic wagon circle for defensive purposes was, however, much less than a Roman field camp. Once a battle had been lost, the wagons offered the survivors fleeing the battleground little protection, especially since they were manned only by women, children, and men no longer capable of bearing arms. Furthermore, they were not a good place to launch a new rally, as the Romans often did from their 'castra'.

Both the weapons and the tactics of the Germans were more suited to offence than to defence. They rejected the breastplates and greaves worn by the Romans. They felt confined and restricted in their movements. In addition, few German soldiers could afford to be fitted out as the Romans, who maintained a veritable armaments industry. Each Germanic warrior had to pay for his own equipment.

If a battle was going badly, the Germans closed ranks and formed a so-called shield wall, rather like a hedgehog, which was very difficult to break apart. Held in front of the mouth, the shield also amplified the voice for battle cries. The long-drawn-out German battle cry which they used going into battle often paralyzed the Roman legionaries. During their attack, the Germans usually carried the 'framea' in their right hand, a 1.8 – 2.4 m long spear with a shaft of ash and a double-edged iron tip, which was suitable both for throwing and for thrusting. The battleaxe and the ironclad were the weapons of choice of the majority of simple Germanic soldiers.

The main weapon was an iron sword. This was more than a weapon, however. It was seen as the symbol of military competence, and was a man's constant companion. Swords were forged by special sword-smiths, and the best of them were in high demand and achieved great fame.

The Germans left it up to the individual to develop skills with weapons. There were no extra training programs or exercises, as the Romans had. Experienced veterans taught the younger recruits, and what the veterans couldn't teach them, they learned for themselves in the course of feuds and raids. The quality of their equipment was vastly inferior to the Romans'. Caesar confirmed this himself in one of his last speeches to his troops, as he attempted to rid them of their 'German complex': "…by now it is clear to everyone that our armour protects our entire bodies, whilst the barbarians are practically naked, and that we fight according to the rules of war and in a prescribed order, whilst they fling themselves at anything in a frenzy of rage and without any order whatsoever."

As far as the rules of war were concerned, Caesar would soon discover that the barbarians had learned quite a bit by the time they met on the plains of Alsatia (Alsace), and that they had a leader in Ariovist whom it would be dangerous to underestimate. Caesar was tricked by a lightning-fast tactical move. The enemy had managed to remain hidden by staying behind the cavalry and by clever use of the terrain, so that they passed by him and attacked from the rear. With that, they had the flow of supplies and reinforcements from behind the lines completely under their control.

Ariovist thus forced Caesar into negotiating, something he was not at all used to. He was now forced by the supply situation, which was quickly becoming threatening, to make every attempt to stop his opponent. Every day for five days he brought his troops into position before the enemy camp in an attempt to force them into battle.

However, Ariovist did not allow himself to be provoked. His plan was to get the Romans to retreat, and then attack them on the march. With their cumbersome baggage train (tross) they would be deathly vulnerable. Until then, he contented himself with sending his 'double warriors' out to fight. This was a special troop composed of a group of cavalry and foot soldiers. They watched out for each other and advanced together, with the infantry soldiers grabbing the horses' manes and letting themselves be pulled along. They pulled back equally rapidly, and fought alternately on horseback and on the ground. The Romans, having nothing comparable to respond with, suffered significant losses day by day, and their position became intolerable.

Caesar's true genius as a commander, in addition to his organizational talents, was shown in his psychological finesse, his contempt for routine and tradition, and the ability to drop a promising plan immediately when he recognized that circumstances no longer favoured it, meeting the new situation with new methods. And this is precisely what he did now. He left the encampment with the main body of his troops and moved 600 paces behind the Germanic line. There he erected a second fortified camp, stationed two legions there, and marched back to the base camp with the remaining four legions. He was thus able to secure his supply lines as well as outflank the enemy camp with two camps of his own.

Whereas Ariovist's move had been daring, Caesar's was a thing of genius. The ensuing stalemate forced a decisive meeting that would determine everything. After Ariovist had tried and failed to storm the smaller camp, and the expected reinforcements failed to arrive, he strode out of his circled wagons and lined up his warriors to their tribes, at equal distance from each other – Suebi, Harudes (Harudi), Marcomanni, Triboci, Vangiones (Vangioni), Nemetes (Nemeti), and Sedusii. The women remained behind on the wagons, raising their arms, crying and loudly imploring their men not to let them fall into the hands of the Romans as slaves.

The Germans arranged themselves into phalanxes, their preferred battle formation. The best-equipped warriors were placed at the tip; these were also the nobility, those with the most possessions. The flanks of the phalanxes were protected by the mens' shields, which they held close together. This formation corresponded to the Germanic strategic philosophy: namely, to ram through the enemy line with a forceful thrust. When they were successful, the enemy line would break, leading to a complete breakdown in their organization. However, if they failed to break through, the danger of being surrounded and annihilated by the enemy's flanks was immense. The phalanx was a purely offensive formation; defensive tactics had no place in Germanic thinking.

The two sides met with such force in this battle on the Alsatian plains in 58 BC that neither side had time to throw their spears,

33

instead immediately commenced with hand-to-hand fighting. Most of the Germanic troops were stuck, but many surged forward and at first they were able to remain in a phalanx. Soon, however, every appearance of order disappeared, and each man fought for himself. Caesar's bodyguards, the famous Tenth Legion, pushed back the Germans' left flank, but soon found themselves threatened on the right, where the ramming manoeuvre had succeeded. The Suebi there worked themselves into the rage of berserkers, in the state of killing intoxication typical for the Germans, which made them immune to ordeal and pain, but which also tired them quickly.

It appeared as though Caesar was about to lose his first battle in Gaul (Gallia), but the luck he had managed to summon so many times before, and which he equated with coincidence, did not fail him this time, either. Fortune appeared in the form of a young, hitherto unknown cavalry officer named Publius Licinius Crassus, who brought his reserve troops in to help the threatened flank without awaiting orders. This was the decisive turning point in the confrontation.

As bold and brilliant as the Germans were in carrying out their attack, they were helpless when it came to defence. They had no knowledge of appropriate formations, never kept troops in strategic reserves, and were unable to organize a retreat. This time was no exception, and they fled head over heels before the Romans, who pursued them tenaciously to the banks of the Rhine where they struck them down or drove them into the raging current. The dead soldiers' possessions were plundered, as was the custom, and the bodies left to the ravages of crows, wolves, and wild dogs. Captured enemies were sold as slaves, whilst the wounded were afforded a mercy killing.

Ariovist had about 28,000 warriors at his disposal during this battle, whilst Caesar had six legions – i.e. 36,000 (a battle-ready legion consisted of 6,000 men). Not only was his equipment inferior, he was also significantly outnumbered by the Romans. The majority of the Germans were killed; only a small remainder managed to flee, amongst them Ariovist. He crossed the Rhine in a small boat and lived for another four years in his homeland on the eastern side of the river, but his Germanic wife was slain by the Romans. His second (Celtic) wife did not survive, either. She was killed by the Romans too, but at least both escaped slavery.

Roman expansion before Christ

Caesar had achieved a complete triumph in Alsatia (Alsace/Elsass), but he did not stop to enjoy it. He never succumbed to the temptation of becoming arrogant or immoderate in the hour of victory. Thanks to his overwhelming supremacy, he was in a position to completely exterminate the tribes that Ariovist had settled around Strasbourg (Straßburg), Speyer and Worms, or send them back to where they had come from. Instead, he did what he had done in similar circumstances previously, giving preference to conquered enemies over doubtful friends, and allowed them to stay where they were. His one condition was that they pledge to defend the Rhine border against all invaders, including their own landsmen if necessary.

The Triboci, Vangiones (Vangioni), and Nemeters (Nemeti) accepted these conditions with the dependability so typical of the Germans. Although they felt a certain sense of commonality with each other, the worst enemies of the Germans had always been found within their own ranks. In the following centuries the Germans living on the west bank of the Rhine were to provide the troops that the Romans needed to defeat the Germanic tribes that continued to storm the borders.

Following the battle in Alsatia, the Celtic Helvetii who had been displaced during the Cimbrian wars returned to the territory of present-day Switzerland. The Helvetii later mingled with the Suebi (Sweben = Swabians) and the newer group of the Alemanni (Alemani/Allmen)

If Caesar thought his victory in Alsatia had taken care of the Germanic threat for a while, he soon learned better – or worse, as it turned out. A mere two years later (56 BC) there was a new invasion. The Usipeters (Usipeti) and Tencteri crossed the Rhine in such large numbers that it alarmed the Roman occupation forces, whilst at the same time giving hope to the occupied Gaul (Gallia).

The Gauls (Gallians) opened negotiations with the Germans with the goal of operating independently against the Romans, but also with the intention of launching a united attack against them.

Thanks to his excellent network of spies, Caesar soon learned the extent of the threat posed by a general uprising in Gaul (Gallia). He knew the Gauls well, and held them to be fickle and undependable. He had no intention of giving up the territory won at the cost of so much bloodshed on the part of his legions, and was not prepared to risk his plans for the future. As soon as the weather permitted, he set off toward the north with his entire army.

By now he commanded eight legions. This was many more than the Senate had allowed, but his success was the more convincing argument, and besides, Rome was far away. In addition, he had 5,000 Gallic cavalry. Although he continued to be sceptical regarding their value in battle, he did not want to do without them.

After several days' march, he met the enemy's advance guard. As usual when the Germans met the Romans, battle was not joined immediately; instead, envoys were sent. The ambassadors of the Tencteri and Usipeti (Usipeters) repeated old demands: they wanted land to settle. They claimed that they did not want it for free, and offered the only thing they possessed in abundance, military services. They added that they had not come of their own volition, rather had been driven out of their own lands by the Suebi, the only group they feared. Caesar objected, and reproached them for demanding others' land when they weren't prepared to defend their own. Furthermore, there simply wasn't any more free land left for settling in Gaul (Gallia), not without infringing on others' rights. Finally, he made them an offer: he suggested that they cross back over the Rhine and settle in the territory of the Ubii. This tribe was friendly to Rome, and could use a few strong arms. He, Caesar, would command that the Ubii accept them. The Ubii lived between the Main and Sieg rivers, and would remain there until they were relocated to the western bank of the Rhine by Augustus (thus, the original residents of Cologne).

The representatives of the Usipeters (Usipeti) and Tencteri demanded three days to convoy this offer to their people, and requested that Caesar refrain from advancing during this time. Caesar refused. He knew that the Germans had sent riders across the Maas (river) to requisition grain, and thought that they had requested the delay only in order to await their return. A short time later the ambassadors returned and brought the agreement of their leaders. Their permission was tied to their renewed demand that the advance be stopped, because now they needed to contact the Ubii.

This all sounded sensible and logical, and was meant absolutely sincerely. But Caesar's suspicion that he was being tricked grew. His experience on the battlefield of Asia as well as in Gaul had taught him not to trust anyone. He simply couldn't imagine that these uncivilized people would say exactly what they meant, since his previous opponents had always intended something quite different than they claimed.

From this point, things started happening all at once. Eight hundred Germanic riders, the remainder of the force which had crossed the Rhine, met the 5,000-strong Gallic cavalry. They pulled their swords and attacked without command. Their leaders were unable to hold them back. Caesar felt that his suspicions had been confirmed, and the next morning, when the princes and elders of the two Germanic tribes appeared in his encampment to try and justify their attack, he had them laid in chains and ordered the horns to play the signal: "Alarm! To arms!"

What followed was no battle, rather a slaughter, a merciless manhunt. The Usipeters (Usipeti) and Tencteri, who had not expected to be attacked as long as their representatives were with the Romans, were trapped behind their wagon circle. Deprived of their leaders, they reacted in panic and were an easy prey for the legionaries. The bloodbath ended at last when all the Germanic warriors had been killed, all their women and children massacred, and the fleeing survivors driven into the river.

The annihilation of the Usipeters (Usipeti) and Tencteri gave the Romans time to catch their breath, but no more than that. The German(ic) border remained a bloody one. The legionaries that guarded the western bank of the Rhine could see the flaming signals on the horizon of the opposite shore during the long nights, and possibly they could imagine what sort of disastrous weather was brewing there. The energy of the youthful tribes strove to be discharged; the power of their people, nourished by an enormous degree of fertility, was like a flood that pounded stronger and stronger against the dam of the Rhine. Again and again groups crossed the stream, both large and small, in order to plunder, to attack Roman troops, and to support the Gauls in rebellions that appeared everywhere.

Caesar saw himself forced to demonstrate the power of Rome in a way he never had before. In order to show the Germans that they were not safe from him on their side of the river, he had a bridge built over the Rhine. Not the usual sort of bridge, built on punts and boats, but rather a more daring construction. His engineers completed the bridge in only ten days. It was nearly 400 m long and 12 m wide, and rested upon wooden posts. These posts had been driven into the riverbed in such a way that their strength increased automatically when the water pressure increased.

Gaius Julius Caesar only stayed on the far shore for 18 days. He contented himself with burning the deserted Germanic villages to the ground and laying waste to their grainfields. He did not dare to follow them further inland where they had retreated.

In the year 44 BC the Romans founded Augusta Raurica, the present-day Augst near Basel. This castellum served to protect Gaul against Germanic attacks.

In the year 38 BC the Germanic Ubii left their settlements on the eastern shore of the Rhine. With the permission of Rome, they were now allowed to settle on the western bank, in the vicinity of what would later be Cologne.

In 16 BC the Sugambri (Sigambri) crossed the Rhine and defeated the Roman governor Lollius. They pressed forward as far as Aachen. This led Caesar Augustus to hurry to the Rhine and establish his headquarters there for three years whilst he planned his retaliation, which would bring him the remainder of the Germanic territory not yet conquered, reaching all the way to the Elbe. He also had plans for the foothills of the Alps, which offered him a further deployment area against the Germans. In 15 BC Augustus gave the command to march. The allied kingdom of Noricum was occupied with hardly any resistance, but the Raeti defended their land stubbornly. The opponents held a bitter sea battle on Lake Constance. The decisive battle was probably held on the Oppidum of Manching in Bavaria. The Celtic tribes were defeated by the superior firepower and tactics of the well-trained Roman legionaries on August 1 in the year 15 BC.

In 13 BC the Romans reached the portion of the Danube that is located in contemporary Germany. They made the Danube the border of their empire in 9 BC. Caesar Augustus could now put pressure on the Germans from the south and from the west. In 12 BC the great offensive began. The commander Drusus began with a naval attack along the North Sea coast and defeated the Batavians (Batavi), Chatti and Frisians. A year later he undertook another campaign against the Germans. Starting from the lower Rhine, he advanced against the Cherusci (Cheruskers) and Sugambri, eventually reaching the Weser. In 11 BC the town of Aquae Mattiacae was founded, which is today's Wiesbaden, the capital of Hessen. In 10 BC Drusus led the first campaign against the Chatti, today's Hessians, from his base in Mainz. He erected several castellae (castells) in the Taunus (-mountains). Starting from Mainz, he then led the second campaign against the Chatti in 9 BC, defeated the Marcomanni, and fought against the Quadi, Suebi, and Cherusci (Cheruskers), eventually reaching the Elbe. On his way back, he fell from his horse and injured himself so badly that he died from his injuries. Tiberius, his older brother, assumed the command in Germania.

In 9 BC the Roman castra Confluentes – Coblence – was built. It was also in this year that the Marcomanni, under the pressure from the Romans, left the Main area for Bohemia, which had been settled several years earlier by the Celts. It was a very long way to travel.

The Roman troops were under Tiberius' command from 8 to 6 BC. During this time there were further Roman advances, from Vetera (Xanten) to the Elbe again. Some of the Germanic Sugambri had settled on the western side of the lower Rhine. After this second Roman advance to the Elbe, the area between Rhine and Elbe was treated as a Roman province.

The Marcomanni, who had been driven out in 9 BC and who had gone to Bohemia, occupied land in 6 BC that the Celts had abandoned, whilst the Quadi (related to the Marcomanni and led by Turdus) occupied Moravia. The leader of the Marcomanni was Marbod in those days.

Between 5 and 1 BC the Roman governor L. Domitius Ahenobarbus undertook an expedition from the Danube to the upper Main, then followed the Saale downstream to the Elbe, through the land of the Cherusci (Cheruskers) on the Rhine. Around this time the Goths, coming from Sweden, settled near the Vistula (Weichsel). They became the neighbours of the first Slavs, who had just arrived from the East.

Arminius (Hermann) the Cheruscus (Cherusker)

We write the year 0

The year 0 is the beginning of the chronology. But Jesus Christ was already born. The Christian chronology was fixed by the abbot Dionysius Exigus, who had adopted as starting point the "Year of the beginning of the human development of Our Lord Jesus". Dionysius Exigus fixed the beginning of the chronology of our time during the erection of the Easter slabs in 532 AD. But Jesus Christ was born some years before, about five or six years before the beginning of our time. He was the first child of Maria and her husband Joseph, a man from Nazareth. His followers in faith founded the new denomination, the Christian Church later. Jesus Christ was executed about 30 AD, he was crucified by Roman legionaries. The judgement on this cruel execution was passed by Pontius Pilatus, the Roman procurator in Judaea (26 – 36 AD).

This year, the year 0 of our time, went on the migration of the Germanic tribes. South of the Elbe, there settled already the Vandals, Burgundi, Goths and Rugii. On the Rhine, Weser and by the North Sea settled the Ubii, Cheruskers (Cherusci), Batavians (Batavii), Chatti, Chauki, Frisians, Saxons, Suebi, Semnoni, Langobardi (Long Beards), Hermunduri, Sugambrers (Sugambri), Brukterers (Bructeri) and the remainder of the Tenkterers (Tencteri) and Usipeters (Usipeti), whom the Romans had very decimated in the last years.

We write the year 4 AD

Tiberius, who became emperor later, started his second campaign against Germanic tribes this year. He made a peace treaty with the Cheruskers (Cherusci) in order to secure another campaign into the region of the Elbe. His brother Flavus and Arminius (Hermann), a leader of the Cheruskers, became officers of the Roman auxiliary troops.

We write the year 5 AD

Tiberius defeated the Langobardi during his campaign in the area of the mouth of the Elbe and subdued the Chauki too. This year got Oppidum Ubiorum (Cologne) also a new name: Ara Ubiorum.

We write the year 6 AD

That year the first big Germanic empire in Bohemia was founded by Marbod. The Marcomanni under their leader Marbod formed together with Hermunduri, Langobardi, Lugii, Quadi and Semnoni a political bloc of power which was a provocation for Rome.

This political bloc of power in the today's Czech Republic and parts of South Germany caused the Roman senate trouble. The rulers of Rome didn't trust Marbod an inch although he had grown up and was educated there, but Marbod followed a strict line between Germans and Rome. Tiberius, the Roman general, ought to annihilate the empire of the Marcomanni now. He crossed on pontoons the Danube by Carnuntum (today Roman ruins by Bad Deutsch-Altenburg/Austria) with ten legions (= 60,000 legionaries) in the course of this year. Marbod was waiting for him with 70,000 foot combatants and 4,000 horsemen. But unexpectedly, there was no battle. In Pannonia a rebellion had broken out and Tiberius had to turn immediately to this trouble spot.

Tiberius put down the rebellion in the plain of Pannonia. Also a young Germanic officer, who had already taken part in the campaign of the year of 4 AD in the north of Germany, had taken part in this campaign - it was Arminius, the leader of the Cheruskers.

When Tiberius returned as victor, but without victory over the Marcomanni, Rome had already finished the occupation of Germania. Between Xanten (Vetera Castra, later Colonia Ulpia Traiana/CUT) and Mainz (Mogontiacum) stretched a line of fortified garrisons in which there were five legions (= 30,000 men). Complete suburbs had been built in the fields before the castells, there were now living skilled manual workers, construction workers, valets, interpreters, writers, physicians, surveying officials, couriers, boilermen and pool attendants; they were the persons who needed a high-technified army. The canabae legionis, as these suburbs were called, were still extended by those persons who always followed the military units too. So there one could see the wagons and shacks of landlords, clowns, showmen, fortune-tellers, gamblers and those girls whose immoral behaviour always raised the morale of the troop.

In Bonna (Bonn) there was already a naval base and Cologne was the religious centre of Germania because it was the seat of the uppermost priest; broad army roads ran through the country, divided up into a wagon's track and a track for a marching column, also a canal connected the Rhine with the Zuidersee (Southern Lake) in Holland, so that the war galleys had a quick access route to the North Sea.

When now Publius Quintilius Varus appeared on the Rhine in order to take over the legions as commander in chief, there was peace. Nobody could foresee that it was only the calm before the storm. The barbarians were trained to be decent people who kept up peaceful trade relations with the Romans. The job of Varus as governor was now, to make a lasting peace in Germania and to convert this underdeveloped country into a civilized Roman province. That meant that there were things to do, so Varus had to organize an administrative machinery, had to adopt the Roman weights, measurer's and coins system, had to develop the economy by building up trade centres and industrial estates, by exploiting mineral resources and improving the agriculture, also he had to adopt Roman law and Roman tax legislation.

The Germanic right consisted of unwritten law, which had the character of proverbs, so they could be passed on easily from mouth to mouth. The Germanic people's and court's assembly, the "Thing", made use of these unwritten laws. But that only happened in case a culprit had broken a most elementary taboo: betrayal or treason, adultery, perjury. If a man took it out on another man and killed him, he wasn't afraid of a condemnation in case he confessed the criminal offence. But they had to be afraid of the revenge of the relatives of the killed man. There was the vendetta, repaying the crime with the same crime. There were also godlike judgements which imposed a certain deed on a defendant in order to prove his innocence, so he had to go on his bare feet over nine razor-sharp plough's blades or to take a ring out of a cauldron, which was filled with boiling hot water or to fight a duel with the plaintiff. If he wasn't wounded it was a sign that the gods had come to his aid and had pronounced him not guilty.

We write the year 8 AD

Arminius (Hermann), the leader of the Cherusci, had come back from the theatre of war on the Balkans and prepared for D-Day which he did with diplomacy and a diabolic cleverness, a talent which one couldn't attribute to a Germanic leader up to now. Arminius, just twenty-four years old, had learnt his lesson, which was given to him under the Roman Eagle. He was a real wizard at the use of the Roman military technique and knew more about tactics and strategy than his teachers, also he spoke Latin perfectly.

Arminius had made out the fact that one could hardly defeat the legions in an open field battle, but if they were combated in the manner of a guerilla war the chance of a victory would be bigger. So as the Illyrians and the Pannonians had done in the rebellion against Rome, being defeated but the Romans sustaining bereavement by killed legionaries there too, so Arminius wanted to do now.

Arminius' slogan whilst he made preparations for the big strike against the Romans was: "Think it over, but don't talk about it." The insider's circle was small, those in the know had to swear to be silent. Arminius travelled through the Germanic "gaus" (districts of the various tribes) and negotiated with princes in order to win many tribes to the participation in the plot against the Romans. Chatti, Angrivarii, Chattuari, Usipeti, Tubanti, Kalukoni, Marsi and Bructeri (Brukterers) offered their attendance at the plot against Rome. Later the Romans were to take it out on Marsi and Bructeri, they were mad at them because of the disgrace of the defeat which they had suffered by Germanic people, and the Marsi and Bructeri were living closer to the Roman frontier than the other Germanic tribes, that was their fate.

Arminius succeeded in uniting the quarrelling Germanic tribes into an alliance. He succeeded also in reaching a masterstroke, namely he deceived Quintilius Varus so that he considered his worst enemy to be his best friend. He made good use of the human weakness to achieve this, the vanity. Varus was vain because of his legal capability, he was a lawyer, and Arminius took advantage of this weakness. He enjoyed the confidence of Varus, the governor of Germania, as bearer of the title "Knight of the Roman Empire." He was often guest in the house of Varus and knew always how to tempt him into speaking about his pet subject, the jurisdiction.

We write the year 9 AD

It was spring time; three legions consisting of 6,000 legionaries each who were fully armed, had left Xanten (Vetera Castra). They had crossed the Rhine and were marching eastward. The flanks were shielded by archers and the cavalry, the military sign of the legions, the Eagle, made from silver, sparkled in the sun, horns and trumpets boomed, in the middle of the train the wagons and loaded donkeys and horses; the heavy catapults left behind deep wheel's tracks, the commanders went on horseback and were surrounded by decorated staff officers – it was an army of frightening greatness.

It was a usual summer campaign. The end of the road of a summer campaign was always the summer camp. A man like Varus, who loved the pomp, a table dished up with exquisite food, and intellectual talks, celebrated his day of court, lived and discussed with his advisers here. In such a summer camp, like the camp in the outer regions of Germania now, he went in for his hobby, the jurisprudence, welcomed the delegations of the Germanic tribes, encouraged the Roman-friendly parties amongst them and tried to put the Roman-hostile parties off.

The factions of pros and cons concerning Rome amongst the Cheruskers had presented their clearest outline. Arminius was faced with Segestes, a leader of the tribe like him, a man of great influence, a giant, eloquent, a man who originally seemed to have had the best intentions although he wanted to take advantage of his friendship with the Romans for the strengthening of his own position. But that Arminius did too, only the other way round.

Segestes was a traitor in any case, caused by tragic involvement, he got caught in the attempt to connect politics with private life. Arminius had kidnapped his daughter, Thusnelda. Thusnelda was intended to marry another man, but that was prevented by the kidnapping now. Segestes hated Arminius, who was actually a political opponent only because of this.

Segestes was the man who came near letting blow up the coup of the Germanic leaders. A Germanic courier, who was instructed by Arminius, reported a rebellion of a tribe some miles away from the summer camp on the Weser that Varus just wanted to leave. Varus took to the bait immediately and decided to put down the rebellion on the way back into the fortresses on the Rhine (the winter camps), so to speak as excursion. That met an important condition of the Germanic strategy; the Germans could dictate to the Romans time and area for a battle. But now Segestes appeared and brought the plot to light. He informed Varus in detail about the plot, but Varus didn't believe him because what he heard seemed to be too fantastic. When Segestes demanded to chain him and to keep him prisoner as long as his words would not yet be confirmed Varus became suspicious, but he eventually refused to comply with Segestes' demand. It couldn't be that Arminius was betraying him, that such a man, a Roman knight, a high-decorated leader of an auxiliary troop, a Germanic prince, who was treated like a son, was a disgrace to him and the Roman Empire.

The auxiliary troops left Varus first. They marched into their base camps, which were spread all over the country. Then the legions left the summer camp, only a small garrison stayed behind. The "tross" (ration's troop, this troop was responsible to the legions for

47

the food), ponderously marching and sore point of each marching unit of the Roman army, was very large this time. Since the officers didn't want to do without comfort in the summer camp they had in the garrisons on the Rhine, the camp was teeming with slaves and released persons, wives and prostitutes and with many other non-combatants.

The march into the death had begun. Varus was ignorant of his last march now as ever. He had not even ordered always to be ready for battle. The column moved forward by keeping dictated distances, 90 centimetres from man to man, in six-men-ranks. These ranks dissolved there, where they were cramped for space, then they mixed with the "tross", built up, stepped out on the sides. This army worm crept through the landscape and was exposed to each sudden attack. But any ambush was out of the question. The Germanic tribal princes seemed to vouch for that. They rode with the group of the governor, accompanied the train for a stretch of many kilometres, but then they reported formally to Varus that they were leaving: They wanted to mobilize in order to come back with their troops later, somewhere on Germanic ground could be the meeting place for the legions and their warriors then, the meeting place for the start of the common campaign against the rebels. But the Germanic troops had arrived already, although not in support of the Roman legions. They had followed in a certain distance like a ghost army, camouflaged by the terrain that they knew extremely well and were waiting for the order of attack, the attack against the Romans. The country between Rhine and Weser was already in an utter turmoil. More and more tribes followed the rebels. The battle against Rome was declared a matter of the Germanic nation, the leaders of the pro-Roman party, as Segestes, were compelled to take part in the rebellion. Also the other members of the pro-Roman party were implicated in the rebellion in the meantime because the Roman legionaries, who were deployed in each tribe, were slaughtered to a man.

The legions continued marching. The terrain had become difficult, wooded, torn by gorges; rain set in, it was the heavy rain, the rain of the autumn, which was lasting for days, the typical rain of this landscape, the rain that Arminius had longed for, the rain that he had taken into his account. Now there was a gale blowing too, a more and more increasing gale, trees fell down and formed obstacles which one could hardly remove, a loamy ground impeded the legionaries marching onward, the wagons got stuck, the sky darkened and turned day into night, legionaries shouted, cursed the situation, then they were suddenly faced with attacking Germanic warriors. These warriors were combatants on feet, quick, dexterous, equipped with light weapons, combatants who made short attacks, then immediately withdrew again if there was resistance and were waiting in the thicket for the next chance for an attack, thus an invisible enemy. It was their goal to break up the marching column, to splinter the Roman armed forces, to chase them away.

Varus kept calm and gave the order "no pursuit of the enemy", he knew the situation, knew the advantage of the Germanic warriors, therefore it was a reasonable decision. At nightfall he let pitch camp. It was the usual Roman camp, a military camp with trench, rampart, palisades, a camp well-tried a thousand times. This camp should encourage the legionaries, should raise their morale. Also Varus optimistically hoped for the arrival of Arminius, who had always been loyal to him, for the arrival of Arminius' auxiliary troops in order to put an end to the haunting savages, the ghosts in the Germanic forests.

But Arminius never appeared again and the following morning Varus knew that he had fallen into Arminius' trap. The sky was dark, the day didn't seem to dawn. Varus saw the worst coming and ordered to burn the train wagons and the baggage, to leave all that behind that wasn't required, that a fighting legionary didn't need. After that he continued marching again, but this time in battle-formation; soon he reached clear terrain much to his relief, there was the possibility that his cohorts could develop their combative strength. Now he expected the Germanic warriors to start their typical attack, an attack in the form of a wedge. But Arminius didn't do him the favour. He let his warriors attack shortly in order to withdraw immediately again then, like guerillas.

Arminius kept the guerilla tactic the next day too, but now there were ten times more warriors than the day before. In the evening Varus had pitched camp again, but now it was a pitiful retreat place only, made from branches and shrubs, the legionaries couldn't take any more, they couldn't do the hard work for a usual camp.

The third day brought the end now. The Roman army, reduced to a few units, got into a marshy wood. A heavy rainfall set in, the visibility was poor, only some metres, and on all sides the war cry of the Germanic warriors was to be heard; they had got reinforcements by warriors who had hesitated up to now, but who saw the chance to make loot now. The Romans fought with courage of despair. There was a multitude of tragedies, so a standard carrier plunged into the swamp with the "Eagle", the holy symbol of his legion, in order not to let it fall into the enemy's hands; another legionary killed himself by making use of a chain, with it Germanic prisoners had been tied up before. The last resistance was extinguished when the Roman cavalry took to flight; but it was only a vain attempt because the Roman horsemen were all captured while fleeing and killed immediately.

Varus was more courageous looking at his own death than fighting against the enemy. He plunged the sword into his body. Also other high officers of the Roman army did the same. Now cruelly mutilated dead bodies covered the ground of the forest by the thousand. The victory of the Germanic warriors was total, only some legionaries succeeded in escaping the slaughter, they fled into the castell Aliso. Arminius, the victor, appeared and could watch the defeat of the Romans, could enjoy his triumph, standing on a hill. He spoke to the warriors and thanked them for their courage that had made the victory over the Roman legions possible.

The Germans couldn't take advantage of their victory. It is true that they could take all castells between Rhine and Weser, but they could not take Aliso, the fortress on the Lippe (river). There, where the remainder of the army of Varus had fled to, they had attacked the walls in vain. They couldn't besiege the fortress because of missing siege's apparatus, thus they confined themselves to blocking up the access roads in order to starve out the garrison. Now and then they carried on long spears the heads of killed Romans along the walls. But the intended shock failed to come. – The commander of the fortress Aliso was a warhorse. During a stormy night he let go his trumpeters through the lines, let blow signal, ventured to do the breakout with his troops then. The signals of the trumpets were intended to make the Germans believe in the advance of auxiliary troops from Vetera (Xanten). The Germanic warriors were taken in by the war ruse and Caedicius, the commander, could escape, but he had to put up with many casualties.

The dead body of Varus was taken to Arminius after the battle; the body was partially scorched, some men of the Roman staff had tried to burn the corpse because nobody was intended to desecrate Varus' dead body. Arminius ordered to behead the corpse, then he sent the head to Marbod, the king of the Marcomanni in Bohemia. He hoped by this horrible trophy of victory to prompt him, the great waverer amongst the Germanic leaders, to a joint action against the Romans.

Augustus, the Roman emperor, was informed about the defeat of his legions in Germania. Marbod had even sent him the cut off head of Varus, he hoped that the Romans would see it as his mark of loyalty to Rome particularly since his warriors hadn't taken part in the annihilation of the legions.
Augustus was badly upset when he saw the head of Varus and heard the message of the annihilation of his legions; he let grow a beard, didn't have his hair cut for months and knocked his head against the door post now and then and shouted over and over again: "Quintilius Varus, give my legions back!" In Rome the day of the catastrophe was celebrated as a black day and day of mourning even many years later.

Germanicus in Germania

We write the year 10 AD

Tiberius became commander-in-chief of the Roman troops in Germania after the death of Varus. He didn't venture on the difficult task to attack the Germans in their own country. He still thought about the thousands and thousands of dead legionaries, killed by Germanic warriors one year ago. Therefore his current campaigns were no real campaigns, he was only pretending. Also his victories were only victory's reports, which were intended to lull the people of Rome. It is true that he crossed the Rhine, but then he contented himself with felling trees and so making forest lanes for an advance, setting fire to villages and devastating fields. He operated with the utmost caution, let always march the column in battle formation, strengthened above all the reconnaissance, held a council of war regularly and never rode without a local scout.

When the legionaries crossed the Rhine he was never too good for a personal control of train wagons; when doing that he had the private baggage and all that seemed to be superfluous thrown into the water without further ado. In the difficult operational terrain on the other side of the Rhine it could be of decisive importance to have a smaller "tross" (entourage) than a cumbersome "tross" that hindered each movement. Since the "Varus Battle" it was the trauma of each Roman commander to fall into an ambush in Germania.

We write the year 14 AD

Augustus died in Rome and Tiberius became his successor. Germanicus, the nephew of Tiberius, took over the command in Germania now. His first action was the raid on the Marsi. He took bloody revenge because of their participation in the battle against the legions of Varus. The honourable appreciation, which the senate had granted him for the annihilation of the Marsi, could hardly please him, being a victory over a tribe, which couldn't offer resistance because its warriors were totally drunk after a sacrificial celebration. So there was no battle, it was a slaughter; no life was spared, also old men, women and children were killed.

We write the year 15 AD

Germanicus went to the battlefield of the biggest defeat of the Romans on Germanic ground in order to bury the mortal remains of the dead. – Publius Cornelius Tacitus (55 – 120 AD; 97 AD consul; 112/13 proconsul of the province Asia), who was a Roman historian (his famous work: Germania – see following section), a hundred years later wrote: "They set foot on the ground of the dark scene, a scene of painful memory. The camp of Varus one could still make out, one could see its enormous extent and the space of the main assembly point, an arrangement that clearly showed the work of legionaries who raised a defensive rampart, the work of three legions. Not far from there a half-finished rampart and a low trench showed that the last reserves had tried to cling to the ground. Between both camps they saw the pale bones of the dead comrades, which were scattered all over the place or piled up onto hillocks, what depended on the way of their death: fleeing or fighting. Between them one could see the fragments of weapons, the skeletons of horses. Skulls of the dead, which one had nailed to the trees, stared out of the tangle of branches. In the clearings of the forest they found altars on which the noble prisoners were sacrificed to the gods.

The legionaries, who could escape the inferno in those days, looked around and told: There, there were killed the generals in action! And here, here the barbarians snatched the Eagle from us! – Then they showed the place where Varus was wounded, and that other unfortunate place where he killed himself, also the hill where Arminius was standing and speaking to this warriors, and they told how many gallows he had to put up and how many sacrificial pits he had to dig for the prisoners.

So they buried the mortal remains of the soldiers of three legions six years after the catastrophe. But since nobody could see whether there were the mortal remains of an enemy or comrade which he covered with soil, they buried all the bones in the good faith they would bury their own relatives, their blood brothers, their friends. All that happened with increasing bitterness to such an adversary, therefore they got sad and mad at the same time.

It was Germanicus who laid out with his own hands the first lawn to the grave hill. He paid with it his last respects to the dead and showed his deference to the sorrow of the bereaved who were standing around him."

The alliance of the Germanic tribes had got rifts after the "Varus Battle". But Arminius could patch them up again and was authorized to take action against the pro-Roman party, which still held a stronger position in his own tribe than in other tribes. The leader of the pro-Roman party in his tribe was Segestes, who put all his eggs in a Roman basket now as ever. He was at a castle now and had a valuable pledge: Thusnelda, his daughter and wife of Arminius. She had fallen by a coup de main into his hands. Now he wanted to take advantage of the arrest of his own daughter. But Arminius appeared suddenly with a troop of select men and besieged first the castle, then he prepared for the assault. Before he could give the orders for the first attack he was threatened himself. That happened by an adversary who was head and shoulders above him, an adversary to whom he had to give way. It was Germanicus. He had heard of the siege of the castle by a courier and had immediately started for it in order to help Segestes. He did it not because he liked him, but the friends of Rome should know that he never would leave them in the lurch.

Segestes was rid of his worst adversary, but he didn't know whether he had found a new adversary now, Germanicus, perhaps worse than Arminius. For he had taken part in the rebellion against Varus, thus sided with Rome's enemies although he did it more under pressure than voluntarily. But Germanicus intended to be lenient towards the family of Segestes. When he heard Segestes' speech now then it was only fair to be lenient to him because for a Roman like him (Germanicus) nobody was to be admired more than a man who had a good command of the rhetoric. That could often save the life of an enemy.

Segestes supplied Germanicus with a masterstroke now. He reported: "I believe it was not the first time that I showed my imperturbable loyalty to the people of Rome. Since those days when I got the civil rights by the immortalized Augustus I have selected my friends and my enemies only according to your mind. That I didn't do out of hatred, a hatred for my native country, because I know very well that traitors also would make persons sick if they sided with them. I did it because I was convinced that Romans and Germans have the same interests and that peace is better than war. – That was the reason I informed Varus about a betrayal and brought an action against Arminius then, the man who had kidnapped my daughter, who had violated the alliance with you. But Varus'weakness kept him from taking action against Arminius, even when I proposed that he could tie me up together with Arminius and his potters. That unfortunate night is my witness and I wish it had been my last night. What was following then I can only regret, but that is impardonable. – But now, since I have the possibility to face you, I want to show that my previous cast of mind is my true cast of mind of today too and not my later behaviour. I don't do that in order to reap any benefit, I do it in order to free myself from the stigma of the disloyalty. As for the rest I feel up to the mediation between Romans and Germans, if there are arguments, but then I hope too, that my people prefer to be remorseful rather than to be rushing into disaster."

The subject of Segestes' son came up; he had left his office as priest of the "Augustus Altar" in Cologne in order to change sides and had gone to the rebels. Segestes said now: "I must ask your forgiveness for the youthful aberration of Segismund."

Now he turned to Thusnelda and said: "As far as my daughter is concerned, so I have to confess that she isn't here of her own free will."

Germanicus granted immunity, Segestes and his family could leave as free people; they went to Gaul (Gallia) and settled on the left side of the Rhine. Thusnelda could also reside there, but she was closely guarded. – Germanicus went back into his headquarters in order to prepare a concentrated advance with the whole of the "Rhine Army".

Germanicus intended to march with separated armies according to the principle: having a separate march, having a common battle. Caecina, an old sergeant of the Roman army, should march with four legions of the Lower Rhine through the country of the Usipeti and Bructeri – the line Xanten-Bocholt-Rheine, the cavalry should take the way through Friesland. Germanicus used the canal from the Rhine to the Zuidersee, the canal built by his father Drusus, in order to take his troops via North Sea to the mouth of the Elbe. The three armies met at Rheine in the country Münsterland.

Arminius was not inactive in the meantime. He tried to win the Germans over again, to win them to a common battle against Rome. His wife in the hands of the Romans, as a slave, that made him race through the country like a man who was quite beside himself. He ran into the "gaus" of the Cheruskers and called upon them to go to war. At the same time he castigated Segestes and Germanicus. "Don't follow Segestes into slavery, but gather round me; I shall lead you to liberty, you will win only fame by me, how in those days when I annihilated the three Roman legions."

Arminius could soon prove that his victory over Varus was not only ascribed to the circumstance that he had outwitted an unsuspecting man. His military genius showed itself in each phase of the combats which broke out against Germanicus now.

Arminius preferred the guerilla tactics now as ever, he avoided to take on the legionaries in an open field whenever there was a possibility, but withdrew after a surprising attack into the forests and swamps, where he knew each way and each footpath. He urged his warriors to attack the auxiliary troops only, who weren't reliable and not well-equipped. He simulated flight and reached by it that the cavalry of the enemy was after him, thus he could attack with the available reserve the Roman riders at the flanks.

How Arminius included the terrain in his strategy is shown by the assault on Caecina. Scouts had notified him of Caecina's intent to withdraw over wooden stick's banks of an extensive moor area. He overtook the Romans on side ways, laid an ambush, assaulted out from the primeval forest then and drove them into the swamps of the moor. A new catastrophe seemed to be developing for the legionaries, and Arminius cheered: "Look! There is a new Varus with his legions and helpless by the same fate!"

But now something showed itself that was the "war abscess" of each Germanic army: lack of discipline. The Germanic warriors pounced on the entourage like barbarians in order to plunder this convoy instead of giving the shaky enemy the death blow. Arminius was powerless, he gave commandos, but he only wasted his breath. Caecina could gather his legionaries in a quickly pitched camp. Now Arminius failed again in his attempt laying stress on his commandos. He knew from his time as soldier in a Roman legion that one could assault a camp only by putting up with many casualties, therefore he advised to wait calmly till the moment when the legionaries were marching again. But "wait" was synonymous with "be a coward", that was not a thing of a proud Germanic warrior. They began the assault on the ramparts and cut off their noses to spite their face. Caecina could escape and reached the castell Vetera (Xanten)But he reached his destination only with the core of his army, he had to mourn the death of many legionaries on the way to Vetera.

Panic had broken out in Vetera because one expected the assault of the barbarians. The legionaries had already begun with the demolition of the bridges over the Rhine. The crossing was intended to make it at least difficult for the barbarians. But now Agrippina, Germanicus' wife, began to speak and demanded of the legionaries to stop the demolition of the bridges, and she succeeded. Thus Caecina could cross the Rhine with the remainder of his troops a short time later.

The result of this campaign was equal to a defeat for the Romans. The loss of human beings and material was enormous. Germanicus depended on voluntary donation of weapons and horses from the other Roman provinces now. He paid for the duty of the legionaries out of his own pocket too, that meant that he gave his entire fortune.

We write the year 16 AD

The conflict with the Germans had become a personal matter to Germanicus in the meantime. He had to be victorious or perish, come what may. Why didn't the Germans give up? What did goad them into offering resistance? On this subject he dealt only with his officers of staff; the result was: one could be victorious over the Germans only if one attacked them on the premises of an open field because in forests and swamps they could gain advantage over the legionaries; also they could take advantage of a winter that set in early. Germanicus also knew that the legionaries had mostly suffered from the endless marches and the loss of their weapons and that the "tross" was especially exposed to the attacks of the enemy. But if he came from the sea, he would gain a foothold unnoticed and begin a new campaign earlier, the train would make good progress without exposing itself to danger and he would be able to save strength, strength of the horses, riders and men of the infantry.

He had built more than 1,000 ships, amongst them landing boats with flat keels, special transporters for the catapults, thick-bellied arks for the horses, for materials to build bridges across rivers, for the rations and weapons. This big fleet left the harbours on the Rhine in the spring, on board an expedition corps of 60,000 men. The ships reached the mouth of the Weser via "Drusus Canal" and North Sea, then they sailed up the river to the Aller (river), there the big sea ships disembarked the troops.

The legions marched upstream now, on the left side of the Weser. Small ships followed them bringing the "tross" to the prearranged place, the planned camp at the "Porta Westfalica". This operation cost the Romans no human life, no horse, no wagon, therefore one can suppose that Germanicus was justified in doing so. But he couldn't know what was going to happen on his way back.

What was following now is remarkable. The self-confidence of the Bructeri and Cherusci had enormously increased in the meantime. Both Germanic tribes, the direct adversaries of Germanicus now, did no longer recoil from an open field battle. Arminius determined even the place of the battle in his favour. That was something unthinkable some years ago.

Arminius got his warriors in the proper mood for the battle against the Romans by the following words: "The Roman warriors here, these are the warriors who first took to their heels, cowards who also would not recoil from a mutiny if they saw only one possibility of shirking the battle. They step up to you without any hope. Some of them show their disfigured backs, disfigured with scars, the others present their limbs which are adversely affected by wind and waves, they present them again to your interest in combat and to the anger of our gods. They have crept in by ships, they did it out of fear to be annihilated whilst advancing and fleeing. But now, when there is a hand-to-hand fight, out of the difficulty neither sail nor oar will help them. Think of their greediness, of their cruelty, of their unbearable arrogance – which other choice do you have but to defend your own freedom or to die before you become slaves!?"

Germanicus also made an inciting speech and described the Germanic warriors as a badly equipped gang, a gang without morale, giving way with each setback. He finished his speech with the words: "Now you are longing for the end of the war, tired of the long march, this battle can bring the end now. We are nearer to the Elbe than to the Rhine and of the other side of the Elbe there is nobody who can frighten us. Therefore help me to achieve the success of a victory. You know, I followed the trace of Drusus, who was my father, and Tiberius, who is my uncle; it is the trace into those countries which they had conquered."

Germanicus was victorious over the Germans by Idistaviso, in the area between Lerbeck and Nammen, only three kilometres away from Porta Westfalica (in the east of Northrhine-Westphalia); there the success of Roman discipline showed again, and the failure of the Germanic foolhardy courage. In spite of the advantage by the terrain – in the own background the timber forest and the hills, the Weser behind the enemy's back – the Cheruskers didn't wait for the most favourable moment for an attack but they pounced on the enemy like a raving man. Now the battle technique of the Romans showed itself: The Cheruskers and their allies, the Bructeri, suffered a crushing defeat. In the middle of the battle Arminius fought, encircled by legionaries. But on horseback he could break through the line of the Romans; he had smeared his face with his own blood before in order to remain unrecognized.

The dead bodies of the Cheruskers and Bructeri covered the ground for miles but in spite of that they attacked soon again. They had still enough warriors to do that the following days. This time they attacked at the so-called "Angravierwall" (rampart of the Angravii), a fortification of the border between the territories of the Angravii and Cheruskers. They drove the Romans toward this rampart that had a height of ten metres and was made of logs and grassy soil after they had them encircled on the sides. This rampart was intended to be the last piece of a big trap, but Germanicus succeeded in putting in action the catapults.

The heavy stone balls had a disastrous effect so that the Germans had to withdraw in spite of their success before. But Germanicus was also weakened, he also had to withdraw and couldn't continue the campaign. He marched back with the remainder of his legionaries to the Rhine.

Rome triumphed over the victory when the good news (good news??) reached them, but a short time later the inhabitants of Rome had to hear also bad news, the Roman transporting fleet of Germanicus was caught in a storm on the way back and many a ship had sunk. The remainder of the soldiers who had survived this catastrophe and reached now their camps on the Rhine, were demoralized, exhausted and psychically washed-out like their comrades who had marched

Germanic Warriors

with Germanicus. Now the mark was overshot. The Germanic chapter was finished. Tiberius came to realize that it would be better to leave the Germans to their own fate, the discord amongst them. This discord he wanted to increase to the best of his ability then, too.

Germanicus came back to Rome that year. Tiberius had given him a triumphal reception. In the triumphal procession in honour of Germanicus went also Thusnelda, at her side went Thumelicus, her son, who was born during her imprisonment in Gallia (Gaul). She was the attraction for the rabble of Rome. She went, leading her three years old son Thumelicus by the hand, before the wagon of the "triumphator" together with other noble prisoners. Perhaps she saw during the march through Rome also a certain guest of honour, Segestes, her father.

After the triumphal procession through Rome Thusnelda was executed; she had to die a sacrificial death, to die in honour of Jupiter, the greatest god of the Roman Empire.

We write the year 17 AD

Arminius had an argument with Marbod, the king of the Marcomanni, this year. The Marcomanni had been deaf to Arminius when he asked them for the participation in the battle against Varus some years before. But towards the Romans they had kept very much in the background too. That undecided manoeuvring between both camps, these politics of fineness or cowardice in the Germanic world, a world of wildness, of patriotic hopes and successes which the people enraptured, were the reason for the beginning of the political end of Marbod. Semnoni, Hermunduri and Langobardi left Marbod, Arminius could win them over to his side.

But also Arminius lost a part of his men, that happened by the desertion of Inguiomer, his uncle, who couldn't bear to think that he was in Arminius' shadow, in the shadow of the fame of his nephew.

The following battle showed the rifts in the Germanic dynasties: not only Germans combat Germans, also Cheruskers combat Cheruskers, Suebi combat Suebi. The battle of Arminius against Marbod had a bad ending for Marbod. He had to beat a retreat; he was desperate and contacted Rome; but now he had to settle an account, an account that was still outstanding since the campaign of Germanicus in the opinion of Rome: The Romans not only refused him the aid, but they financed a plot against him. Their own fellow countrymen drove him out of the land. That was just what the Romans would have done. But now they gave him asylum in Ravenna, a generosity in their opinion, because he wasn't entitled to any obligingness in their eyes. That was the final political end of Marbod. He vanished into thin air too, nobody knows his last whereabouts.

We write the year 21 AD

Arminius couldn't enjoy the fruits of the victory over Marbod. He wanted to extend the position, which he had reached by the victory and rise, he wanted to be an autocrat. The authority, which a leader of the army had only for the time of a war, should be effective during the time of peace too. Personal ambition and fascination, signs of power, played a great part, but also the feeling that only a strong man could weld together his fellow countrymen, that only in this way the fight against Rome could be successfully continued.

Arminius became too mighty for the Cheruskers. So they soon found a man who killed him. The life of a hero of German(ic) history came to a bad end in this way.

Rebellions in Germania

We write the year 28 AD

This year the Roman tribune Olemnius appeared in the coastal region of the North Sea, between Zuidersee and Weser, there where the Frisians settled, in order to negotiate with the chiefs of this tribe. Friesland was on friendly terms with Rome; the Frisians had a so-called "clientele relationship" with the Roman Empire. Friesland was under Roman protection and had to do war service for it, also it had to pay a yearly tribute. The tribute consisted of a certain quantity of skin of oxen. Olemnius, warhorse but no expert in administrative affairs, ordered that the skins the Frisians had to deliver had to meet the size of a "Bos primigenius" (wild ox) in future. That was a very hard demand because the wild "Bos primigenius" was larger than the domestic ox. The Frisians had to give little by little their entire livestock because it was impossible to kill so many wild oxen. Since the demand was not yet fulfilled with it they also exchanged their fields and meadows. But Olemnius was merciless now as ever and said: "That is not enough!" The members of a Frisian delegation met with a rebuff although they tried to explain that Frisians had saved the Roman navy from sinking, that Frisians had not taken part in the rebellion of Arminius and had often proved their friendship to Rome. They had to leave the camp of Olemnius under his brusque words and his threats. Olemnius instructed his soldiers to collect the tax debt by using brutal force too.

It seems to be incomprehensible what the Frisians did now: They weren't outraged, they didn't stand as one man to drive the Romans away, no, they moved with their women and children to the nearest Roman trading place and sold them into slavery. The proceeds were intended to finally meet the conditions, which Olemnius had laid down, a new norm that they had fulfilled now, so they hoped. But the Romans wanted more, because it was not yet enough. Now the Frisians flew into a rage and rose in arms.

The Romans had to mourn many casualties, killed in action during the combats. Olemnius now feared that he would meet the fate of Varus, therefore he gave orders to leave Friesland. The Romans left the country and never returned again. Friesland belonged to the free part of Germania from now on.

We write the year 41 AD

In the Roman province Noricum, the greatest part of Austria, which belonged to this province, many settlements received town right that year and later, till 54 AD. That happened under the reign of the Roman emperor Claudius. So belonged to the new towns also Aguntum (Lienz), Brigantium (Bregenz), Juvavum (Salzburg), Teurnia (St. Peter im Holz) and Virunum (Zollfeld).

We write the year 50 AD

Also some settlements in Germania received town right now, so this year Ara Ubiorum. But with town right the name was changed, too. The new name of Ara Ubiorum was now: Colonia Claudia Ara Agrippinensis (Cologne). Now also the Roman governor of Lower Germania (Germania inferior) had his seat in Colonia (Cologne).

This year the Chatti (the Hessians of today) invaded the region of the Main (river) and destroyed many Roman settlements there. But they couldn't withstand the Roman counterblow, the Roman legionaries pushed them back again. Now the Romans were left in peace for years to come. Domitian was the next one to take action against the Chatti some years later. He started off his attack from Mogontiacum (Mainz), the capital of Germania superior (today capital of the German country Rhineland-Palatinate).

We write the year 57 AD

The Romans needed time and again gladiators for the combats in the arenas. The prisoners of war, who were necessary to the combats, were bought on the spot or on the slave markets. One of the best places for public sales that year was Aduatuca. Aduatuca, the Belgian town Tongern of today, was in today's Flemish district Haspengau.

The Aduatuci were the descendants of the 6,000 Cimbri and Teutones who were left behind in the region between Maas and Shelde before their people had started off their big march southwards. They ought to guard the "tross" and the loot that their people had stolen in Gaul (Gallia). After they had heard of the annihilation of their people they had fought for a new home and mingled with Celtic inhabitants of the Flemish region in the course of some decades.

We write the year 58 AD

This year some Germanic tribes on the right side of the Rhine, the northern flat region, accepted the Roman supremacy.

We write the year 69 AD

This year another Germanic woman entered the field of vision of the history, it was Veleda. She was a woman from the tribe of the Bructeri, one of the most bellicose tribes of Germania. They had taken part in the rebellion against Rome under the leadership of Arminius, they had conquered the "Eagle" of the nineteenth legion, they were Germanicus' favourite goal for his campaigns of revenge. Germanicus had several times devastated their country, he could also bend their will of resistance but never break it. When the Cheruskers had almost exterminated one another by a constant fratricidal war, the Bructeri already played a leading part again in a new rebellion this year. It was a rebellion, which one year later came to an end.

This war caused many Roman casualties, like the battle of Varus. Castells went up in flames, camps of the legions were destroyed, Roman ships were captured on the Rhine. This rebellion against Rome was led by the Batavian prince Julius Civilis, who could only achieve his successes by Veleda.

Veleda possessed might and had far-reaching influence, a result from an ancient belief of the Germans. They believed some women to have second sight and a godlike capability. Valeda's reputation increased even, because she had prophesied the victories over the Romans and the annihilation of their legions.

Veleda was the intellectual head of the national uprising, an extraordinary woman who had parapsychological ability, there's no doubt about it, but this ability she often put into service of politics. Her prophecies were coordinate with the interests for reaching one goal only, the foundation of a Germanic kingdom under the leadership of Julius Civilis. Therefore all Germanic tribes should submit to Julius Civilis.

A present shows how much the Batavian prince esteemed her service; this present is suggestive of the head of Varus, the grand head of a barbarian that Arminius had sent to Marbod. But this time the head was still on the shoulders of a living human being, it was Munius Lupercus, a commander of a legion and now a noble prisoner of war of the Germans. But Veleda didn't know what to do with him. Perhaps she should get married to him; but she was a fortune-teller and a female fortune-teller had to be a virgin. But Munius Lupercus never had the occasion of making her happy too because he died already on the road to her.

But Veleda seemed to be receptive to presents. Since it went wrong with the noble Roman officer the Batavii presented something else of the Roman camp now. They had taken a suicidal action against the Roman fleet. Their frogmen let drift toward the Roman galleys, which rode at anchor to the north of Colonia Claudia Ara Agrippinensis (Cologne), in a night without moonlight and captured the flagship. But the new commander of the fleet, Petilius Cerialis whom they wanted to take prisoner, wasn't on board; he enjoyed sleeping with the pretty Claudia Sacrata in a luxurious tent on the riverbank.

The Batavii were content with the magnificent ship, they sailed down the river up to the mouth of the river Lippe, there they rode at anchor not far from the tower of Veleda now. Veleda lived on the last floor of the tower, there she could be nearer to the stars and was far away from the common people. She had announced by her confidant – she never appeared in person in order to keep the image of a godlike being – that she was willing to accept the present.

Veleda no longer had luck on her side because one could not even transform her visions into successes from a certain time. The allies were victorious in many battles but they had never won a war. The Romans got the upper hand more and more. Then in the year of 70 they won the last battle of this war. But this victory before the castell Gelduba (today Krefeld-Gellep) they didn't use in order to gain any advantage over the enemy, they had grown weary of war, they wished for peace. Thus they made an offer of peace of their own accord. The Romans also esteemed the spiritual capability of Veleda and her influence, therefore they asked her for an intercession with her people. Cerialis intimated on this occasion that he considered her to be a personage but her art would be a deception. He knew very well the practices of his own priests, the Auguri, who interpreted the future according to the bird's flight, the intestines of sacrificial animals or the voraciousness of the holy chickens. So he asked, using a certain cynicism, for some favourable signs of the barbarian now; there would be no harm for her in doing that.

Nobody knows Veleda's answer, but she played a decisive role in reaching the peace. She went to Rome as leader of a delegation. There she negotiated the final peace treaty, but she showed that she knew all the tricks of the diplomacy too. The Romans showed mercy, normally they weren't in the habit of doing that. The status quo ante became effective again, the former territorial proportion was accepted and the former laws were re-established.

The Batavian warriors had grumbled about the peace treaty: "…if we are free to choose our master, then it is more honourable to bear a Roman emperor than a Germanic woman." Here they surelmeant Veleda. Some years later a Roman poet wrote in his poem: "The requests of the caught Veleda." Perhaps she was at Rome's mercy, a prisoner of the Romans because her own people had turned their backs on her. From now on nobody heard anything of her; her trace vanished into thin air.

We write the year 73 AD

The Romans crossed the Upper Rhine this year. They annexed the so-called "Agri decumates" and the area on the Neckar (tributary of the Rhine). By that they met the requirements for the construction of the limes Rhine-Danube.

We write the year 77 AD

The Bructeri rose in arms again this year, but the Romans were victorious. The Bructeri had to suffer a crushing and bloody defeat.

We write the year 83 AD

The Chatti had risen up against Rome and inflicted some bloody defeats on the Romans in the last months. Now Domitian, the new Roman emperor, was on the Rhine. He was also commander-in-chief of all Roman legions in Germania. In the fortress Mogontiacum (Mainz) he prepared for the campaign against the Germanic rebels. Soon an endless train of wagons, loaded with a supply of provisions and stockpile of weapons, left Mogontiacum through the big gates of this fortress. The wagons had loaded wheat from Egypt, salted beef and venison, vegetables in olive oil, chickens which were still alive, Italian wine, Gallian beer, dried apricots, figs, peaches and apples. Special transporters had loaded the expensive delicacies for the imperial escort: finest olive oil in amfores, wine from Chianti, the best fish sauce from Spain, living thrushes and quails, perches and eels, all these delicacies were prepared by the imperial cooks with exquisite ingredients. The cooks also dished up the meals with rare fruits, amongst them the much loved honeydew melons.

There was no remarkable situation at the beginning of this war. The Chatti hardly offered resistance when the legionaries began to construct roads through the Taunus (-mountains). Military scouts crossed the Rhine as vanguard under the cover of riding troops. They fixed the course of the roads, determined the places for fortresses and watchtowers. Along the roads signal towers were erected at regular intervals of a third of a mile. The guards of the towers used a signal system that Domitian had thought up himself.

The legions were divided into cohorts of 480 men each, who began to clear the forest for attacking lanes, which ran parallel to the roads. That all happened in order to conquer the hill's fortresses of the Chatti. If the Chatti attacked a working troop the Romans could call for reinforcements by fire signals. The troops of reserve were left behind on boats on the Rhine; the intention was to take them immediately to the places where combats had broken out. The territory of the Chatti was impenetrable and extensive. Domitian knew that the barbarians never would take on the Romans with their whole army, then, if they did it, his legionaries would have a clear advantage. Therefore he had no choice but to spread out his troops over a big area, which he also had to do for strategic reasons.

The Chatti weren't rich, they didn't possess things which were concentrated in certain places, as it was usual in other countries where might and riches one could find mostly in the towns. The strong point of the Germanic nation was in the first place its human beings. That was the reason why Domitian gave orders to kill all enemies without pity if the legionaries reached a little village from which the inhabitants had not yet fled. The legionaries normally hated to carry out such orders because they had never killed children of the civilized world. But they had no liking for the Germanic barbarians. Many legionaries believed, that the Germans had not even to a language. It is true that children produced pity, but that didn't necessarily mean that that applied to Germanic children too. In the eyes of the Romans, Germanic children were only the youngs of wild animals. The legionaries knew that animal mothers always protected their young generation, but they also knew that human beings never protected the youngs of wild animals.

The Romans thouroughly destroyed the fortresses of the Chatti. They burnt down the wooden gates, emptied the wells and destroyed the ramparts. This strategic line of action earnd the legionaries the praise from the imperial staff, but also from the critics in their own country. The legionaries said that the emperor would prove to be dignified towards his guardian goddess Minerva, the goddess of the tactical warfare and he did not think much of Mars, who drove the human beings into blind combats and sacrificed them for himself. Domitian was at a loss for the words of his legionaries because he knew for certain that their admiration wouldn't go on for a long time.

We write the year 85 AD

Whilst Domitian prepared the second campaign against the Chatti, the Chatti gathered round their leaders far away from him in the north. They had pitched their tents in the region of Biebertal (Hessen), the tents of 80,000 warriors. Day after day fugitives came from the south who reported on clouds of smoke and villages, which were burnt down, villages where women and children were slaughtered like animals.

The Romans came to an agreement with their gods, but the Chatti were frightened and confused, they implored their war god like children who implored the fathers. The famous Roman war strategists calculated exactly the day of the victory, whilst the holy women of the Chatti, who looked ahead harmonizing with the nature, heard death in the rustling of the leaves of the old elms.

It was to be no great victory of Domitian over the Chatti, because he couldn't annihilate this tribe, he wasn't in the position to do that. The Chatti had offered great resistance and recovered quickly from their defeat in spite of many casualties. Thus Domitian had to plan a new campaign against the Chatti in order to reach a final success.

Domitian knew that one could hardly train the Germans to be a peaceful nation. Therefore he gave the orders for the construction of a border fortification. So this year one began with the construction of the limes on the right side of the Rhine. – Limes: It was a border fortification, which was intended to safeguard against attacks of the Germans. The Upper Rhine limes, which was built by Domitian, had a length of 382 km. It began by Rheinbrohl on the Rhine, on the other side of the mouth of the Vinxtbach, a little creek (stream) close to Andernach (Antunacum), the future border between the Roman provinces Germania superior and Germania inferior. This limes ran through the hills of the Westerwald and Taunus along the Wetterau (a region in Hessen) to the Main (tributary of the Rhine), from there through the hills of the Odenwald to the Neckar (another tributary of the Rhine) and then southwards to Lorch. In Lorch the Raetian limes began. – At the beginning the limes was only composed of wooden towers, which stood as watchtowers within sight; later under the reign of Hadrian it was additionally secured by a palisade's fence with a lane that ran along this fence. After the first invasions of the Aleman(n)i, at the beginning of the 3rd century, the palisades were replaced by a stone wall, one metre thick and three metres high. During the 3rd century in Germania superior a trench was dug in the shape of a V behind the palisades; the soil of the trench was used in order to raise a rampart then. This rampart one can still see in the area today. Only some kilometres behind this line the legionaries of the border protection were deployed in castells made of soil and branches, later then there were castells of stone. One of the known castells is the "Saalburg" by Bad Homburg vor der Höhe in Hessen. It was reconstructed according to ancient data. – The Romans could hold the limes of Germania superior till 260 AD, the limes in Raetia even till 400 AD; by it they brought about peace for the hinterland.

We write the year 89 AD

A new campaign against the Chatti took place. This time Domitian
wanted to be successful and force them to give up their combats.
He crossed the Rhine by Mogontiacum again and worked his way
through the Taunus without meeting with worth mentioning resistance of the Chatti. They had not yet succeeded in replacing the
many casualties of the last years in spite of their successes over the
Romans. Now they were pushed back and had to mourn over many
killed warriors again. Many Chatti fled into the territory of the Hermunduri, their brother's people. Domitian returned as victor. Now
in Mogontiacum he was immediately busy with another crisis centre, whilst the Chatti kept quiet for many decades.

Since the year 85 the Romans had to combat other tribes in the
middle Danube area. The Sarmati, a tribe of the Skythi (Skoloti),
and the Daci, who were a tribe of the Thraci, all these tribes were
non-Germanic tribes, and the Marcomanni had conquered the Roman castells of the whole of the middle Danube area. Now the combats lasted already four years. During this time the Romans could
only achieve partial successes, therefore they were compelled to
make peace, but it was a peace of compromise; by it the Marcomanni could reach a strengthening of their present position.

We write the year 90 AD

This year the two army districts of Germania became official Roman provinces. Thus there were the new provinces with the already
known names Germania superior with the capital Mogontiacum
and Germania inferior with the capital Colonia Claudia Ara Agrippinensis (the town of Agrippina; 15 – 59 AD; Augusta - empress
- and sister of emperor Caligula and wife of emperor Claudius, who
was born in this place).

We write the year 98 AD

In this year Tacitus, the famous Roman historian, began with the notes of the armed conflicts between Romans and Germans. By his annals we get to know much about Germania in the time between 14 and 69 AD. His main work, the histories, cover the years between 69 and 96.

Tacitus mentioned the first time a "saltus Teutoburgiensis", the "Teutoburger Wald" of today (Teutoburg Forest). But the Teutoburg Forest for many centuries bore the ancient Germanic name Osning before it was changed. Tacitus also for the first time mentioned the term "Teutonicum" for the Germanic territory to the north of the Alps. From now the Germans were the Teutones, the "Teutschen" (what was their name still 200 years ago), today the "Deutschen"; only the English name was never changed, the Teutschen or Deutschen were always the Germans although there are many other German(ic) nations.

We write the year 99 AD

Trajan, since 98 emperor of the Roman Empire, founded the town on the Lower Rhine, which was to bear his name: Colonia Ulpia Traiana (CUT). Today this new town bears the name Xanten, the town of Siegfried, the hero of the German legend. Before the gates of Colonia Ulpia Traiana there was the military camp Vetera, from where Varus began his march into the death.

Germani ante portas

We write the year 100 AD

Rome is at the height of power. It could after crises and wars always build up its strength in the course of the history, also it could master foreign challengers by reforms. Now a century began in which the Roman Empire threatened to break down.

This year Rome began to build some great buildings to the north of the Alps. So for example in the country of the Treveri, in the province Belgica, the amphitheatre of Augusta Treverorum/Trier. – Trier didn't belong to Germania in those days.

Now, with the beginning of the second century, the towns on the Rhine saw a great economic upswing. Since there was found fine quartz sand, the glass industry could develop, above all in Cologne; pottery, for example in Tres Tabernae (Rheinzabern), reached a heyday because there was found suitable argillaceous earth in the environs. Use was made of the limestone quarries too, which lay in the Metz area. Also an own style of art developed in the provinces, so in Gaul and on the Rhine. There were made excellent products. The quarries of volcanic stone in the Brohl Valley (Eifel) were extensively exploited, that happened also to the trachyt quarries of the "Drachenfels" in the Rhine Valley. The Romans also worked sandstone in order to meet the demand for making sarcophagi, that happened for example in Kriemhildenstuhl by Bad Dürkheim in the Palatinate. Granite pillars from the rocky sea of Felsberg in the hills of the Odenwald were fetched. The production of basalt lava for making millstones played a great part. This basalt lava came from the Mayen area in the Eifel (-mountains in western Germany). Also the trade was important in those days; it extended up to England that was reached from the mouth of the Rhine.

We write the year 117 AD

In this year Publius Aelius Hadrianus became emperor of Rome. The following settlements received town right under his reign: Carnuntum, also called Cetium (St. Pölten in Austria), Ovilava (Wels in Austria) and Vindobona (Vienna, the capital of Austria today). In 112 AD Hadrian had the limes reinforced (fortified defensive line on the border) of Germania. He carried out a military reform too. He strengthened the officials of the knight's class, improved the public finance and the legal procedure and fitted out both of the Germanic provinces with roads and water pipes. There it remained peacefully to the end of his life in the year of 138. That year, the year of his death, he had the castell Saalburg in the Taunus (-mountains) extended.

We write the year 150 AD

This year already showed the first signs of the big Germanic migration of peoples. There began the biggest threat to the Roman Empire. Whilst the people still conducted themselves peacefully on the Rhine, there were already troubled times on the Danube. The Goths, who came originally from southern Sweden, settled first on the island Gothland and then at the mouth of the Vistula, had left the Vistula and started their long march southwards. Their goal was the Black Sea that they reached many decades later.

We write the year 162 AD

The Chatti broke through the limes in large numbers. They moved plundering through Upper Germania and Raetia. The Romans could chase them away only with difficulty. The Chatti fought hard back before they were driven out of Germania again.

We write the year 165 AD

The Chauki worked their way through to the Lower Rhine and attacked Roman settlements there. But the Romans could repulse
their attacks and expelled them from the region of the Lower Rhine.
The Chauki settled by the seaside of the North Sea, between the
rivers Ems and Elbe. They had been integrated into the "Roman
Clientele States" by Tiberius in the year of 5 AD and had taken part
in the campaigns of Germanicus. They had plundered the coast of
Gaul under the leadership of Gameascus around 47 AD. Gameascus
was a Cananefat. The Cananefati were a nation which was related
to the Batavians (Batavi) and Chatti. They settled in the region between Waal and the Iyssel Sea in the today's Dutch province South
Holland. They were subdued by Tiberius in the year of 8 BC.

Back to the Chauki it's to say that they managed agriculture and
stockbreeding. They integrated into the Saxons later. Their staple
food was oats and barley. They already used the turning plough in
the field, an appliance that the other Germanic tribes didn't know.

There were troubled times in the middle of the Danube this year.
Some Germanic tribes, amongst them Goths, crossed the river and
attacked the Roman settlements in the provinces Noricum and
Pannonia. These attacks were to increase in number in the following years. The peaceful period, the "Pax Romana", drew to an
end during the winter time 166/67 AD. The Marcomanni attacked
along a broad front line. Vandals and Langobardi, both peoples had
advanced from northeast Germany to the Danube in the meantime,
and also Hermunduri followed the attacking Marcomanni. Then in
167 AD there were heavy combats between Romans and Langobardi on the Danube.

We write the year 170 AD

The Marcomanni and the following Quadi and other Germanic
tribes, broke through the limes in the next months and soon reached
the Adriatic Sea. Now the Romans had to pay dearly for the doctrine

Marc Aurel, the victor over
the Marcomanni

of the "rigid frontiers", because there were not enough legionaries in the hinterland who could oppose the enemy. Thus the Roman emperor Marc Aurel had to stop the advance of the Marcomanni with the last reserve he had; also he had to recruit veterans, slaves, gladiators and even criminals for the big battle by Opitergium. Here by Opitergium the Marcomanni suffered a crushing defeat now.

We write the years 178 – 180 AD

Marc Aurel and Commodus could push back the Marcomanni, who had risen in arms again in spite of defeats during the last years, over the Danube and occupy Bohemia and Moravia. In 180 the victory had such a lasting effect that Marc Aurel, the philosophical emperor as he was called because of his profound contemplation, considered making Roman provinces from Bohemia, Moravia and the northern part of today's Hungary. But he couldn't realize his intention, he died of the plague in 180 AD. That happened in Vindobona (Vienna). The new Roman emperor Commodus made peace with the Marcomanni after the death of Marc Aurel and had the limes, which was adversely affected by the combats of the last years, repaired again.

We write the year 200 AD

The Romans had extended their influence on Bohemia, which led to the fact that the Aleman(n)i (All Men) left the original areas of their settlements. The Aleman(n)i were a new mixture of peoples, the core formed by the Suebi who had marched to Moravia under the name Quadi. Other Germanic tribes follwed this mixture of peoples now, thus also Semnoni and tribes from Thuringia and Saxony. This mixture of peoples, called Alemani (All Men), moved over the northern part of the Main (-river) in the direction of Southwest Germany.

We write the year 213 AD

The Alemani (All Men) reached the Rhine this year. Here there were the first repulse battles of the Romans against this new mixture of peoples now. – The Roman border guard had reported on the appearance of Alemanian riding hordes on the borderline, the limes. Rome saw the invasion's danger for the "Agri decumates" (Tenth Land = land which had to pay the duty in kind; here the southwestern part of Germany, the upper Rhine Valley. – Tenth = the people had to pay a tenth of their income as tax, mostly natural produce). The "Agri decumates" was the most vulnerable sector of the northern border of the Roman Empire. Emperor Caracalla went to Raetia himself. At Aalen he activated an army for the big preemptive strike. On 11 August the Romans crossed the limes and defeated the Alemani close to the river Main. Now Caracalla adopted the title "Greatest Victor over the Germans". – In 260 AD the Romans lost the "Decumation Land" for ever, the Alemani became the new possessors.

Whilst the Roman legions combated the Alemani on the Rhine, severe fighting took place between Goths and Romans on the lower part of the Danube too.

We write the year 222 AD

Rome had a new emperor, it was Alexander Severus. Under his reign the legionaries of the border troops on the Rhine received land now; they became military service farmers.

We write the year 234 AD

Alexander Severus faced an Alemanian invasion, but he didn't fight, he negotiated with the invaders. He could reach an agreement about peace. But the peace lasted only into the following year. It was the year when Alexander Severus was murdered. He became

The "limes" the Roman border fortification in Germania. It was a protecting bulwark till 260 AD, then the first Germanic warriors overran it. The remainder of this bulwark one can still see in the forests of Westerwald and Taunus the mountains between Rhine and Main.

victim of a mutiny under the leadership of Maximus Thrax, a simple soldier.

We write the year 235 AD

Maximus Thrax, the head of the mutiny against Alexander Severus, became Roman emperor. After the coronation he had to manage immediately the defence north of the empire since there was unrest on the Roman-Germanic borderline. In three quiet sectors hard fights had broken out. The Alemani broke through the limes for a stretch of many kilometres between Rhine and Danube. They destroyed the Roman fortifications and settled in the region of the Upper Rhine that had become ownerless. It is true that Maximus Thrax was victorious in some battles against the Alemani, but he couldn't expel this Germanic tribe from the Upper Rhine. After his death in the year of 238 AD new hard combats arose again on the limes.

We write the year 248 AD

The Roman province Moesia on the Balkans was threatened by the Goths this year. Emperor Philippus sent Senator Decius to Moesia therefore. He was to protect this province from an invasion of the Goths.

We write the year 251 AD

Decius became Roman emperor in the meantime; but his reign didn't last a long time. He was the first Roman emperor who was killed in action during a battle against the barbarians. The Goths had invaded the Roman provinces Moesia and Thracia and devastated them. During a battle Decius was then killed there.

After the death of Decius, Trebonianus Gallus, the governor of Moesia, was proclaimed emperor by the legions on the Balkans. He had to pay a high price for the peace by granting a yearly amount of money. In 253 AD he was murdered by his legionaries. Also the fate of his successor, Aemillianus, was sealed this year (253 AD), he was murdered too.

We write the year 257 AD

A new mixture of peoples crossed the Rhine between the tributaries Lahn and Sieg and attacked the towns and centres of commerce. The attackers called themselves "The Frees" (Francos/Franconians = Franks). They were a Germanic union of small Istvaeonian tribes (= Istjaivi, after Tacitus one of the three Germanic tribes' unions). To this union belonged the Salier (Salii or Salians), Chamavi, Chattuari, Brukterers (Bructeri), Sugambri, Usipeters (Usipeti), Tencteri and Amsivarii. The Batavii (Batavians) followed them later. Also other tribes were to unite with the Franks (Franconians) in the course of time.

Rome was in a critical situation. The border troops on the Rhine and Danube had diminished in numbers. Many legionaries were needed in order to put them into action during the power struggles of the aspirants to the Roman throne. They had to fight for one or the other party. Legionaries were also needed in order to drive Persian invaders out of the Roman province in the East. The auxiliary troops from Britannia (Britain), fetched in a hurry, filled the gaps in the border securing only at some points. The resistance on the border, where the Franks broke through the limes, had broken down. The Franks could cross the Rhine unhindered. Then they marched to Tarraco (Tarragona in Spain) and plundered this town. After that Tarraco was completely destroyed by them.

This year was a very terrible year for the Roman Empire. The Goths forced their way deep into the empire. They reached Macedonia and plundered this Roman province. And the invasion of the Saxons played havoc with the Atlantic coast between Germania and Aquitania (up to the Spanish border of today).

We write the year 258 AD

The Germanic leaders were well-informed of the quarrels and power struggles in the world empire. They took advantage of the quarrels and struggles by invading the empire; they made use of the weakness of the border defence and attacked when the Roman legions had withdrawn there. The "green border" opened the door to espionage. Many Germanic legionaries of the Roman army willingly informed their tribes about military details.

The stubbornness of the Roman Empire to get the last territories back was remarkable. So Gallienus left Germania in order to put Ingenius, his army commander and antagonist in Pannonia, in his place this year. Gallienus had hardly left Germania, when Cassianus Latinius Postumus proclaimed himself counteremperor and declared Colonia Claudia Ara Agrippinensis (Cologne) capital of a new Gallian Empire (in 259 AD). Casssianus Latinius Postumus was governor of the provinces on the Rhine. Now in Cologne he appointed a senate according to Roman example and kept also a praetorianus' guard (imperial bodyguard). The Gallian Empire continued also under his successors Victorinus and Tetricus. Tetricus declared Treverorum (Trier) the new capital of the Gallian Empire in 271 AD. The rulers over the Gallian Empire could also seize the power of Hispania (Spain) and Britannia (Britain). Cassianus Latinius Postumus and his successors withstood all attacks for 15 years, also the attacks of the Franks, who became allies and supplied auxiliary troops for the combat against other Germanic invaders in the end.

We write the years 259 – 261 AD

The Alemani devastated the ancient capital of Helvetia, Aventicum. After that they invaded Italy and marched to Mediolanum (Milan). The Romans were surprised, they hadn't thought of an invasion of Italy by the barbarians. Rome panicked, "Germani ante portas" echoed through the streets, but the Germani, amongst them Juthungi (a Germanic tribe; the Juthungi formed one nation with the Alemani later), didn't risk to take Mediolanum by storm. For plundering the open country was easier for them.

The Romans defeated the wild barbarian hordes before Milan now. After the bloody battle they drove the remainder of the warriors of the Alemani and Juthungi out of Italy.

We write the year 265 AD

The Franks settled on the left bank of the Rhine for ever now. This region became the basis for the great Franconian Empire. – This year the emperor in Rome had to approve the Gallian Empire and also the Franconian reign over the land on the right side of the Rhine.

We write the years 268 – 270 AD

Gallienus was murdered by his generals in 268 AD. The new emperor became Claudius II. The battles against Germanic tribes went on all the time of his reign. First he defeated the Alemani, who had invaded Italy again. The decisive battle took place on Lake Garda in the southern Alps. Then, in 269 AD, he was victorious over the Goths in the battle of Naissus (today Nisch or Nis in southern Serbia). He bore for this reason the epithet "Goticus" from now on. But in the following years the front line was shortened on the middle Danube. The Romans had to abandon their province Dacia since the Goths had attacked this province over and over again.

We write the year 274 AD

In Gallia (Gaul) a huge army marched up under the command of emperor Aurelian. Tetricus, the emperor of the Gallian Empire, saw no chance of resisting this army. He gave up and the Gallian Empire became part of the Roman World Empire again. But it was to be a long time before this fertile province could be integrated economi-

Roman villa in the Ahr Valley

This villa was discovered in 1980 during road construction and excavated by archaelogists until 1991. The entire system was in the 5th Century already ruinous and was buried by a landslide, conservation seen a godsend. So could murals be preserved in their unusual colour. Today you can wonder through the mansion of the villa rustica, including bathhouse. With the construction of the villa one began in the 1st Century, until the year 270 the villa was then enhanced. End of the 3rd Century was built a hospice/roadhouse.

The image shows a reconstruction

cally, militarily and administrative-organizationally into the Roman Empire again. The Franks and Alemani took advantage of this phase of rearrangement and attacked Gallia one year later. They destroyed 60 – 70 villages and towns during their raids.

We write the year 276 AD

Franks and Alemani were still moving plundering and killing through Gallia. But now stepped in the happenings the new emperor Probus. He attacked the invaders by Lyon with a concentrated army power and pushed them back over the Rhine, Neckar and the Swabian Alb in the following months.

We write the year 278 AD

In the meantime Vandals and Burgundi had invaded Raetia and devastated this Roman province. The Vandals were a Germanic tribe from Jutland, they had settled on the mouth of the Vistula for some time and then occupied Silesia. In course of time they had forged ahead up to the southern part of Germany, then they had devastated the Roman province there. The Burgundi came from Scandinavia. They had settled many years between Oder and Nogat. Then they had moved slowly, over many years, toward south into the region of today's South Germany. But also the Burgundi had wreaked havoc there in Raetia.

Probus defeated these invaders this year. He could drive them out of Raetia again. The northern border on the Danube could so be secured for many years. In Augsburg an inscription was found of the year of 281 AD, there was given a mention that "Probus was a man with farsightedness, a renewer of the provinces and fortresses who excelled as brave general all the former emperors."

We write the year 286 AD

The Germanic tribes remained restless in spite of the victory of Probus. In Rome reigned Diocletian now. The Germanic invasions were lasting during his time of reign. Saxons and Franks invaded Gallia (Gaul) and threatened Treverorum (Trier) one year later. Dioclatian, the last soldier's emperor since 235 AD, was worried about the development on the border north of his empire, on the Rhine and Danube. He found himself compelled to continue the reforms of Probus too. The growing pressure of Germanic peoples and the tensions in the centre of the empire urged him to do that. Thus he tightened up on some measures for the centralization of administration and government, he introduced a new system of government, the "Tetrarchie", the "four-sovereign government" of two Augusti and two Caesari. An imperial conference of 288/89 AD, which was called in a hurry, decided to strengthen the borderline between Rhine, Danube and Iller. This line, which was permanently threatened by Germanic tribes, should become the best-secured border of the Roman Empire. The work lasted more than 100 years, it was finished only in 401 AD. But the Germanic tribes showed flexibility: they avoided the border on the Rhine, they took the sea route. Now they terrorized more and more the coastal strips of Gallia, Belgica and Britannia. Above all the Saxons knew to lead brilliantly such a war from the seaside.

We write the year 289 AD

Alemani, Burgundi and Heruli crossed the Rhine and devastated the regions on the left side. Diocletian had appointed Maximian fellow emperor in the meantime. Maximian was the man now who could drive the barbarians out of the regions on the left side of the Rhine.

One of the Caesari who were appointed by Diocletian, Constantius Chlorus (since 293 AD already emperor of Hispania, Gallia and Britannia), declared Treverorum (Trier) capital of the western part of the Roman Empire this year.

We write the year 298 AD

Constantius Chlorus, son-in-law of the fellow emperor Maximian, had led an army detachment through Alemanian territory some months before the beginning of the year of 298 AD. There on Alemanian ground the legionaries plundered and killed Germanic people in the region between Mogontiacum (Mainz/Rhine) and Guntia (Günzburg/Danube). During the raid a chief of the Alemani, head of a Gau (border district), fell into their hands. Constantius Chlorus took him prisoner to Rome, what happened in a triumphal procession and was a provocation to the Alemani they couldn't tolerate. They plundered all regions up to Langres this year, a region 150 km away from their tribal territory. Constantius Chlorus took them on by Langres and inflicted a crushing defeat on them there. It is supposed that nearly 60,000 Alemani were killed. But the Alemani recovered quickly from this disaster, they soon threatened the Roman World Empire again. With them also other Germanic tribes attacked this empire.

The last great time of the Roman Empire

We write the year 300 AD

This year the Langobardi, the "Long Beards", forced their way southward. For the Langobardi, a Germanic tribe from the northern Elbe, it was to become a long way, because they reached their destination, the northern part of Italy, only more than 150 years later.

The Caesari and Augusti of Diocletian succeeded in being victorious in some battles. So Caesar Galerius was victorious over the Persians and obtained the supremacy over Armenia. Thus he made the securing of the eastern defence line of the empire possible. This line was named then "strata Diocletiana". Diocletian's partner Maximian strengthened the limes in Germania and Diocletian's Caesar Constantius Chlorus put down the rebellions in Britannia.

The Roman Empire, which was in danger on all sides before the reign of Diocletian, became a closed whole again. The legions of the standing army were always ready for a powerful repulse of each attack of a restless neighbour. Magnificent palaces and administration buildings were erected in the capitals; also in Rome, that seemed to have fallen into oblivion, monstrous public baths were built.

A population's unrest spread out more and more in spite of the successes of Diocletian. The well-being of the population, decreed by the emperor, was without breath. Decrees, which were chiselled in stone and visible in all places, weren't observed since the fixed price limit chased away the products from the markets, the black marketeering flourished and the people made fun of the laws of the emperor. Who was to blame for it? Who was responsible for the miserable failure? The answer was clear for the Romans: The Christians. Their faith was subversive. The fact that their faith was only tolerated, hampered the necessary adoption of a united faith for the Roman Empire.

The famous Roman wine ship
of Neumagen on the
Moselle

Diocletian ordered the persecution of the Christians now. The measures of this persecution were reckless or gentle, it depended on the opinion of the local governors who had to carry out the order. The only high ruler who didn't persecute the Christians was Caesar Constantius Chlorus, the imperial defender of the Roman border against Germanic attackers.

We write the year 305 AD

Diocletian resigned voluntarily his post as emperor this year. His Augusti and Caesari took over the power now. They reigned independently over their territories from now on. In Hispania (Spain), Gallia (Gaul) and Britannia (Britain) there reigned now as ever Caesar Constantius Chlorus, the ruler over the western empire.

We write the year 306 AD

Constantius Chlorus died during a campaign in Britannia. The legions proclaimed Flavius Valerius Constantinus (Constantin) emperor now. Constantin I was the son of Constantius Chlorus, his mother, Flavia Helena, was a Christian. Galerius, the Augustus of the East, immediately recognized Constantin as new Caesar of the western empire. Also Maximian, the former fellow emperor of Diocletian, accepted Flavius Valerius Constantinus (Constantin) as Caesar of the western empire one year later. But the other rulers didn't follow this example. Diocletian, the former emperor, tried to reach an agreement during an imperial conference in Carnuntum (Roman military camp on the Danube, also capital of Upper Pannonia; today ruin's town in Lower Austria); he made every endeavour, but he failed in his attempt to reach a result. So everything remained as it was, the other rulers didn't accept Constantin.

Constantin didn't make use of the decrees of Diocletian, the persecution of Christians, either. Thus great Christian communities developed in the western Roman Empire now.

Constantin's residence was Treverorum (Trier) in those days. That it was still in the beginning of his campaign against Maxentius, the Augustus of Italy.

We write the year 312 AD

Constantin is in Italy. There, at the Milvian Bridge before Rome, the battle against Maxentius now took place. Constantin's legions were successful, they defeated Maxentius. Constantin was the ruler over the whole of the western part of the Roman Empire. His "cross's vision" before the battle against Maxentius ("You will be victorious under this sign") caused him to adopt the cross's flag with the monogram of Jesus Christ. Constantin was victorious because he fought against Maxentius with Christian legionaries from Germania. He marvelled at their combat courage under the symbol of the cross, he filled himself with enthusiasm about their devotion to God and his Son also during the battle, a battle against pagans.

The hour of Constantin's victory before Rome, a great hour for the world history, this hour of the decisive battle in the name of God can be interpreted as dividing line between antiquity and Middle Ages. Thus Constantin, who was a sun worshipper, made a career for himself between two eras. He became a Christian only on his deathbed.

We write the year 313 AD

Constantin agreed with Licinius, the ruler of the eastern part of the Roman Empire, on a religious programme that assured the Christians of freedom of worship like the followers of other religions. That agreement was reached during a conference in Milan (the "Edict of Milan") – Constantin vested the church with state-jobs and rights, he declared Sunday a public holiday and began with the construction of the Lateran Church in Rome.

We write the year 324 AD

There were time and time again conflicts between Constantin and Licinius in the last years. Thus there were two battles this year. Constantin defeated Licinius first by Adrianopel in Thracia (today Bulgaria) and then by Chrysopolis in Bithynia (today Turkey). After that Constantin was an autocrat. He came back to the hereditary monarchy by the appointment of his sons as Caesari.

We write the year 325 AD

In this year the council of Nicaea (a former Roman town in Asia Minor) took place. Constantin standardized the different Christian communities by putting his foot down during the council of Nicaea. He made the Catholic confession of faith possible by it. Constantin completed this political measure by making a state religion of the Christianity and by forbidding the exercise of other creeds. By it he succeeded in realizing the great administrative reform, which Diocletian had already intended, but in a reversed sense. At his standardization of the faith Constantin took into account the circumstance that the most important pillar of his might were the Germanic legionaries who were enthused about Christianity or could get enthusiastic about this religion. He also obliged the legionaries of a different faith by such supplements and extensions of expression of faith, which the Christians could still accept. So he gave the sun worshippers the day of rest, which was designated also in the Holy Scripture, as ceremonial Sunday. He allowed to practise every faith only in such a manner that people of a different faith weren't offended by any mixing of adoration.

Constantin punished everybody who held on to obstinate departures from the standardized faith, the faith he wanted the empire to adopt. There was above all the "Arianism", the Christian doctrine of Arius (260 – 336 AD), who was a Christian priest from Libya.

During the Council of Nicaea (today Iznik/Turkey) the argument about the question: "homousios" or "homoiusios" (same or similar) flared up. The bishop of Alexandria explained at the council: "God exists all the time, the Son exists all the time. The Father was present at the same time as the Son. God had led the way neither by a thought nor by one moment only. God exists all the time, the Son exists all the time. The Son is God himself." Arius answered: "That is hardly bearable to hear such unscrupulousness, even if the heretics threaten us with thousand deaths. What we say and believe, what we teach and have taught is, that the Son was born by God's will and advice and that he hadn't existed before he was fathered, created and intended for the existence. We get persecuted because we say, the Son has a beginning and God has a beginning." Constantin had to decide now at the council which of these contrary opinions ought to come into force as Roman right. The content of the faith didn't touch him, therefore he decided against Arius with the majority of the present bishops although he was enthusiastic about the personality of the priest. But personal affection had no influence on Constantin's decisions; he was a strong-willed auto-crat, he always made his decisions by cleverness and had applied his strength to the standardization of administration and faith. He was the omnipotent "dominus", the omnipotent ruler. He was the ruler over Rome in all matters of importance. But what was Rome? The capital of the past. Constantin wanted to build a new capital, the capital for the future, he wanted to erect a monument to himself, a monument to the eternity.

Constantin had secured the western part of the Roman Empire. There he was friend of the Germanic people, who had become his peaceful neighbours. The most influential members of the admin-istration, the most important commander of the legions were his Germanic friends: Men from Britannia and from the Rhine, Ale-mani and Franks. These men represented his military superiority, they were in command of the moving army and the border troops. His bodyguard came from amongst their ranks. Also both com-manders of the legions, his military substitutes, were Germanic men. He could strengthen his power by it in the western part of the empire.

We write the year 326 AD

Constantin wanted to demonstrate his enormous might by the foun-dation of a Christian capital, a capital for the future, his capital, Constantinopel.

On the ground of Byzantium, this ancient city by the Bosporus, Con-stantin laid the foundations of a new world city, a city which bore his name till the end of the First World War (but I will use the an-cient Greek-Roman name Byzantium, at least in the following sec-tions). Kemal Atatürk, the founder of the modern Turkey and presi-dent of the Turkish Republic since 1923 AD, changed the name of Constantinopel, it is Istanbul today. – Now the grey fortress, which was always an important site, became a magnificent residence of the imperial court that displayed an unimaginable splendour there.

We write the year 330 AD

Constantinopel became officially capital of the Roman Empire this year. Treasures of art from all regions of the empire were taken to Constantinopel (Byzantium). The Romans robbed the Greek temples and holy shrines of their valuable monuments and ornaments in order to decorate the new churches and palaces now. All valuable things of the whole of the empire, which could make Constantin happy, should be in his city; by all the treasures he wanted to demonstrate the glorious time of his reign; Constantinopel should be the centre of the Christendom too.

All that seemed to be so too, although the bishop of Rome, who was the head of the western Christendom, and the bishop of Alexandria, the most influential opponent of Arius, had held the intellectual leadership of the ministry. The bishop of Rome bore the honouring title "papa" too. Later was only awarded to him the name "Representative of Jesus Christ on Earth" which all popes bore as successors of Saint Peter.

Constantin tried to clear the controversial issues that split Christendom up into two irreconcilable camps, by threat of violence and by encouragement. He had also banished Arius, but then sent for him again. He needed Arius, because a great part of the Germanic tribes, friends of Rome, leaned more toward Arius than toward the confession of the bishops during the Council of Nicaea.

Constantin's endeavour failed because of this conflict. There was no possibility of using the Christian faith as common and peace-preserving connection between inhabitants of the Roman Empire and its Germanic neighbours. But Constantin ignored that as long as he lived; his power extended not only to the worldly affairs, but also to the religious affairs, he was the "Dominus", the personification of the "pax Romana". He was the emperor who was so high-ranking that he was above all human beings and near God.

Constantin had committed indecent assault on many human beings on the road to his successes, so he had his wife murdered and his eldest son Crispus. Whilst the Cristendom of the East split up with the Roman-Catholic Church as a result of the schism later and Constantin was worshipped as holy man in spite of his crimes, only then he was called "the Great" in the western part of the Roman Empire.

We write the year 332 AD

Constantin had militarily taken action against the Goths who settled by the Black Sea. The region of the Black Sea had become a trouble spot in the last years, caused by the Goths there. Therefore he had to pacify this region again. He defeated the Goths and forced them to offer their military service.

We write the year 335 AD

Constantin couldn't remove the constant threat at the frontier in spite of the frontier protection. This year he had to give up the upper Germanic-Raetian limes for ever, the border troops withdrew and went across the Rhine and Danube. Now the commanders of the Roman legions were content with putting the adversary in his place. Another time began, a time like already many years ago, the time of plundering, scorching, murdering, taking of hostages and paying of fine; all these actions were always mutual.

We write the year 337 AD

Constantin (the Great) dies. The discord, which followed now, began in his own family. Before his death he had decided as ancestor of a ruling dynasty to share out the empire amongst the family as follows: His three sons should be Augusti, both his nephews Caesari.

He had hardly departed this life when his sons first got rid of the two Caesari and then were at war against each other. Each of them wanted to stand his ground and become autocrat, autocrat like the father, a ruler over the whole of the empire.

The fratricidal war had not only a stimulating effect on the Persian king, but also on the Franks. The Persians attacked the Roman Empire in the East and the Franks short time later in the middle of Europe. They had taken advantage of the discord of Constantin's sons.

We write the year 340 AD

The decisive battle of Constans and Constantin II, the two broth-ers, took place by Aquileia now. Constantin II was killed in action. Constans lived ten more years after that, then in 350 AD he fell victim to a rebellion of the Frank Magnentius. The only surviving successor of Constantin the Great, Constantius II, had reached his goal after the death of his brother Constans. He was autocrat to the end of his life in 361 AD, but he wasn't a ruler of the united and peaceful empire his father had been thinking of.

We write the year 341 AD

Wulfila or Ulfilas, who lived 311 – 383 AD, became bishop of the Visigoths (Westgoths) this year. In those days the Goths still settled by the Black Sea. Wulfila (Ulfilas) translated the Bible from Greek into Gothic. He made with it a contribution to the conversion of Germanic people, who were not yet Christians, to the (Arianian) Christianity. His translation of the Bible is the first Germanic liter-ary monument; greater parts are included in the "Codex argenteus" (today in Uppsala/Sweden), which came into being about 500 AD.

We write the year 347 AD

Constantius II leaned toward the Arianians (Arianism), but he didn't radiate the reputation of his father that had impressed the bishops. It was also of no use to Constantius II that he banished Liberius, the bishop of Rome, because he had spoken for Athanasius (295 – 373 AD), the patriarch of Alexandria and opponent of the

Arianians. The Church congress of Sardica, which was called in order to compensate the contrary opinion between West and East, awarded to the bishop of Rome highest-judicial authority. The episcopal seat of Saint Peter was the rock on which the Church was erected. Rome remained the centre of the ecclesiastical power although it had lost the political power.

The partition of the Roman Empire had not yet taken a final shape, but the partition, which Diocletian had made in order to reach a better administrative machinery, turned out to be a military necessity under the reign of Constantius II. He was forced to repulse himself the attack of the Persians in the East. He had no choice but to entrust his cousin Julian with the repulse of the Franks and Alemani who invaded the empire by crossing the Rhine.

We write the year 350 AD

Whilst the bishops of the Christian world quarrelled with each other Julian had apostatized from the Church and prepared the reinstatement of the deities in Germania and Gallia (Gaul). That did not happen as superstitious symbol, but within the scope of philosophic interpretation. He wanted to become again a non-Christian emperor later.

This year again the war torches on the Rhine and Danube burnt. By the combats of the usurpators in the interior of the Roman Empire troops were withdrawn from the border north of the empire. That couldn't happen in secret. The reconnaissance patrols of the Germanic tribes saw immediately the weakening on the border and informed their tribes about the situation there. The Franks stormed ahead on all fronts now and ravaged the regions to the south. Some years later followed the Alemani and ravaged the region of Southwest Germany.

In the East the Eastgoths could expand their empire from the Black Sea to the Baltic Sea, that happened under their king Ermanarich.

This empire was the largest Gothic empire that ever existed. After the death of Ermanarich in 375 AD it was destroyed by the Huns.

We write the year 355 AD

The Franks continued to rage in Germania. They destroyed Cologne and ravaged many other Roman towns in the Rhineland In the meantime other Germanic tribes followed the Franks so that their military power had considerably increased.

We write the year 357 AD

The Alemani advanced westward this year and devastated the region between Mainz and Basel. Julian, the cousin of Constantius II, took steps against them now. The Juthungi, an Alemanian tribe, had so wreaked havoc in the last years in Raetia that only fortified mountain settlements had got over the havoc. Now Julian defeated the Alemanian warriors under the leadership of Chnodomar in the battle of Strasbourg (Straßburg). Chnodomar was taken prisoner and Julian pursued the fleeing Alemani without the slightest hesitation. Whilst doing that he devastated their country too. Now he also forced the Alemani to release their Roman prisoners, soldiers and civilians. After that he let erect again a camp of the auxiliary troops, which was burnt down during the reign of Trajan. After the completion legionaries demonstratively marched in there. In full view of the Roman power the Alemanian leaders asked Julian for peace now. They were namely informed that the Romans had brought the Franks to their senses in the meantime too.

Julian, the victor over Alemani and Franks, moved to an old military bivouac on the Seine after his victories. There he began with the extension of this bivouac; later it became a World City, Paris.

We write the year 361 AD

Constantius II wasn't up to the difficulties of the Persian campaign and died suddenly there in the East. Now the Gallian legions proclaimed Julian emperor according to the ancient tradition in Paris. He was to be the last heathen emperor of the Christian Era. His only deed in Germania during his short time as emperor of the Roman Empire was to erect again the buildings in the towns, which the Alemani and Franks had destroyed. This towns he had fortified too, because there were attacks expected of Germanic tribes in future.

Julian was called "apostata" (apostate) in history. The fame he had also acquired by victories over the Persians was clouded by measures against Christianity. He wanted to reshape each faith into philosophy, he was in favour of an agreement amongst the denominations in order to clear the differences. He entitled not only the Christian communities to give their opinion on religious affairs, but also the Jews to do that.

The interlude of Julian's reign was kept like an only holiday in Rome. It might be died out in the greatest part of the ancient senators' families, but the nouveaux riches and the nobility had continued to live in their palaces and gardens. There they lived splendidly as though it was a sacred tradition.

Rome was neither the seat of the military power nor the seat of the political power, but remained the centre of the economic life of the empire. Its businessmen saw to it that the wealth not only survived but also increased. And the very rich idlers of the uppermost classes, whose possession was conducted by employees, saw to it that Rome's inhabitants could enjoy the loved fights of the gladiators, the circus and theatre performances. They shouldn't become aware of the political and military turmoil in the empire. The rich paid for the pleasure of Rome's inhabitants out of their own pocket; that they did only in order to receive a cheering welcome by the masses. But a short time after the death of Julian, who was killed in action during the battle against the Persians in 363 AD, the first dark clouds were already to be seen on the horizon. The new ruler

Jovianus, who was proclaimed emperor by the legions in Asia Minor, had to capitulate soon to the Persian king Schapur. – Jovianus reigned over the Roman Empire only some months.

We write the year 364 AD

Jovianus died on February 17th in Dadaszana and Flavius Valentinian(us) became new emperor of the Roman Empire. He came from Illyria like all the emperors since Diocletian. He took over the power in the western part of the empire, his brother Valens in the eastern part. Flavius Valentinianus continued to extend the limes on the Rhine, that he did above all for the protection of the Gallian "praefectur" (the residence of the highest Roman government official in Gaul). Three big Alemanian hordes roamed about this year in Gaul (Gallia), they plundered, violated and destroyed the villages there. Flavius Valentinian(us) had to stop that now, but only two years later he was successful and could drive the Alemani out of Gaul. Valentinian personally supervised the work on the fortresses of the limes in the Rhine area, therefore he moved house from Milan to Trier. On the limes were renewed the old military camps, were erected new defence buildings and bridgeheads were built on the other side of the Rhine, which were fortified by towers and walls. Ferries made a quick transport for a counterblow possible. Valentinian's conception of a quiet border on the Rhine came true, and by 375 AD, the year of his death, there was peace in Germania Secunda.

Ausonius, Waltrauda and Egonimus

A funny story about a hike through the Dog-Back Mountains (Hunsrück)

Long time ago, the time of the Romans in Germania, the time of the wild Germans, some hundred years later the time of the knights, the time of the castles, in those days we are now. Waltrauda and Egonimus went on a ramble through the time of those days now, a hiking tour through the Dog-Back Mountains near Augusta Treverorum.

It was a good day to go hiking! "Good morning, Egonimus!" "Haaa?" "I said good morning!" "Haaa?" "Isn't your brain clear? Brain storming or didn't you have a good rest in the night?" "I dreamed of Ausonius, my yardstick!" "I thought he was dead!" "No, no, no! We'll see him later in the forest!" "You are sure?" "Yeee, I'm more than sure" "Ok. It will be a surprise; I think so!" "Wife, be quiet!" "Ok, ok, then let's go!" – So both started off on their hiking tour. It was a cold morning in the spring time when they left the village Doina, that little village that the people called Gräfendhron later on.

Waltrauda and Egonimus wanted to follow the trail of Ausonius. A short time later they went over a Roman bridge; it was the bridge over the river Doina. Where was the Roman guard? They could see nobody there. The day was too cold for the Romans, therefore the guard had given up watching over the bridge on that day. Thus Waltrauda and Egonimus could pass the bridge without hindrance. The way was steep now and the mountain high. But where was the Roman road? Nothing of this road they could see! But it was a good way and some minutes later they saw the head of Ausonius on a tree. "Hello Ausonius, we are glad to see you here!" "Egonimus, it is only his picture! Drunken?" – Many minutes later then the next picture of Ausonius on a tree. "Egonimus, pssssssssssst! It is only his picture again !" – And half an hour later, the way finished in a thicket. "Egonimus, where is our way ahead now?" "I don't know!" "I thought Ausonius would show us the way!" "I thought so too. But where is Ausonius?" "You saw him always! And now?" "There, look at the tree; I can see his head there." "Ok, then we go in this direction!" "Ooooooh… Aaaauuuhh, shit...Brennnnessssel!" "What do you mean?" "Breeeennnnnessssel!" "I don't understand what you mean!" "Brrreeeennnnnneeeeessssselllll!" "What?" "Stinging nettles!" "Now I know what you mean!" "But we have to go through that what I feel in this moment in order to find the right way. Shit!" "Ok, you first!" "I ??? I've had enough of feeling these plants here!" "Yes, you first, and don't make such a fuss, go now!" "When we have problems, then always I first" "Yes, that is life!" – "Yeee, through the thicket and the stinging nettles!" "So it's right! Now it's my way free. The nettles are down and I can walk like Ausonius." "And my legs?" "These are your legs and not mine. I repeat: That is life!" – Some minutes later. "Hi, Ausonius, we are happy to see you again. Now show us the way like before!" – And Ausonius showed the way through the dense undergrowth and the nettles. In this case the lances (walk sticks) helped to beat the way free.

On the way further on, Ausonius was smiling from a tree. "Hi, walkers, I hope you will have a good hike today! When you started off to go hiking, the weather was bad; now I promise that it will be better later on! So, my friends, good bye." – "Waltrauda, what do you think about Ausonius?" "He is well and you are dreaming, because he died a long, long time ago. Now go on, we have still a long, long way!" – So Ausonius (his picture) showed them a good way through the deep forest again. After one hour they reached the ridge and left the forest. In front of them was the old village Hagum. Here they hoped to have a drink in the tavern of an old village woman. But all the people of this area knew that this woman often closed her shop. So she shut up the door always in the noon too. "Waltrauda, what time is it?" "Twelve o'clock in the noon!" "Oh dear, she has shut up the door!" "What would Ausonius do if he were thirsty?" "He was always lucky and was a famous man; so all taverns opened their doors for him!" "And where is our luck? Please make her open the door!" "Ok., I try, but help!" Thus they knocked at the door; later they trod and kicked against the door! But the old woman was deaf; she kept the door shut. "Shit!" Waltrauda's back ached because she was missing a good seat to have a rest up to now. And this bad luck now! Thus they had to go further on. In far remoteness they saw the castle of the old Hunold, an old Germanic warrior. That was a goal at least. But first the way guided down into a deep valley. On the way down into the valley they intended to have a rest within a small lateral meadow valley. A rest would be necessary, because Waltrauda had more and more back-ache now. The reason for this was walking over pavement of the last part of the ancient Roman road. Now they were on a loamy public way. But when both of them reached the small meadow valley they had to settle with the fact that the resting-place was engaged by Romans on hiking tour. Oh, oh, poor Waltrauda, no possibility for resting again. Thus both of them had to continue the way. More down in the big valley there was an old wooden bridge over the Doina and some metres before that the longed for possibility for resting, a seat. No other Roman or Teutone close by.

Waltrauda and Egonimus enjoyed the silence and the "met" (stupis!!!) they had with them for quenching the thirst if they didn't find an open tavern. – The way to the castle was very hard for hikers. And now, what a surprise! The old castle of Hunold, the Germanic warrior of the Dog-Back Mountains, was only a ruin and was conquered and destroyed long, long ago. Nobody built up again this ruin. And the knight Hunold had died a long, long time ago too. But in the nearness there was a Roman manor house!? Egonimus and Waltrauda were despairing; with the last effort they went further on.

In the meantime the sun appeared and it wasn't so cold as before. Soon they saw a group of trees on the meadow hill, behind this group a building. When they approached they saw the manor house and its adjoining buildings, cows grazed beside it and (modern) wagons parked near this. Were these Roman and Germanic tourists? – Now Waltrauda and Egonimus had reached the manor house. It wasn't a Roman manor house, it was a Germanic one. Germanic meal and beer? So to go in quickly! – Old Germanic furnishing and how fine, Germanic meal, an "urig" (earthy) meal for Germanic gourmets. So they could start off a short time later on their way home. The sun was favourable, too. Half an hour later on they had a stop on a deep-green meadow. From here they had a wonderful view over the hills of the Dog-Back Mountains. It was quiet, slightly windy with the scent of wild springtime flowers. A stop to enjoy the nature! – One hour later they started off again on the way home. No Romans, no

Germanic people they met on the way. So they reached again the valley of the Doina. Here they had to cross a creek over a wooden bream. The old Roman bridge was destroyed and no Roman legionary had renewed it. The following meadow valley offered a fantastic view. Inviting for staying, but Waltrauda and Egonimus didn't have time enough because the evening drew near. Soon they had reached the next bridge over the Doina. It was an old Roman bridge again but without guard. Thus they could pass unprevented from doing it. From afar they heard the wild howling of some Germanic people. When they approached they saw a Germanic festival taking place with much "met" (old Germanic beer). Egonimus and Waltrauda didn't have the possibility to evade this hospitable place. They were already bowling welcomed. "Hi you both! Romans or Franks or...?" "We are Franks from the north." "Hey boys, they are Franks, our brothers! And where are you coming from?" "What do you mean? From here or where we are living for the other time? Because we are tourists !" "Where do you live the other time?" "In the Franconian province North-Rhine." "So you are Merowingians?" "No, no, we would say: Cherusci or Cheruskers." "Like Arminius?" "Yes, that you can say so!" "Boys, these are our friends, because enemies of the Romans too, so they are ok. Have a drink? Stupi or our met? You can choose, met or draft beer, how do you say in the north today?" "Waltrauda, what do you wish?" "Draft beer! Is better for us now!" "Ok, boys, two glasses of draft beer!" – Thus Waltrauda and Egonimus enjoyed this very good beer, or better, Germanic met. "Boys, thanks for these drinks, the best of today and good bye." "Good bye, friends!"

No sooner Waltrauda and Egonimus had left this hospitable place than they saw the picture of Ausonius again. Now he showed them the way home. Some minutes later on they crossed the next Roman bridge close to the village Doina. – "Waltrauda, what do you think, is Mrs. Circleear waiting for us?" "I think so, because we are very late back." "Tired?" "More than tired! I need a bed! I'm kaputt, down!" "You have still to wait some minutes, then you'll have the possibility!" "The last hours it was also too hot! So I thought, it would be better winter time!" "Like the time with the kids in the Alps?" "But a little bit warmer, then ok!" "And Mrs. Pignest is waiting for us with a Jagertea!" "No, beer is better now!" – "Hi, Mr. and Mrs. Herring,

I was worried because you are so late back!" "Oh – Mrs. Circleear, we had some drinks with some Franconian friends close to here. The best draft beer of the world." "Ok then. But I heard that some wild Huns are in our forest. As you know, long, long time ago our people built stone ramparts for the defence against the Huns. These ramparts you can find everywhere here today." "Yes, we saw them. Therefore perhaps the other name for these mountains:
Huns' Back Mountains." "Right; here it's usually to say Huns' Back Mountains; only some people say Dog-Back Mountains." – "You said 'wild Huns'. But we think that we have another time today." "It's right, but enough wild people too. – What do you think, a good supper now? I think that you are hungry!" "Yes, yes, a good idea, a typical Germanic supper, that is what we need." "Egonimus, stupis and schnapps and then good night, with a good bed, that's what we need now too." "Ok, ok, Mrs. Circleear, I think that you heard what my wife wants more." "Of course, you are my guests!" – "Waltrauda, a good pension here!" "What do you mean?" "I said, a good pension!" "I don't know, what you mean!" "Pension is like guesthouse." "Please, so say guesthouse and not pension." "Sorry, we are in Germania here and therefore I say pension." "But pension is like money for the retirement!" "Yes, in England, but not here." "England is an Anglo-Saxon land and thus a Germanic country too." "Yes, Germanic a long, long time ago!" – "So, now I have my supper." – Later: "Good night, Waltrauda, have a good rest night!" "Thanks, you too!" – So the day had gone.
(stupi = a little bottle of beer; a word of some people in the western mountains of the Hunsrück)

Ausonius has lived indeed. Decimus Magnus Ausonius was born 310 AD and died about 393 AD. He was teacher of the grammar and the rhetoric in Bordeaux (France), later then princes' teacher in Treverorum (Trier). He wrote the poem "Mosella", a river boat trip on the Moselle, and "Bissula", a poem's cycle. Also he often went on a ramble through the Dog-Back Mountains near Treverorum, therefore a hiking way from Trier (Moselle) through the Hunsrück to Bingen (on the Rhine) was named after him too. Of course Ausonius could profit by the well-finished Roman military roads on his hike through the dense primeval forest of this area of those days.

The beginning of the great Gothic period

We write the year 375 AD

Gratian, the son of Valentinian and just 16 years old, became new ruler of the western part of the Roman Empire. Some years ago the commander of the army of his father, Severus, had ambushed the invading Saxons and inflicted a crushing defeat on them in the area of the mouth of the Rhine. Thus the northern flank was no longer threatened and Gratian could turn to the Alemani and Juthungi, who still operated separately from the Alemani. Both tribes now invaded as ever the regions on the other side of the Rhine and Danube. Gratian took on the Alemani now by Colmar in Alsace (Elsass) and inflicted a crushing defeat on them too. Only 5,000 Alemanian warriors survived the slaughter, more than 35,000 Germanic warriors were killed in action. The young imperator pursued the pitiful remainder of the once so proud Alemani, after the battle. While doing that he annihilated all that was in his way, a way full of cruelty up to the Black Forest, deep on Alemanian ground. But that was to be the last campaign of a Roman ruler on the right side of the Rhine.

This year was to become an important year for world history too. A Turkish-Mongolian steppe's race, the Huns, had invaded Europe and had annihilated the empire of the Alani (Iranian steppe's people who settled to the north of the Caucasus, in South Russia). After that they had subdued the Eastgothic Empire, the great empire of Ermanarich.

The Goths, this Germanic tribe from Scandinavia, had already split up more than 100 years ago. Both Gothic parts, the Westgoths (Visigoths) as well as the Eastgoths , now settled in South Russia by the Black Sea.

The Eastgothic Empire was destroyed and the people had to perform war service for the Huns Now the Westgoths (Visigoths) were in danger of suffering the same fate. Athanarich, the king of the

Westgoths, found himself compelled to lead his people into the Balkans now. In those days, 375/76 AD, there was an exceptional pressure on the Roman frontier, caused by the Westgoths who crossed the Danube and marched southwards. On the Balkan Peninsula they asked the Romans for protection under their weapons; that was the only chance to save their lives, the only chance that they saw in this situation.

The Romans took advantage of the situation of the Goths, they integrated the fleeing Westgoths into their defence system on the Balkans. The Huns, who overran the Goths, could be a danger to Rome sooner or later, therefore the Romans provided shelter for the Westgoths now, but for it they had to renounce heathenism. Gratian in the West and Valens in the East saw in it the main reason of the warlike behaviour of the Germanic tribes. That was understandable. Now Christianity was state religion in the Roman Empire, but the heathen time was not yet so long ago that heathenism could be considered to be completely wiped out. There was an example only some years before, during the reign of Julian. It was a risk to integrate big heathen units into the Roman defensive alliance for the frontier on the Danube at that time.

We write the year 376 AD

The Westgoths had reached their goal and settled on Roman ground to the south of the Danube, but that they only reached proving their Christian faith before. They had been able to pass the frontier by behaving like Christians, in this way they had convinced the Romans of their real faith too.

We write the year 378 AD

The Westgoths had two leaders who weren't friendly facing each other. Both leaders, Athanarich and Fritigern, were equipped with the strongest authority amongst a group of "gau-"princes. But Fritigern's group was especially hard exploited since settling in the eastern part of the Roman Empire. It is reported on their exploitation: "It happened to them, as it not seldom happened to people who are not yet resident, that they were struck by a heavy famine. Fritigern, Alatheus and Safrak, who ruled as princes and dukes over them, had pity on their people who suffered from the considerable lack of food, therefore they tried to establish trade relations with the Roman leaders Lupicinus and Maximus. But what satisfies the damned hunger for gold? The Roman commanders sold to them for a high price, full of greed, not only the meat of sheeps and cows, but also carrion of dogs and other animals. So they demanded one slave for one bread or ten pounds meat. When the household effects ran out the Roman businessmen, exploiting the predicament, demanded the children. The parents accepted that worrying about their descendants since they were convinced that it would be better to lose their freedom than their lives. Also it seemed to be less cruel for them to sell a member of the family, and so to take care of him, than to hold him back and to leave him to death from starvation then."

Here was reported that last crisis of the Westgoths during the reign of Athanarich and Fritigern, which led to the establishment of a single kingdom, but also to a deep hatred of Romans that was in no way inferior to Attila later. Athanarich, the wiser and older of the both leaders, had no illusions about the inhabitants of the eastern part of the Roman Empire. He knew that hungry Goths would be an object of merciless exploitation for Levantinians, Greeks and the whole of the Byzantinian mixture of peoples. So the Romans first allowed only women and children to cross the Danube, by it they were namely at their mercy, an object of their business. After that they demanded of the Goths to hand over their weapons, then they made them an offer of dead dogs as food, that the Goths had to pay in gold as an offset. The hunger must have been dreadful, all people seemed to be finished, they couldn't take any more, then never else they would have put up with this shame.

However, the Goths could reach to keep their weapons, they had enough weapons for an attack of defence. When Athanarich had gone into the mountains because he had a grudge against Fritigern, the Goths turned to Fritigern who soon was to have every reason to be in possession of weapons. So there was reported an occurrence: "In this hard time the Roman commander Lupicinus invited the Gothic prince Fritigern to a banquet. He intended an insidious murder as the course of the day showed. Fritigern came with a small escort to the banquet without dreaming that it was intended to kill him. Whilst he dined with the governor in the official house, he heard the shouting of his men who were intended to be murdered miserably; they were shut in another part of the palace of the governor .Fritigern saw the insidiousness now, he drew his sword, escaped with great boldness and quickness and snatched the threatening death from his companions."

This occurrence enraged the Goths so much that they attacked the Romans at Adrianopel (Bulgaria, near the Turkish frontier) this year. Ammianus Marcellinus, a Chief of Staff in the army of Valens, reported the battle, a battle which Valens took alone because he feared he had to share the fame with the fellow emperor Gratian. Ammianus Marcellinus said: "From everywhere clashed weapons with weapons, and missiles flew through the air. The war goddess Bellona, more raving than any time before, let the trumpets horribly ring out for the annihilation of the Romans. Our legionaries still offered resistance cheered up by encouraging shouts, but the battle spread out like a sea of flames and frightened all combatants on the battle ground when some of them were hit by whirling lances and arrows. Now both battle ranks clashed like ships with beaks, as a result they were thrown around. Our left flank approached up to the last Gothic defence line formed by wagons. Our legionaries certainly would have penetrated through this line if there was any support, but the remainder of the cavalry left them in the lurch. Thus the legionaries of the left flank were crushed as if they were hit by the mass of a collapsing dam by the Goths, the remainder was separated by the enemy then. Now the foot troops were without cover and their detachments stood so closely packed that each legionary could hardly draw his sword. Nobody could see the sky because of the raising dust, only the ghastly shouting echoed from there. Thus the fatal missiles, which were flying on all sides, hit definitely every man and caused deep wounds. One couldn't see them coming and take cover from them."

Here Ammianus Marcellinus surely described the annihilation of a great part of the foot troops in the hilly environs of Ardianopel, where the defeated army of Valens could not any more retreat to. Each ravine was a trap and the Romans, who had to combat crowded here, were at a mortal disadvantage compared with the moving Germanic warriors who could use their spears and slingshots.

Ammianus Marcellinus continued with his report as follows: "When now the barbarians, pouring into immense crowds, man and horse trampled down and there was nowhere a possibility for a retreat of the compressed detachments, a dense gathering rather robbed us of the last possibility of escaping too, put down also our combatants the fear of death, they took the swords again and massacred the attackers. There one could see some barbarians who clenched their teeth in proud defiance, with cut hollow of the knee or cut off right hand or pierced side still let their wild gaze wander for a short moment before their death. But the wild combatants fell to the ground during a hand-to-hand fight, so that the ground was covered all over with their dead bodies. The lamenting shouting of the dying warriors sounded horribly. In the middle of this big chaos and general muddle the foot troops were limited to the efforts and danger; there were missing strength and determination for another methodical line of action. The majority of the lances was broken by the constant clash, so the Romans had to seek refuge with the drawn swords and to throw themselves on the dense lot of enemies with defiance of death – because they saw blocked up each escape route everywhere."

One can get no general idea of the arrangement and course of the battle by this report, but there was said in plain terms that the Roman army was completely encircled and compressed in the hilly area. Valens had underestimated the Goths. Only Victor, a general of the cavalry, had warned against the Goths and their combat strength; he had got into trouble with them several times, therefore he advised Valens to wait for the reinforcements from the western part of the empire and to keep the Goths on a string till then. But Valens saw it differently, Victor was only a pessimist for him who didn't see the certain victory, therefore he cast Victor's advice to the wind.

The Romans seemed to be in the dark about the numerical strength of the (West-)Goths too. A man of the reconnaissance patrol had reported wrongly there would be (only) ten thousand Gothic warriors; that lulled Valens into a false sense of security now, he had about 15,000 combatants at his disposal, experienced legionaries, an army of soldiers coming from several legions. But the Westgoths had 30,000 warriors at their disposal indeed.

The Westgoths went all out by Adrianopel, they had mobilized all men who could bear arms. It was a political war, their victory was an absolute victory because Valens didn't survive this black day of his army. But he didn't die like a hero whilst fighting against the enemy. Ammianus Marcellinus wrote about his death the following words: "There was said... Valens hadn't immediately done his last breathe, but some bodyguards and eunuchs had carried him into a near country house because a wound caused by an arrow had prevented him from going. This house had two floors and was fortified. Whilst one took care of Valens' wound he was besieged by the enemies, who didn't know about his person there; so he could escape from the disgraceful captivity. When now his pursuers tried to break open the barred door and were bombarded from an "altan" (balcony, buttressed up by pillars) with arrows, they collected in a hurry, in order not to be hindered in plundering by delaying tactics, straw and dry twigs and set fire to the heap before the house then, so that it was on fire too. All what was inside was burning now. Only one bodyguard could escape the flames by jumping through the window. But he was taken prisoner by the barbarians and told them who had been in the house. Now they regretted Valens' death very much because they had cheated themselves out of the fame, they could have captured the emperor of the (eastern) Roman Empire. The bodyguard, who could escape the flames, came back to our line later and reported how Valens died."

The Westgoths were very annoyed at the missing ransom, but here they had let a good opportunity slip because the rich inhabitants of

112

Byzantium should have had to pay in gold for their emperor and that accordingly to his weight. But this date, the 9 August, brought yet enough loot for the Goths, and there was above all the end of the Roman resistance, all regions up to the Bosporus were abandoned, they were occupied by the Westgoths. The exceptional location of Adrianopel on the three rivers Tundža, Arda and Merìca the battlefield had narrowed down so that the vehemence of the Westgoths had to triumph over the legions. There was no regulated retreat of the units, also Victor, who wanted to help the emperor out of his situation, didn't find anyone who could follow him. – Only one third of the proud Roman legions had survived the slaughter, fleeing in all directions of the wind.

Ammianus Marcellinus still reported how the Westgoths tried in vain to conquer Adrianopel and how the officials, citizens and a part of the remainder of the defeated legions defended the town. Their own wildness, mixed with hatred for the Romans, robbed the Westgoths of the fruit of their victory, of the loot which they could have in the rich town and the treasure of Valens, when three hundred defenders formed up and broke out of the own lines in order to desert to them (the Goths). But they were slaughtered without mercy by the warriors of Fritigern. Since the other defenders saw the fate of the deserters, none of them followed the traitors. Now all defenders combated with utmost bravery, they knew what was in store for them.

The Westgoths finally grew weary of the bloody assault on the town walls and joined their companions who had devastated the flat country long ago. There was a horror, which was no longer described by Ammianus Marcellinus. He finished his book of history with the chapter of the death of Valens and the words: "So I have as only soldier and Greek, beginning with the ruling period of Nerva and finishing with the death of Valens, reported the course of the events correspondingly to my modest talent; I believe to have also never knowingly lent my name to the distortion of a work, that only seemed to correspond to the truth, by keeping silence or saying the untruth."

113

Fritigern gave the Romans time for the recovery from the shock. The Romans called an experienced veteran back, his name was Theodosius, who should combat the Westgoths now. One year later Theodosius became emperor of the eastern part of the Roman Empire and Gratian accepted him as Augustus of the East.

We write the year 380 AD

Theodosius shook hands with the Westgoths and reached an agreement. He awarded the Roman provinces Dacia and Moesia as permanent settlement's area to them. But the Westgoths had to obey the command of the Roman army leaders for it.

We write the year 381 AD

Athanarich, who had gone into the eastern Carpati with a small part of his people, was driven out of these mountains by their own tribal members. He, who had always shown an irreconcilable behaviour towards the Romans, went to Constantinopel (Byzantium) and made it up with Theodosius. But some days later he was dying already. Then on 25 January he was at his last gasp and died in the course of this day in the imperial city. Perhaps an obliging eunuch had brewed a fatal drink to the best man of the Gothic camp; nobody knows that because the phalanx of the praise's singers was greater at the court of Theodosius than at the court of Constantin the Great. And now God did Theodosius another favour too; in the following year Fritigern died, the big adversary of Byzantium, and Alarich, the conquerer of Rome later, was still a child and so there was no danger for the empire at the moment.

We write the year 395 AD

Since many years the Salians, the Franconian group of the Lower Rhine region, had settled in Toxandria (northern part of Brabant, today a province of the Netherlands). That they did in agreement with Rome. But now they threatened again the Roman Empire, so that the Romans felt insecure in their northern provinces, and gave up Treverorum (Trier), their important residence town in Belgica. Also the Vandals were to threaten soon both Roman provinces of Germania. They had already started their big migration from Hungary, where they were the neighbours of the Westgoths, and were marching westwards now. Also the Burgundi sowed again discord, they moved towards Upper Germania, it was an endless train of people who soon reached this Roman province.

In 394 AD Theodosius could unite once more the Roman Empire. Now he died on 17 January in Milan. The Roman Empire was divided again. Arcadius, the son of Theodosius and just eleven years old, became heir of the eastern half of the empire, and Honorius, just ten years old, inherited the western half. But in Rome ruled Stilicho indeed, who was a Vandal. He substituted for Honorius, the minor emperor. The death of Theodosius was a great moment for Stilicho. Theodosius had put him in charge of all troops of the western half of the empire just before his death. Amongst them were also the victorious legionaries who had defeated the counter-emperor Eugenius. The control of the entire army was the decisive fact now that Rome had furnished a man with might, who was to be superior opponent of Alarich, whose reign over the Westgoths had begun this year too.

Stilicho should prevent the separation of both parts of the empire, that had been the intention of Theodosius. He had not been able to find a better man for this job than Stilicho, because each other man would have taken a risk of great significance if he had made it his business to do that what Stilicho did. Also Gainas and Bauto, two educated Germanic commanders of the Roman legions, had not the capability of Stilicho, only he was the great warrior, great commander and statesman, thus a man who was needed for each alarming situation.

Stilicho descended from a princely family of the Vandals. His father was already a high commander of the legions, so that Stilicho could receive an excellent Roman education. But he had never forgotten his Germanic descent. He spoke three languages: General-German-ic, a general Germanic idiom, the so-called lingua franca of the migration's tribes, then Latin (West Rome) and Greek, the language of the eastern half of the Roman Empire.

Stilicho rose quickly because of his bravery and became favourite of the emperor. In 383 AD he was sent to Persia as head of a delegation, then he was about twenty-five years old, so he was not yet forty years old when Theodosius died, a man in the prime of life.

Stilicho didn't oppose the main rival for the power after the death of Theodosius, he knew Rufinus and his dangerousness, but he left Italy in spite of the risk of losing control over the empire by a plotting Rufinus. He went with a small troop into the Rhine area, an unrest had broken out again there. Now he showed his talent, his quickness and cleverness during a campaign against the Germanic nation and excited admiration. He must have impressed the Germanic tribes on the Rhine by his personality and his words, because after the conclusion of a peace treaty the Rhine region was at peace for many years.

We write the year 396 AD

Back from the Rhine region, Stilicho immediately turned against the east; there the Westgoths under the leadership of Alarich sowed discord, roaming about they plundered above all in Greece. Perhaps he had found out that Rufinus' estates had been spared the plunders by the Westgoths, which was suspicious. Alarich was no blindgreedy barbarian. He was clever enough to know that he could tip the scales in favour of his own interests, that he could play with Rufinus, the imperial administrator in Byzantium and right hand of Arcadius (emperor of the East) and Stilicho.

When now Stilicho met Alarich, it was a bizarre situation, two Germanic men of royal lineage were at war with each other on Roman ground, a Vandal led Roman legionaries against Goths.

Alarich, who had been commander of the Gothic army since 391, was proud that he had pulled the chestnuts out of the fire for Theodosius, the Roman emperor. The Westgoths had fought in the first front during the battle in 394 AD, the battle against the counteremperor Eugenius, who was defeated by their bravery. When Theodosius died in January the year before, Stilicho, his imperial administrator and general, had released the Gothic troops. The Gothic warriors had withdrawn after that, they went into the region, which the Romans had let them have, the landscapes of Lower Moesia, the long stripe of land between the confluence of Save and Danube in the west and the today's Dobrudža (Dobrogea) in the east. The Goths had hesitated to get down to doing farmer's work again, first they grumbled then they did it yet so far away from rich towns, which they had seen during the war, towns that ought to be their property; they had merited them by rights because they had had hardly possibilities of plundering, which was very disappointing, which racked their brains, more, they got furious, no, they were seething properly with rage.

Now the Westgoths moved plundering through Thracia, Macedonia and Thessalia. But Stilicho didn't intend to let put at risk his great goal, the power over the whole of the Roman Empire, by the dissatisfied Goths from Lower Moesia. His troops had encircled the Gothic fortification of wagons before Alarich could say Jack Robinson; there was every indication that Stilicho could reach a great success, the Goths, who were belligerent shortly before, scoured in vain the slopes of the mountains for an escape now, but then came the rescue at the last moment. A horseman, a courier of the emperor of Constantinopel (Byzantium), had a message for Stilicho: The young emperor, a lad under the care of Rufinus, ordered Stilicho to leave again the ground of the East Roman Empire, because he, the emperor, hadn't sent for him.

Stilicho knew, these weren't the words of the twelve years old emperor, these were the words of Rufinus, his opponent in Byzantium. Stilicho followed the order and withdrew with his West Roman troops, thus Alarich's life was saved and the lives of the encircled Goths.

The troops of the eastern Roman half were under the command of Gainas, a Germanic man like Stilicho. Now these troops came from the front without having fought there. Rufinus had to meet them with a splendid reception now, because they had been victorious for Theodosius once. So Rufinus and his young emperor rode to meet them. Rufinus wore a Germanic fur, by it he wanted to honour Gainas, the Goths. He wore it over the shoulder like a Germanic prince too.

Rufinus personally welcomed all known officers with flattery. Soon he was encircled by Gothic captains, atrocious faces of barbarians, who attacked him with their swords. He had no longer a chance to call for help. Arcadius didn't hear nothing, nothing of the last gasp of a dying man, his imperial administrator. Stilicho had an opponent less, but he was many days' marches away from Byzantium; he saw no possibility to take over the power there too, then there was suddenly a new opponent, a eunuch, Eutropius, who became successor of Rufinus.

Another man was glad about the intrigues at the court of the Roman Empire, it was Alarich, the young king of the Westgoths. The West Roman troops left the Balkans and were on the way to their Italian garrisons, in the eastern part of the empire ruled a greedy slave, who had put the pretty Eudoxia into Arcadius' bed in order to keep the emperor busy. The Westgoths had to show no consideration for anyone now, Greece was ahead of them, they could soon plundering and stealing penetrate the holy ground like their fathers and grandfathers, who penetrated Anatolia and had plundered in the eastern region of the Mediterranean Sea.

The Roman emperors after Caesar

Augustus	27 BC–14 BC
Tiberius	14 BC–37 AD
Caligula	37–41
Claudius I	41–54
Nero	54–68
Galba	68–69
Otho	69
Vitellius	69
Vespasian	69–79
Titus	79–81
Domitian	81–96
Nerva	96–98
Trajan	98–17
Hadrian	117–138
Antonius Pius	138–161
Marc Aurel	161–180
Lucius Verus	161–169
Commodus	(177) 180–192
Pertinax	193
Didius Julianus	193
Pescennius Niger	193–194
Clodius Albinus	193–197
Septimus Severus	193–211
Geta	(209) 211–212
Caracalla	(198) 212–217
Macrinus and Diadumenianus	217–218
Elagabal	218–222
Severus Alexander	222–235
Maximus Thrax	235–238
Gordian I	238
Gordian II	238
Pupienus	238
Balbinus	238
Gordian III	238–244
Philippus Arabs	244–249

Decius	249–251
Tebonianus Gallus	251–253
Volusianus	251–253
Aemilianus	253
Valerian	253–260
Gallienus	(253) 260–268
Postumus (only in the Gallian Empire)	259– 68
Claudius II, Goticus	268–270
Victorinus (only in the Gallian Empire)	268–270
Quintillus	270
Aurelian	270–275
Tetricus (only in the Gallian Empire)	270–274
Tacitus	275–276
Florianus	276
Probus	276–282
Carus	282–283
Numerianus	283–284
Diocletian	284–305
Maximian	286–305
Carausius (only in Britannia)	286–293
Allectus (only in Britannia)	293–296
Galerius	305–311
Constantius Chlorus	305–306
Flavius Severus	306–307
Maxentius (Usurpator in Rome)	306–312
Maximinus Daia	309–313
Licinius	308–324
Constantin I (the Great)	(306) 324–337
Constantin II	337–340
Constantius II	337–361
Constans	337–350
Julian Apostata	361–363
Jovianus	363–364
Valentinian I	364–375
Valens	(364) 375–378
Gratian	375–383
Magnus Maximus	383–388
Valentinian II	(375) 383–392

Eugenius	392–394
Theodosius the Great	(379) 394–395

Emperors of the West Roman Empire

Honorius	(393) 395–423
Constantius III	421
Johannes	423–425
Valentinian III	425–455
Petronius Maximus	455
Avitus	455–456
Maiorianus	457–461
Libius Severus	461–465
Anthemius	467–472
Olybrius	472
Glycerius	473–474
Julius Nepos	474–480
Romulus Augustulus	475–476

Alarich in Rome

We write the year 400 AD

Between the end of the fourth century and the beginning of the fifth century the kingdom of the Hermunduri in Thuringia was founded. They were the neighbours of the Chatti . That was also the birth of a new Germanic tribe, the Thuringi (Thuringians), who came into being by the fusion of the northern part of the Hermunduri into the Anglo-Saxons and Warni (a small insignificant Germanic tribe).

This year Greece was far away from those virtues by which it had won eternal fame in the fifth and fourth century before Christ. The Greeks didn't even try to stop Alarich's troops in the pass of the Thermopyls, which they could have defended easily. The Greek towns negotiated immediately about contributions at the sight of the attackers. Also Athens, the dedication's place of the Romans who sought Greek education and culture here, capitulated. But the Goths made merciful stipulations. The inhabitants of Athens had to hand over a part of their possession, which they had accumulated in many years, only. They were no people of thinkers in the meantime, they were people of business and shipowners now. Alarich went on horseback and as victor with a small escort only into this famous town. His Gothic warriors protected the town gates during his stay there. The inhabitants spoiled him and could soon find out that he, a king of an unknown nation, had an impeccable behaviour at the table and good manners. But there was great grief in the many burn-ing villages and in the families. They were at the mercy of the Goths and weren't spared cruel deeds. The female prisoners came under martial law, because to have the pleasure of enjoying the beauty was the reward for bravery. There was no resistance of the Greeks, also Sparta, the most martial town of Greece, capitulated without resistance.

Greece was past help, the disaster had happened. Now one had to punish the malefactors only to put the Goths off. Stilicho therefore came running up with West Roman troops. The new imperial mentor, the eunuch Eutropius, had called for help. So Stilicho could be at war on East Roman ground. He pushed his way directly into the happenings by disembarking before Korinth. So his troops didn't get all the bad breaks of a troublesome advance. Stilicho defeated the Goths. His success was due to a surprise attack. He also knew that plundering armies fought badly. He knew too that Germanic warriors could part badly with stolen things, what made them awkward. Therefore he could gloat at his victory over them now, because it was a genial prank again. Alarich was suddenly surrounded on a plateau without water. Arcadia seemed to become a Walhall (Valhöll = in the Germanic mythology the residence of Wotan/Odin, the head of the Germanic deities) for him, when Stilicho decided on a kind of pressure in spite of the loyalty of Byzantium. He gave Arcadius, the emperor of Constantinopel (Byzantium) the ultimatum to send Eutropius into the wilderness and then to confide in him. When Arcadius refused, Stilicho declared Alarich as new ally, although he was defeated by him. But now he couldn't let him die of thirst.

Eutropius was very much annoyed at Stilicho's ultimatum. He declared Stilicho a people's traitor and confiscated his possessions. On the other hand, Stilicho let his arrested adversary escape to win him over again as ally. Now Eutropius began a war against Stilicho; first he entered into a treaty of cease-fire with Alarich, then he was looking for other possibilities to do Rome harm. But he couldn't crack down on him by force of arms, then he would expose himself to danger. He was also aware of the fact, that Germanic men and Huns, the only available troops, would never go to war under the command of an eunuch.

Italy with its towns was always dependent on grain deliveries. These deliveries had come from Alexandria for a long time, but also from the Black Sea, since East Rome grew stronger but more and more from near North Africa. A leader of the pirates, like Sextus Pompeius, could put Octavianus Augustus under pressure, because the hungry Roman rabble coped quickly with an emperor who didn't supply bread. Also now, under the reign of Stilicho and Honorius, Libya was an Achilles's heel of the western empire again. Stilicho

123

had taught the Goths a lesson, therefore he could suppose that they would try to take pleasure in a peaceful country life for some time. But in Libya ruled Gildo, who was a Moorish man. He was in the true sense of the word only a governor of Rome, but he lived pompously like a great king in Carthage.

It seemed that ten years of the most curious excesses had weakened the intellect of Gildo more than his courage. He had taken the creation of a new human race into his head. This race should be piebald, therefore he copulated the prettiest white women and girls of his pirate loot with black and brown athletes. Since these creatures were unicoloured, he thought up the craziest technique of sexual intercourse. So he hoped to create the stain pattern, which he had longed for.

Gildo was an extreme like Eutropius. Therefore it was easy for him to submit himself to the order of Eutropius too, particularly since he hadn't a hard time with the thick sissy of Byzantium who ruled only nominally. Gildo saw that the grain ships to Rome didn't leave the harbour. Now Rome would have been hard-pressed if Stilicho hadn't supplied with lightning speed grain from Gallia. So Rome had enough to eat as long as the conflict was lasting.

Stilicho didn't take the trouble to go to Africa because Gildo had made an embittered enemy by his senseless cruelties. He had his brother's sons killed because he was worried about his throne. Now his brother, his name was Maskezel, thirsted for revenge and Stilicho came to his aid with a legion although he had wanted to avoid trouble before.

Gildo had fought bravely in a Roman legion and gained a high military rank. So he had been a superior adversary to each landing corps, which had to be small of necessity. But by the many years of excesses he went mad. He forgot who his adversary was too. He underestimated the five thousand experienced combatants from Gaul (Gallia), although he was head and shoulders above Stilicho.

Seventy thousand half-naked, shouting and gesticulating combatants encouraged one another when the legionnaires advanced

Castell Saalburg
A reconstruction of an ancient Roman castellum in the mountains of the Taunus

according to their tradition with quiet step. Without shield, half-naked and roaring, so no Roman could be defeated. When Gildo's cadet was cut off the arm and the colours sank down into the sand, the battle was already over. Gildo's combatants scattered to the four winds and Gildo committed suicide in a cave. Stilicho was triumphator again.

We write the year 401 AD

Alarich, the king of the Goths, hadn't made the triumph easy for Stilicho. He was in Epirus, an ancient landscape of the southern part of Illyria, and lurked like a beast of prey. This barren but rich country wasn't enough for the West Goths, therefore Alarich contemplated revenge. He had taken advantage of Stilicho's absence and settled in the region of Epirus. But he didn't know what to do with this mountainous country south of Albania and north east of Greece. The valleys were so separated from each other that there were little principalities until the beginning of the modern times. Alarich considered this country only to be a waiting site for a great action. He negotiated with Byzantium about means for a war against West Rome. The Goths had enough skilled manual workers who accompanied them also when they carried out a raid. The Roman province Illyria supplied moreover tools and iron. So there resounded the hammers in all valleys, sounded clearly the made swords and spears. It was a treasonable noise: Alarich prepared for the great march to Rome and the great fight against Stilicho.

One cannot imagine that a nation making a living by being at war, by stealing or putting mercenaries in action, returned in between to peaceful activity again, that men became farmers and stockbreeders, to say nothing of the wars, which didn't break out when the farmers could just take time for them as soldiers. That was the biggest weakness of the new Roman principle, to take powerful and young people from the infinite reservoir of barbarian vigour into the Roman Empire, to settle and to incorporate into the legions. That didn't go off well with the Goths, because one couldn't expect the life of a homeless leader of mercenaries of Alarich, who had fought at the side of Stilicho and had obtained a high military rank.

Alarich had marched westward. What made him do that? One can be sure the court of Byzantium didn't make him do that. It was his own will, his desire for increase of the already reached advantages, it was the thirst of action of the young and heroic human being aware of his ability. Alarich was certainly glad that a pang of mounted robbers of the Danube area had started to move westward in the first years of the new century, the fifth century. Idle mercenaries of the Huns had joined forces with Alani, with dispersed Eastgoths and other Germanic men and sowed discord. That was no danger for Stilicho; nobody knew better than Alarich, who had experienced the skill warfare of the great Vandalian commander for himself, but he could get some air for the deployment of his own troops in

Dalmatia, a difficult region. Alarich could break out of the barren mountains between Istria and Görz. In the plain of Venice he could supply his troops with provisions now. That was possible because it was a long time ago that there were enemies in the plains.

Since Stilicho was still held up in Pannonia, Alarich effortlessly could defeat Rome set against him. He marched into the Po's plain; he was yearning over and over again for the rich towns there during the hard winter of Epirus. Now he had reached the land of his dreams after the famine on the Balkans. He came before Milan, the residence of Honorius, the imperial town, and surrounded it without respect. Stilicho already cautiously concentrated troops from Gaul and Britain whilst Alarich, the young Gothic leader, roamed about as new ruler over Italy as though Stilicho didn't exist. Stilicho seemed to be ready for risking nothing now: Alarich must fall. But the young Gothic king had learnt in the meantime, and the flat region of northern Italy wasn't comparable with the Peleponnes. When Stilicho finally approached with all his might, the Goths found their way out escaping to Genoa. They seemed to want not to go back into the Krâs/Carso (the barren mountainous region on the peninsula Istra/Istria by Trieste).

We write the year 402 AD

At the beginning of the year Stilicho had to continue his march, wheeling about furthermore, because the Goths could also take the way along the coast of the "Mare Tirreno" towards the south. When the fast Gothic troops had first invaded the Italian Boot then things were looking bad for Stilicho and he had sustained a loss of prestige. Therefore Stilicho, the Vandal, hurried up his scratch troops. As quickly as he had managed the crossing over the Addua when he had saved Milan, he blocked up the way towards south for the Goths now. By Pollentia there was the battle of Easter now.

The Goths had marched from Epirus into the area of Turin, a small migration of peoples. They had marched through ancient Roman territory many hundred kilometres, fighting, conquering and plun-

127

dering. That was an alarming sign, therefore the defeat of this bold invader had to be as impressive as his raid through the original land of the Roman Empire. On 6 April, it was Easter Sunday, both armies met.

To the south of Asti, on the little river Tanaro, where the battle took place, still exists the village Polencia, also called Pollentia. There the ground of a good many vineyards, which contribute to the fame of the "Asti Spumante", covers a number of dead bodies of Gothic warriors and legionaries of Stilicho. Alarich's troops had slopped their plundering advance on Easter Sunday in order to keep this day holy. Stilicho saw his advantage and the carelessness of the Goths and attacked the Gothic bivouac with a small army of selected legionaries. He captured many Gothic warriors, many Gothic women and children went into slavery. But the real armed conflict was settled on the banks of the river, there where the Gothic cavalry could develop, and not in the hilly area, there where the Romans would have had advantages. This battle remained without result for both sides. But Stilicho had achieved that the Westgoths stopped their advance southwards, in direction to the defenceless Eternal City. They had received free withdrawal after the battle but hadn't left Italy. They stayed in northern Italy, there was to be unrest soon.

We write the year 403 AD

Alarich had started going to war again and marched to Verona. But there he was beaten. It was a bloody battle before Verona, the river Adige (Etsch) coloured red with the blood of the killed soldiers, many dead bodies were carried into the sea by the running water. Alarich couldn't reach a free withdrawal after the lost battle, he had to retire into the mountains, into the Roman province Noricum at that time.

Honorius, the young emperor of the West Roman Empire, felt no longer secure in the residence Milan. But which town presented security? Where could people pay their court to him without running the risk of being attacked by marauding Germanic hordes?

Mediolanum (Milan) was too close to the Germanic people, who were sowing discord, and Rome was hopelessly past. So one had to look for a new capital, a safe site, and Honorius made his choice, Ravenna. He had chosen well, because Ravenna was protected landward by swamps and lagoons and seaward by sandbanks.

Now Honorius entered into negotiations with the Westgoths/Visigoths from Ravenna. The stay in the Alps wasn't exactly pleasant to Alarich. He was glad to have the opportunity of leaving these mountains. But Stilicho had blocked up all ways southwards. By the negotiations new possibilities were presented. Alarich could obtain free withdrawal to Illyria by surrender of his fortresses in the region of the Adriatic Sea, so for instance Aquileia too. Honorius promised money, which he urgently needed. Money was very important in order to buy food and material for the new armament. But Alarich should keep still for the aid and agree to go to war for West Rome. That proviso showed why Stilicho had spared Alarich's life, why he let him escape during the massacre on the Adige (Etsch). For Stilicho knew that a strong Roman party agitated against all Germanic people at the court of the emperor, above all against Germanic men, who held a high office. Thus it would have been a half suicide if Stilicho had annihilated Alarich, the mightiest man of the Germanic nation. There could come a situation in which only Alarich was capable of helping Stilicho out. Stilicho had foreseen such a situation and spared Alarich's life therefore. But it didn't work out when the situation was really coming now.

We write the year 404 AD

Alarich had withdrawn. He had reached an agreement with West Rome. For the time being he took no longer interest in conquests. It required much money and many good words amongst old friends and proved enemies to reach that. But Alarich didn't want to be caught between two armies, which moved toward each other. He didn't want to be between two fronts, between two camps. Because there was an adventurer, a man like himself, a Germanic chief named Radagis, who marched with two hundred thousand Alani, Quadi, Eastgoths and Vandals towards Italy.

We write the year 405 AD

The Germanic troops of Radagis had crossed the Danube and the Alps. Nobody could stop their march southwards. Their march southwards was like a flight from a horror, which they had left behind their back, their settlements in which the Huns had caused havoc. There the wild Huns had been merciless, therefore they were it now too. One town after the other fell into their hands. It was more than a campaign of conquest for the Germanic tribes under the command of Radagis, it was a raid too. Only one man could save the West Roman Empire now: Stilicho.

The battle by Fiesole in Tuscany, which Stilicho, the great "Condottiere" of the world history, presented to Radagis, who was with his army head and shoulders above Stilicho (he had ten times more warriors than Stilicho!), lasted only some hours. In the end of the battle the Germanic troops were completely annihilated. Before that, Stilicho had had to withdraw all Roman troops from the Rhine in order to have enough legionaries for the big battle against the Germanic hordes. The Rhineland and with it both Germanic provinces of the West Roman Empire were without military protection now and exposed to any Germanic attack. But Stilicho had won in style the battle and now once more achieved a great success. Also he could take Radagis prisoner and take him to Honorius, chains at hands and feet.

All threats seemed to be eliminated. The surviving Germanic warriors had retired, crossing the Alps again, after the battle. Now it was necessary to strengthen the borders of the remainder of the West Roman Empire, to call up new legionaries and to train them for the next battles. Stilicho, an old hand, had to show that nobody would have a chance of winning a battle if he attacked Roman legions. But it wasn't allowed to underestimate one adversary: Alarich, who was waiting for his chances to come. Stilicho was standing up for holding Alarich peacefully by money and presents. But in his opinion that was only necessary to the moment he was so head and shoulders above Alarich, that the Gothic king was no longer representing a threat for the empire.

We write the year 406 AD

It is true that the Germanic warriors had retired after their defeat, but they had formed a new community this year too. The Burgundi had just founded a new empire on the Rhine, their capital had become Worms, when Vandals, Suebi (who had freed themselves from the Alemani in the meantime again) and Alani invaded together Gaul and devastated this country whilst Vandals, Alani and Suebi went to Spain later, the Burgundi for the time being stayed in Rhineland. Here came into being the German(ic) legend, the "Nibelungen Lied" with Kriemhild, the daughter of the king of the Burgundi, with Siegfried, the king's son from Xanten, who had killed the dragon and was murdered by Worms. Here, close to Worms, the treasure of the Burgundi is said to be buried in the water of the Rhine, from here the Burgundian heroes went to Hungary, to king Etzel (be meant for Attila, the king of the Huns) who had them killed. Only a legend? Perhaps a little bit of truth too!

We write the year 407 AD

Rome withdrew its last troops from Britain in order to protect Italy against the barbarian invasions. So Britain was exposed to Germanic attacks because of missing military protection. As first Germanic tribes invaded the Saxons, then followed the Angli from Schleswig-Holstein, who founded their new country later then in Britannia (Britain), Angloland/England. – After the withdrawal of the Roman legions came into being the English legend too, Arthur and the table knights, Prince Ironheart. Only a legend? Perhaps a little bit of truth too!

We write the year 408 AD

That year was a decisive year: Stilicho got down to his work strengthening of the West Roman Empire. But soon came a bad piece of information to Honorius' ears. His advisers were whispering that Stilicho, who was also his father-in-law, spared no effort to make his own son an emperor. Honorius therefore ordered to kill Stilicho. Stilicho's vassals were certainly able to expel the men, who should carry out the order, without effort, but he preferred to let kill himself.

The message of the arbitrary execution of his friend and enemy was a sign for Alarich to take the offensive. He had marched with his warriors to Carinthia in the meantime. And now some opponents of Stilicho at the imperial court made his work easier. They murdered commanders of the legions, who were friends with Stilicho, because they dreaded their revenge. The ranks mutinied and went over to Alarich, who demanded money from the emperor now, four thousand pounds of gold. But Honorius refused him the payment. Now Alarich stole all he could on the well-known way to Rome by way of compensation for the refused payment.

The Roman senate, which had had no say for a long time, assembled now. During the solemn session the widow of Stilicho, who was in Rome, was found guilty of having sent for Alarich as her helper. She was executed too.

Alarich took revenge for the death of the innocent widow. He had marched for the first time before the walls of Rome at the end of the year, but he didn't force his way into the Eternal City. He didn't want to walk into a death-trap. He saw to it that Rome's supply with foodstuffs was interrupted and was waiting out of the city, in sight of the walls.

The famine the siege involved was terrible. Inhabitants of the Eternal City reported later that many people ate human meat to survive. The senate sent a delegation to Alarich. The high men in their crimson togas asked Alarich for giving the conditions to the surrender of the city. One senator, who wanted to relieve Alarich of making his conditions, mentioned self-confidently that one million Romans were ready to offer resistance. Alarich roared with laughter: "The denser the hay the better it is to be mowed!" But he said too that he would agree to retire with his troops if the city handed over all gold and silver and all movable precious objects.

"What is left for us then?" asked the senators. Alarich answered: "Your life". Now he received five thousand pounds of gold, thirty thousand pounds of silver, four thousand silk togas, three thousand furs and three thousand pounds of pepper.

We write the year 409 AD

Alarich still besieged Rome. But now he was as rich as no other ruler of those days. But what now? Whilst Alarich thought over his next move, where he could go to, Honorius sent an army, made up in a hurry, under the leadership of Sarus, an Eastgoth, against him.

Now caution and patience of Alarich had reached the end. Italy was the country of his dreams, the country of his kingdom. He repulsed the attack of Roman legions and turned again to Rome.

In the course of this year also Vandals, Alani and Suebi reached Spain. Now we are in the middle of the period of the migration of the peoples.

We write the year 410 AD

Alarich was before Rome again and besieged the Eternal City. His headquarters were situated before the Porta Salara near today's Monte Pincio, since there the walls were weak. But the city wasn't taken by storm, the city fell by betrayal. There was a strong barbarian party in the city, slaves and minor people, who weren't willing any more to eat rats and human meat and put up with epidemics in order to save the lives of the riches only.

133

In a night of August the Goths were secretly admitted. Only three hundred selected young warriors are supposed to have entered the city. They threw fire into the houses near Porta Salara, diverted the attention from the defenders by it and made possible that other Goths could force their way into the city during the general confusion.

The Goths raged three days together with Roman slaves in the Eternal City; nobody impeded their doing that. They stole all valuables. Statues were smashed to pieces, and should they be made from precious metal, they were melted down. Jugs, pitchers, pots, furniture, glass ware and so on, thus all articles, which were breakable, were smashed to pieces too. Who resisted the robbery was killed. The slaves violated the wives of their owners. The dead bodies piled up in the streets. Only two buildings were spared the devastation: the Peter's Church and the Paul's Church. People who had taken shelter there survived.

Alarich himself didn't take part in the devastation. But he didn't prevent his warriors and the slaves from doing that too. It was good enough for him having kept his word: They were victorious. Each of his Goths was a rich man now. He called his warriors to order again and left Rome with thousands and thousands of prisoners, amongst them was also Galla Placidia, the half-sister of Honorius. Alarich marched southward now. He wanted to conquer Sicily – after that all of the West Roman Empire. He put down each resistance on his hurried march. But then he suffered an attack of fever during a short rest. The long march through Europe and all the campaigns had spared him death, but now it was approaching.

Alarich died in Cosenza. The slaves who had followed him detoured the course of the river Busento. That should make it possible to dig a spacious grave in the ground of the drained river. There in the dry riverbed of the Busento Alarich was buried. After that the Busento was detoured again, into its former riverbed. All slaves who had done the work were killed. Nobody except the most devoted vassals should know the burial place of the great king. This place should be hidden forever.

The Huns

We write the year 411 AD

Athaulf is the new king of the West Goths. He was still in Italy, with it the West Goths now as ever were a danger for Honorius in Ravenna. But it was a good choice to make a capital of Ravenna. The swamps and lagoons which surrounded this town guaranteed a reliable protection. They were the best legion for Honorius. A conquest of Ravenna by a coup de main seemed to have been a lost cause also for Alarich. But Athaulf, his brother-in-law, who was his successor, didn't try to continue Alarich's campaigns on Italian ground now. He preferred to negotiate. He wanted to have finally suitable areas for settlements to his people. Since he was head of a family and had six adolescent children he was in search of a place of residence of his own.

Athaulf made already out during the first meeting with an imperial delegation that he possessed a valuable pawn, Galla Placidia. The Romans showed no interest in the return of the stolen treasures, but for an assignment of suitable areas to the Goths they made it a condition that Galla Placidia, the half-sister of the emperor, had to be released from prison first.

The negotiations dragged on. The more urgent the demands of the imperial negotiations the more stubborn Athaulf showed himself. Which country should be assigned to the Goths? The territories where they were living before? No! There they went hungry. But the lack of foodstuffs they felt in their present-day camps too. They wanted to set out in any case. But Athaulf gave up Alarich's idea to take the way southwards, to cross over the sea to North Africa, because he was missing of the needed fleet. He didn't have the needed raw material for the shipbuilding and the skilled manual workers for it neither. Also he was in a hurry now.

We write the year 412 AD

Athaulf led his Goths northwards. The Roman province Gallia was always mentioned during the negotiations. The imperial negotiators couldn't keep secret that the "Limes" (a protecting bulwark) on the Rhine was already broken through at many points by Germanic tribes. Athaulf had got to know about rebellions in the northern Roman provinces too. The Romans had sent out some imperial legions therefore. Now the negotiators let him know, if he followed these legions with his West Goths then the emperor in Ravenna would agree to supply grain for his people, provided that Galla Placidia is released from the imprisonment. By this comment on the pretty princess Athaulf became suspicious from negotiation to negotiation. The emotional coldness of the emperor was known. Honorius probably didn't set great store by the release of his half-sister. The Gothic king soon found out that Flavius Constantius, the new adviser of the emperor, wanted to imitate the career of his predecessor, Stilicho, in every respect. Also Constantius wanted to enter in relationship to the emperor. By it he would have not only great influence, but also a claim to the imperial dignity after the death of the childless Honorius. What Flavius Constantius could do, Athaulf could do as well. He approached Galla Placidia to show her his honest intention and rejected his wife and his six children.

The big tribes of the Vandals and Alani had marched through Gaul in the meantime. This West Roman province was in a turmoil in those days. But that was no obstacle to both tribes, also the West Roman legionnaires who advanced in a hurry. Both tribes reached the Pyrenees and invaded the Iberian Peninsula, where there settled the Suebi (it was a part of this Germanic tribe only, the greater part still settled in South Germany and Switzerland in union with the Alemani). When the restless hordes could conquer (North) Africa, West Rome lost its most important possession and its granary too. Now there were open questions. Would Honorius flee to Byzantium and ask for help or even demand of his relatives to be a party to their reign there? Or would it be better to help him, if there was a possibility to help him at all?

It seemed that there was no possibility to help him. Honorius stuck stubbornly to his unfortunate leadership of the state. He was no man who was once bitten twice shy. He recruited warriors of his enemy as auxiliary troops and refused to believe in their disloyalty. It is true that they were at first victorious in his name, but they soon changed sides.

We write the year 413 AD

The negotiators of Constantius really succeeded in putting into action Athaulf and his Goths against the Vandals and Alani (non-Germanic steppe's people from Asia) who still occupied a part of Gaul. That warded off the most pressing danger. But Athaulf was backed up in the negotiations with Constantius by his military successes. Therefore he had made a plan too. If the West Goths settled in the regions, which they had freed from the occupation of Vandals and Alani before, and founded an empire of order in Gaul, then he could be sure to reach what Constantius, his rival in love, strove for, to be in favour with Galla Placidia. He could acquire the claim to the throne by marriage to her and then try to get through this claim by action of his Goths.

We write the year 414 AD

The news of Athaulf's marriage to Galla Placidia shocked the imperial court in Ravenna more than the plunder of Rome by Alarich some years ago. – The marriage was performed in Narbonne, where the Roman wedding customs were carefully observed. Galla Placidia wore a Roman wedding dress, a Roman wedding round dance moved through the halls, and Athaulf had changed his traditional costume, he wore crimson men's dress like a noble Roman now. He took moreover the second seat during the ceremonies. By it he wanted to demonstrate that Galla Placidia, the "imperatrix", was the future empress and the Gothic king the lawful ruler over the Roman province Gallia (Gaul) by virtue of this marriage. His marriage should symbolically show a deep merger of the Romans into the

West Goths, who were the representatives of all Germanic persons who were living on Roman ground.

Honorius agreed to the marriage of Galla Placidia to Athaulf. For he saw a possibility to rule under the strong protection of Athaulf, therefore he didn't want to be at war with him too. Also it was all the same to him whether Constantius or another man was the head of the government. When Stilicho was still alive, he hadn't to be worried about anything. Why shouldn't Athaulf play the part of Stilicho now?

Honorius was too weak to act against the will of the members of the court. He consented to a campaign of Constantius against Athaulf. The war began. In Gaul Athaulf had immediately cut off his supplies of foodstuffs from Italy and Africa. The Goths were no farmers. They were unqualified for the cultivation of farmland, therefore it lay fallow. Athaulf's only way out of a battle was to go to Spain. It had been the way of the Vandals and Alani before. – He crossed the Pyrenees and made his home at the north of the Iberian Peninsula. In Barcelona Galla Placidia gave birth to a son. His name was Theodosius.

We write the year 415 AD

Athaulf and Galla Placidia hoped that owing to the birth of Theodosius, who bore the name of his grandfather, Honorius would make it up with them. But Theodosius died whilst Athaulf's negotiators were still on the way to Ravenna. Theodosius was buried in a silver coffin. Some days later Athaulf was murdered. The murderer was Eberulf, a slip of a Gothic man. Athaulf had made fun of him, therefore he was killed by him during a drinking bout.

Athaulf's successor became Sigerich. But also Sigerich was killed soon. That happened already seven days after his coronation. Wallia, the brother of Athaulf, became king of the West Goths now.

We write the year 416 AD

Wallia was a wild king like some kings before. He forced his way through Spain, a country which was big but sparsely populated. It would have suited him best if he had had the possibility to cross the sea and to land in Africa because there the feeding of his Goths was better guaranteed. But in the autumn Africa was out of his reach, storms dispersed the transport fleet and he couldn't reach Africa any more. Wallia didn't give up, Spain was big and he had a powerful army. He fought with perseverance and energy, so that the emperor in Ravenna got into a sweat.

In Spain Goths fought against Vandals and Alani. That was just what Honorius would have done. But Honorius knew, if he let Wallia have his way only for some months, then Wallia would be the ruler over Spain too. Honorius gave the order therefore that the Goths had to leave Spain again, had to cross the Pyrenees and settle in Aquitania where they had settled before. Then, in Aquitania, they should wait for new imperial orders.

It was a hard decision for the Goths to leave a country that had a luxurious vegetation like Andalusia or the region of Cartagena where they had fought against Vandals and Alani and where they got ready to drive the Suebi out of the Spanish province Galicia. But they followed their king Wallia back to Aquitania. There imperial ships were waiting with breadgrain; grain that Honorius had also sent for them to Spain but wanted to send no longer now.

Constantius was the winner of this haggling about grain. He had so successfully taken action against usurping men that Honorius couldn't refuse him the hand of Galla Placidia now. Galla Placidia was twenty-five years old when she got married to the old Constantius. She was only an object of exchange now, grain for marriage, not more. Before she had lived with a young Germanic man, therefore she struggled against this marriage too. But Honorius did what he could to convince Galla Placidia of the advantage of this marriage.

We write the year 417 AD

Galla Placidia got married to Constantius on 1 January. It was the day when Constantius became consul too, the title "patricius" he held already. Galla Placidia didn't love her husband, but it made her do that he seized the opportunity to become Augustus and co-emperor later. That was the compensation for her, for a marriage without love. In September of the year of 421 AD Constantius died, having been Augustus and co-emperor for just seven months.

Galla Placidia had two children with Constantius. Her daughter Lusta Gratia Honoria was already born that year. On the 3rd of July followed Placidius Valentinianus, who got immediately awarded the title "prince" by Honorius. By it he was candidate for the throne.

We write the year 418 AD

Wallia wasn't fate to become emperor or to be frightened of the murder weapon of an emperor like Stilicho or Aëtius later. Wallia had grain and a little bit land. So he consolidated his reign in To-losa. But there he survived only some weeks, then the little kingdom around Tolosa had a new king, it was Theoderich I who took up the office as king that year.

We write the year 425 AD

Honorius died on 15 August 423 AD in Ravenna. His successor became first Johannes, but this year followed the little son of Galla Placidia, Valentinianus III who had been Augustus since 421 AD. But Galla Placidia took over the power for him. Since 421 AD she was Augusta too. She could settle quarrels and differences of opinion with her relatives in Byzantium only with difficulty. It had required her powers of persuasion to put the leading statesmen of Byzantium off ruling themselves over West Rome, which would have been better in their opinion. They disapproved of a reign of a child and a young woman. The thought of a united Roman Empire came back. It was clear that the past greatness could get restored only if all available forces were united in one person. Advocate of this line was Aëtius, a nobleman from the East Roman empire. The Huns took him prisoner when he was still a child. During his youth he was at the court of Rua, the king of the Huns, as hostage. There he had made friends with his nephews Bleda and Attila. When he came back to Byzantium after the releasing from the hostage custody his knowledge about the Huns was of advantage to him. He reported that the king of the Huns didn't want to continue the migration. But that only as long as his people had suitable areas for their settlements and pastures for their cattle in the conquered territories. They would also keep quiet if the payment of tribute was guaranteed for a long time.

Aëtius was promoted. His ambition increased with each rise in rank. Galla Placidia had made out his talent during some awkward talks. She needed such a man who was young and experienced. She made him the offer of the post of the governor of Gallia. That was a great chance to him, he couldn't let this slip. He accepted.

In no time Aëtius succeeded in throwing the Franconians and Alemani back. They had to retire from the Rhine and to go into the awarded areas. Also the West Goths, who had occupied new areas in the meantime, had to withdraw again. Aëtius was raised to the head of all legions of the West Roman empire after these successes.

The head of all legions was an office, which offered the possibility to realize the plan of his friends in Byzantium. He flirted with the idea of a reversal of roles. He wanted to guide Galla Placidia and not to be guided by her. Galla Placidia was wary against him. She had a presentiment of Aëtius' intention. Therefore she wanted to replace him by Bonifatius, the governor of West Rome in North Africa. But events, which she hadn't expected, prevented her from realizing this.

We write the year 427 AD

Bonifatius wanted to imitate Aëtius's cleverness. He wanted to use the aid of Germanic auxiliary troops too. Therefore he needed the Vandals who were living next and disposed of the numerous ranks.

Wallia, the king of the West Goths, had pushed the Vandals by order of Honorius and his adviser Constantius into the southern province of the Iberian Peninsula many years ago. There in the south they were living now, in Vandalusia (today Andalusia), the country that was named after them. But there in (V)andalusia they were condemned to inactivity. Now they were asked for aid by Bonifatius. But they couldn't yet decide on a campaign in Africa. However, they thought it over this year, the situation was changing some months later.

We write the year 429 AD

Since 428 AD Geiserich was the new king of the Vandals in Andalusia. He was the son of a slave. The Vandals crossed the sea to Africa now. That happened under the leadership of Geiserich. But the Vandals didn't come as allies of Bonifatius, they came off their own bat. The Moorish people (Mauritanians), the native population of the Roman province Mauritania (the inhabitants were named Mauritanians therefore too), welcomed the Vandals. The Mauritanians thought that the Vandals would help them with the elimination of the Roman oppression. Therefore their mounted troops followed the eighty thousand warriors of Geiserich. Also the remainder of the Alani, who had suffered a crushing defeat by the West Goths, were at Geiserich's command. These Alani merged completely in the population of the Vandals, what meant that this tribe ceased to exist.

The concentrated troops of Bonifatius, what happened in a hurry, suffered a crushing defeat by Geiserich. Bonifatius retreated into the coastal town Hippo after a vain attempt to stop the advance of Geiserich.

There he could withstand the siege of Geiserich for fourteen months. The bishop of Hippo, Saint Augustin, tried to help him out of the difficulty by cheering the inhabitants of this town up.

We write the year 431 AD

This year finally ferried task forces of West Rome to Africa. Geiserich was compelled by it to stop the siege. He resisted the arrival of the West Roman empire and defeated its legions. The imperial envoy agreed to an armistice now. He also accepted the conquests of the Vandals on African ground. That was the beginning of a new empire in Africa, the empire of the Vandals there.

Bonifatius, who was no longer governor of Africa, was called back to Ravenna. There he should help Galla Placidia with getting rid of Aëtius, who became high-spirited and too strong in the meantime in spite of the trouble in which he was.

Whilst Geiserich extended his conquests without disturbance, Aëtius fled to the Huns. He succeeded in getting an auxiliary army, for it he promised to let them have the lowlands of Pannonia (today Hungary).

We write the year 432 AD

Aëtius rode hurriedly to Ravenna at the head of the hordes of the Huns. There he wanted to regain the power he had lost, by force. But his campaign against Ravenna came to an end by the lost battle of Arimium (Rimini). Bonifatius had set a combat troop of experienced legionnaires against the Huns who unrestrainedly pushed ahead. He could beat back their wild attacks and then start a counterattack. Bonifatius was killed in action, but Aëtius lost this battle in spite of that. But Aëtius, the loser, became also winner by the death of Bonifatius. He could force the reconciliation and his friendship upon Valentinianus and his mother now.

We write the year 434 AD

Aëtius rose to the highest rank of the Roman empire, he became "patricius". This title was equivalent to the job of an "administrator of the empire" and gave him the same authority Stilicho had held in the West Roman empire.

It was a high but also an ungrateful office. Aëtius had to come to an agreement with the king of the Vandals, which wasn't easy. Geiserich was in a better position than Aëtius, he had covered his sites in Africa against attacks so well that an East Roman auxiliary army had to withdraw even without having achieved anything. Aëtius had also problems in Gaul, there where he had established order with great difficulty. It had become a loot of Germanic tribes.

Aëtius proved his worth again. He succeeded in reaching an agreement that the supply with grain from (North) Africa wasn't interrupted. For it he had to admit only the claim of the Vandals to Africa, which was in their possession anyway in the meantime. But with the Germanic tribes in Gaul he had trouble in spite of his cleverness. The West Goths had extended their empire and had become the most dangerous enemy, more dangerous than the Burgundi who had advanced from Worms to Trier, the ancient imperial town Augusta Treverorum.

The Burgundi were a belligerent nation. Aëtius wasn't a match for them. It is true that he disposed of some legions but that wasn't enough for a campaign against the strong Burgundi. So he tried to make use of troops of the Huns again in spite of the defeat by Rimini. The mounted hordes of the Huns galloped towards west again. But Aëtius had learnt from his mistakes. He put the mounted Huns so into action against the Burgundi under their king Gundikar during the battle that they caused a cruel massacre. Gundikar was killed in action and with him his next of kin. But Gundikar became immortal as king Gunther of the German(ic) legend (the "Nibelungenlied") In "Nibelungenlied" is mythically reported on him, but in another coherence. But the Burgundi weren't completely exterminated. A part escaped after the battle and migrated westwards. They found

The Huns in Europe

new areas for their settlements in the region where today the famous burgundy comes from, the wine land Burgundy, and above it up to the river Saône. In 443 AD Aëtius gave them permission to settle in the so-called Sapaudia, to the southeast and south of the Lake Geneva, in Savoy (La Savoie). There they founded a new empire that existed till 534 AD.

Now, after the defeat of the Burgundi, Aëtius ventured to attack the West Goths. He was successful and could put them out of action by some short combats. They had to withdraw into their awarded region. But Aëtius assured them of peace and friendship and admitted their claim to independence.

Aëtius was looking for further allies now. He wanted to reach more security for the West Roman empire. But he had to abandon hope to get support by troops of Byzantium. His friends, the Huns, had destroyed that. After the death of Rua (433 AD) Bleda and Attila, his nephews, became kings in the territories between Don and Danube. That meant that they ruled not only over Huns but also over Germanic tribes there.

The name Attila stands for "loving father" in the Gothic language. To what extent this tender name really means that or is an ironic name only is left open. But the Gothic historian Jordanes wrote: "Attila was a man who was created to shock the world, he was the horror to all countries. He frightened all nations by his terrible standing. He walked proudly along and let his gaze wander. With it he wanted to show his power also by his deportment. He liked the war, but was guarded himself. His strength was his intelligence. He didn't stand firm if there was someone who had a favour to ask of him. But it had to be someone who had already submitted himself to his reign. He was short, broad-shouldered, had a big head, but small eyes, thin growth of hair, a flat nose, deep colour of skin and wore men's dress of his country of origin."

The capital of Attila, who was named Etzel in the German(ic) legend, was a big village on the Danube, perhaps Buda, a district of Budapest today (Hungary). The inhabitants of Buda still called their district "Castle of Etzel". There was a palace made of wood during Attila's reign. This palace was furnished with valuable furniture and carpets. This village should also be a site to Attila where he could reign over his great empire like a European king.

We write the year 439 AD

This year Geiserich conquered Carthage, the most important town of West Rome on African ground. With it the Roman province Africa was completely under his control.

We write the year 445 AD

Only some campaigns of the Huns took place on European ground during the first years of Attila's reign. The first campaigns were the two campaigns, which Aëtius had arranged and led too. In this campaigns the Huns took part only with auxiliary troops. But other campaigns of the Huns, by which they had also reached the Rhine, were led by Attila or Bleda personally, who was murdered by Attila this year. Now Attila could reign over the giant empire alone as he had already intended to do all the time.

We write the year 448 AD

This year the Huns crossed the Danube and threatened the East Roman empire (Byzantium) Theodosius II, Pulcheria (P. Aelia Augusta, Roman empress and daughter of emperor Arcadius and the sister of Theodosius) and their ministers set an army against the Huns. But this army was defeated and the emperor and his sister, empress Pulcheria Aelia Augusta, had to make peace. By the assurance of the payment of a high tribute the Huns agreed to withdraw again. That saved Byzantium because it was without protection against the Huns after the defeat. Attila had showed humanity, he was merciful to Byzantium in this case.

Another campaign of the Huns took the opposite direction, towards South Russia. The Huns invaded Scythia, pillaged seventy towns there and took the men prisoner. The women of the defeated were put on an equal footing with the women of the Huns. The copulation of Huns with European women produced human beings with Mongolian characteristics now. But the warlike operations of the Huns hardly differed from operations of other nations before. Therefore they don't justify the bad standing of Attila.

What was the reason for Attila's bad standing? What was the reason that Germanic tribes like Anglo-Saxons crossed the sea to avoid a battle with the Huns? Some historians are of the opinion that the Anglo-Saxons had come to the southern part of Great Britain to help the Britons with their repulse of the enemy from the north, the wild Pictian and Scottish warriors. Also there is the question whether Attila, the "flagellum Dei", really had the intention to exterminate Germanic tribes. But there is nevertheless some truth in it. The Germanic tribes knew about the fate of the East Goths and some other tribes who were enslaved and whose men had to fight in the army of the Huns. There they formed the greatest part too.

Attila had more than half a million warriors under his command. This huge army was to march westwards three years later. The West Roman empire was weak. An alliance of Geiserich, the king of the Vandals, and Theoderich, the king of the West Goths, had meant the end of this empire. An attack from south and a coup de grâce would annihilate the few West Roman legions if no exceptional event was taking place. Where could Aëtius recruit new troops? The emperor of Byzantium didn't want to be at war. He had more than enough problems with the Huns to whom he had to pay a high tribute each year.

The Germanic nations in the middle of Europe were mostly pro-Roman or they received money. The southwest of Gallia was ruled by the West Goths. Also the most important regions of the Iberian Peninsula were under their sovereignty. There in the west the Suebi ruled over today's territory of Portugal. It is true that the Franconians in the northern region of Gallia (Gaul) had accepted the Roman sovereignty, but there is still an open question: How much longer will it take to the moment they formed an alliance again to attack the Roman empire? Another problem for Rome were the Vandals who settled to the south of the Iberian Peninsula and in the northern regions of Africa. Also the south of Italy was a problem to Rome and Aëtius. There he couldn't recruit legionnaires. The raids of the Goths had also weakened the population there. So Aëtius had to take a martial risk, which was equivalent to suicide. He tried to convince the European nations that Attila was the flagellum of the world, that it would be better now to form an alliance against the wild Huns who wanted to subdue all people like the East Goths or even to wipe out populations.

149

Aëtius had already used a bait to prevent Geiserich from attacking the West Roman empire. He promised him the daughter of the emperor, with it the claim to the imperial throne and Geiserich took this bait. Now he thought that he could do it the same way with Attila without getting into trouble with him.

There presented itself an opportunity now. Honoria, the imperial princess, had been involved in a love affair. There was a scandal at the court of Ravenna and Honoria had to leave the court of this brother, Valentinianus III, after the death of her mother, Galla Placidia. In Byzantium she met with a friendly reception. Pulcheria, the empress there who had married Marcianus belonged to her next of kin. Theodosius II had died in the meantime and Marcianus could ascend to the throne by marriage to Pulcheria. Now in Byzantium Honoria sent a ring to Attila with the request of help.

We write the year 449 AD

Honoria was compelled to marry, not Attila but Herkules Bassus, who was an obscure creature. She despised him from the beginning of her marriage. Now she was full of hate for all men too with the exception of Attila. He was the only man who could take revenge on her adversaries.

We write the year 450 AD

Honoria wasn't the only motive for a campaign towards west, there were also the West Goths. Attila wanted to defeat them at all costs. There were quarrels about the succession to the throne amongst the West Goths. It is true that Theoderich I was still alive, but there were still two of his sons. The eldest son of Theoderich I wanted to call Attila for help, the younger son, who had been adopted by Aëtius many years ago, wanted to get support by West Rome.

Attila made a conciliatory offer before his campaign in the direction of West Europe: He would only rule in Gaul as a good friend of the

Merovech, the progenitor of the Merovingian Frankish royal family. He reigned over the Salian Franks in the years 447 - 457. According to legend, he originated from a sea monster that has the shape of a bull. This being fertilized his mother, the wife of King Chlodio (425 - 455) who just bathed in the sea.

Roman empire if he got Honoria. But Honoria was in Byzantium. So he started the campaign indeed. Whilst the Huns were on the long way to the Rhine the moment of truth to Aëtius had come. He had two possibilities: He could combat the West Goths with the help of the Huns or he could call upon the West Goths to attack the Huns, what had to happen under his command then. But he succeeded in realizing the last possibility not before the following year. Then he called upon the European nations to resist the Huns with the following words: "You are the bravest people of all nations, you must make a common cause of the fight against the tyrant who wanted to enslave the world." Theoderich I answered now: "Romans, you've reached your goal, Attila is our enemy."

We write the year 451 AD

Attila's huge army moved towards west. Aëtius tried once more for a peaceful solution by negotiations. But the negotiations couldn't avert the disaster although both sides put the best diplomats in charge of this case. Aëtius wasn't afraid to send his son Carpilio, who had lived at the court of the Huns for some time, to Attila.

Carpilio travelled with Cassiodor. Cassiodor was father of the famous son of the same name, who was the secret writer of Theoderich the Great later. Carpilio and Cassiodor tried to make something clear to Attila, namely that he got a clear idea of the difference between the Asian and European kind of rule and why the West Roman empire wasn't a private property but heritage and order. But they failed in their attempt.

Attila sent a little part of his huge army against Byzantium. The order of these troops was to keep the East Roman legionnaires back from taking action against Attila's army in West Europe. These troops first met an East Roman legion in September and were defeated by Marcianus.

The main force of the Huns marched along the Danube upwards at the beginning of this year. With the forces of the Huns marched all

Germanic vassals and allies who hadn't made raids for more than three years. The most powerful troop of the allies had the Gepidians under their king Ardarich. Attila could trust them blindly, therefore they marched independently as vanguard or as rearguard. The next powerful force were the East Goths under their king Valamir (Walamir), then followed the Skiri under Edekon, who was a Hun, the Rugii, Heruli, Quadi and on the right flank the Thuringians. The Ripuarian Franks came along later. They belonged to the Franconian tribes of the east, their leader laid claim to the Franconian throne. The Burgundi and the West Goths were on the side of the Romans and combated Attila.

The big war of the century had begun. All of Europe was called upon to fight. The enemy came from the east, in the west nobody believed it and hesitated still. Nobody knew exactly the route of this enemy who advanced with nearly 500,000 warriors.

The Alemani were between the fronts. In those days they showed already as third force that they knew the importance of neutrality. The Huns and Gepidi (Gepidians) couldn't break through their bulwarks on the Rhine, there where the Alemani had founded their empire in 436 AD. The Black Forest and the Vosges were hardly to capture. Attila's army, which wormed its way through the land, had to divide. The fast Gepidi made a south turn, they crossed the Rhine close by Kaiseraugst, a site by Basle (Switzerland), and met the main force after Besançon again. The main force had made a north turn. So Attila's warriors could avoid an attack of the Alemani. They crossed the Rhine by Coblence and more down the river.

The valley of the Moselle presented difficulty for the Roman road constructions by the dense forest and the meandering river. Therefore roads were lacking. So the Huns could only load up barges with their siege's equipment and then haul these barges by horses or men's strength up the river ("treideln" to say it by one German word only). The warriors marched on the ancient Roman roads, one part of them from Andernach to Trier (Treverorum), the other part from Bingen through the Hun's Back Mountains to Trier. – Many people fled from the Huns into the dense forest of the Hun's Back

Mountains (Hunsrück, also named Dog Back Mountains because of the form of their highest mountain, the Erbeskopf). There on and near the Erbeskopf they built so-called "Hun's Rings", (mostly round) defence ramparts of stones for some persons only. Today the remainders of these ramparts are still to be found deep in the forest.

The Alemani had saved their mountains and valleys. But for Trier that was a bad thing. The town was taken by storm. The Huns and their allies plundered, violated the women and killed many inhabitants of the town. Then they set fire to the buildings so that the town was a sea of flames only. But many years later there were people living again, so it is safe to assume that a great part of the inhabitants could escape the massacre in the nick of time. Perhaps they fled into the Hun's Back Mountains and found protection in the "Hun's Rings" there.

By Trier converged the Roman roads and formed one great army road towards south, to Divodurum, the name of Metz in those days. The horror of war came to Metz before Easter. On 7 April, it was a Sunday, the Huns took the town by storm. They set on fire the houses, killed the inhabitants by the point of their swords and murdered also priests before the altars. They left behind only ruins with the exception of the prayer's house of Saint Stephanus, which is nearing a miracle.

The Huns marched in the direction of Paris now. They made quick progress because nobody offered resistance on their way. The people took flight or prayed for their salvation. But Paris was situated on the "Ile de la cité" making a conquest difficult for the Huns. Also the Vikings couldn't conquer this town later, although they came on a few hundred ships. The Huns had to besiege the town but that wasn't their strong point. Thus they gave the siege up because they couldn't take it by a coup de main.

Whilst Attila was in the Reims area the Thuringians marched northward through the country of the Franconians, today's Belgium. Here the big catastrophe befell the inhabitants. Not the Huns caused the catastrophe but the Thuringians (Thuringi), a Germanic tribe like the Franconians who were living here. This catastrophe exceeded the worst expectations. The inhabitants of Tongern tried to make the enemy lenient, brought food, offered hostages and hoped for peace but without success. The Thuringians killed the hostages and attacked. They took the possessions of the inhabitants of Tongern and hanged the boys from the trees. For it they used their own shank's sinews. Also two hundred girls were cruelly murdered. Their arms were tied to the necks of two horses. The horses were startled then, so that they scattered in two directions and tore apart the girls. Other girls were laid on the ground, their arms and legs were tied to stakes, then heavily laden wagons overran their bodies. After that the Thuringians fed dogs and birds with the dead and squashed bodies of the girls. Those were the worst tortures, which human beings had to go through. The Huns as riding people had never spent their time on such a cruel show. Their main weapon was the fastness, they appeared, attacked and disappeared again. Thus the atrocities of the Thuringians stuck more in the mind of the people of Franconia than the Huns' storm, which had broken on France those days.

Châlons-sur-Marne was threatened by the Huns on their way to Paris. Paris escaped the Hun's threat with a fright, also Châlons-sur-Marne was to be lucky, the fate meant well by this town. – This town was full of fugitives. The herds were released, the stove's fires extinguished, the churches and cloisters abandoned. Now many people took refuge in Châlons-sur-Marne, but also in the fortress Mont Armé (Mont Aimé) people found refuge from the Huns. This fortress was also immediately attacked by the Huns and conquered after a short combat. Some hundred persons were killed, some thousand taken prisoner. That showed that the Huns were still advancing, and they did it without hurry. There was nothing to be seen of Aëtius, of the West Goths, of the Franks of the dynasty of the Merowinger (Merowingian Franconians). Only the inhabitants of the towns and villages offered desperate resistance. The death was before their very eyes, they fought for some minutes of their lives because they knew that they were going fast.

Châlons-sur-Marne got off lightly. Perhaps it was the nearness of the fortress, which made the peaceful character of the town to the Huns too. The town had an intercessor, it was bishop Alpin who was especially skilful in banishing and exorcizing. Attila, the suspicious king of the Huns, had heard of this strength of the young praelatus.

Alpin succeeded in convincing the king of the Huns of the usefulness of an occupied town instead of a town that lay in ruins. That happened during a talk before the town wall. Attila also agreed to release the captured women of the town now. But Attila's warriors protested, they didn't want to give their loot back. But just in this moment the possessors of female loot were attacked by dreadful stomach-ache and cramps. It concerned a gastroenteric influenza or a food poisoning. But the Huns thought that only Alpin was to blame for it. They had to be prepared for the worst, therefore they released all female prisoners of Châlons-sur-Marne. The women of this town were saved.

The Huns crossed the Marne at various points and continued marching southward. Some towns, like the wonderful town Troyes, were lucky, because Saint Loup, the great bishop, who was already over 60 years old, was a courageous man and entered a special relationship with Attila.

The way of the Huns led via Agedincum, the today's Sens, to Orléans. On the entire way they had fought and plundered, had taken possession of towns, had taken fortresses by storm, had crossed rivers with an army of 100,000 men. Now they reached Orléans in the first half of June. The warriors immediately started with the siege.

Whilst the Huns tried to take the town by storm the citizens prayed to God and went on the walls to look out for rescue. When they were already desperate they suddenly saw how far away a cloud rose from the ground. That they reported to their bishop, who said to them: "That is the aid of the good Lord."

In the meantime the walls trembled by the assault's blocks and threatened to collapse. But now Aëtius and Theoderich with his

Attila, the king of the Huns

son Thorismund appeared at the last moment before the town walls. They could throw the attacking enemy back and chased him away. Attila moved into the Mauriacian plain. There he prepared for the big battle now.

Orléans was an outermost town of the Westgothic Empire and was situated on the Loire. With approval of Theoderich this town was administered by Sangibanus, a prince of the Alani. The possession of the bridges near Orléans was decisive for the conquest of France and Orléans was a pledge for everyone who wanted to compete against the Westgoths.

Aëtius had to win over the Westgoths, to win over for the great battle against the too strong enemy, the Huns. He had to appear as a strong adversary somewhere in Gaul, therefore he needed additional strong military forces, forces the Westgoths had. For, on the Rhine, the Romans had suffered a bitter defeat.

Aëtius and his diplomatic helpers had to talk like angels with the Westgoths because he was their favourite hate. He had been at war against them for years and had even set the Huns on them. Also the Burgundi hated him because he had thrown them to the Huns as easy prey. The Burgundi first saw the new threat by the Huns when they could get a clear idea of the route of them, when they saw their goal, Aureliana, the town Orléans on the Loire. Merowech, the young prince of the Salian Franks certainly desired to combat Gundebaud, who led the Ripuarian Franks in the wake of the Huns to Gaul.

Thus there was the core of defence: Westgoths with Theoderich I as leader, the Roman troops from the garrisons of northern Italy under the leadership of Aëtius and the Salian Franks under the command of Merowech, who was the son of king Chlodjo who died in 448 AD.

Before Orléans the Huns were caught between two fires. It was even said that there were combats in the town when the Westgoths and Romans approached. The Huns were surely not prepared for a repulse because it became a surprise victory to Aëtius. But before Orléans, the town on the Loire, there were only parts of the armed forces of the Huns, thus the victory was only a quick bite into the neck of a beast of prey. It is true that Attila couldn't cross the Loire because there would be no return, but there were many other possibilities: withdrawal with rearguard actions, quick flight without combats and the big field battle.

Attila decided on the big field battle. He had two reasons for it: Only a great battle could ultimately guarantee a great victory. He knew that if he lost this battle it would be only a long but profitable raid and he had to fight his way through somehow toward east, what he had to do otherwise, too. But if he won the battle, then there was anything still possible in this huge game for the power over Europe. He would be in possession of the rich Roman province Gallia (Gaul) with the West Roman Empire as appendage then too.

The Goth Jordanes wrote about the second reason: "Attila even thought of flight, which was worse than death. Thus he decided to question the clairvoyants about the future. After their examination on the intestines of animals according to the tradition they prophesied a disaster for the Huns. But simultaneously they gave them at least one comfort: They announced that the highest leader of the enemy army would be killed in action and his death would deprive the other side of the fruits of the victory. Since Attila wanted at all costs the death of Aëtius, who was in the way of his future plans, he put up with a defeat too. But he was also circumspect in warfare. So he started the big battle first around the ninth hour of day (after sunrise), because he wanted to make good use of the night in case of a defeat..."

These words reflect the hardest hour in the life of Attila. But here, on the withdrawal from the Orléans area, was the point to put up with a defeat, a defeat that was avoidable. But Attila wanted at all costs to get rid of Aëtius knowing that Rome without Aëtius was without a leader and thus an easy loot for the Huns. Attila did not yet know much about Marcianus, the new ruler in Byzantium; he knew more about Galla Placidia in Ravenna. But Galla Placidia was only a woman and the present emperor in Ravenna was a weakling. Thus the adversary in the fight for the world domination was

Aëtius. Therefore a defeat was not too high a price for the extermination of Aëtius. But the defeat shouldn't be a débâcle, the night should prevent that.

Also on the side of Aëtius and Theoderich not everything was clear. It may be possible that Thorismund, the son of the Westgothic king, had fought before Orléans, but the units and allies of the adversaries of the Huns seemed to gather first little by little for crossing the Loire. Aëtius was also on the point of following the Huns without hurry.

The Huns moved in the direction of the Troyes area, northeast of Orléans. They took time for that, what calmed down the troops and gave confidence after the disappointment of Orléans. Troyes, the town of bishop Saint-Loup and rich in art treasures, was in any case traversed. The Huns were doing that without stealing anything. The legend says: sans toucher même à une poule. But Saint-Loup had to go with the Huns, as hostage. Thus the inhabitants of Troyes knew that they couldn't rise against the Huns, because if they did the life of the Holy Man of the Champagne would be in danger.

There was nevertheless a bloody incident, not with the Huns, who were calmly led by Attila, but with the Gepidi who formed the vanguard together with the Ripuarian Franks under the command of Gundebaud. They should safeguard the passage over the little stream Aube.

Ardarich, the king of the Gepidi, and Gundebaud had taken up their quarter in the little town Brolium, Saint-Mesmin of today. They knew that they were in the land of an enemy, but there they had lived together with Christian parishioners for many months too. They saw that these parishioners had gained an inexplicable strength from their faith and from the adoration of their priests. Only that can illustrate the nervousness and panic, which were caused by a small delegation of priests under the leadership of the diacon Memorius. They had approached the Gepidi, who were on horseback, without fear. A sunbeam was broken so unfortunately on the monstrance, which was carried ahead by a priest during this walk for grace, that a high officer, a relative of Attila, couldn't control his dazzled horse. The horse reared, but the Gepidi saw only the priests and feared that these magicians would harm Ardarich or Gundebaud and drew their swords. Six priests lay dead on the ground, but the seventh could escape to Troyes with serious wounds.

This day, it was September 7, remained unforgotten to date, and the place was called Saint-Mesmin or Mémin a short time later, Mémin after Memorius who was killed. But the bloody daybreak took shape to the first big battle.

The Huns had kept marching in the direction westeast on their way from Orléans to Troyes. The distance covered 200 kilometres and that without trouble, which was worth mentioning. The enemy, Aëtius and his Germanic allies, had reached Orléans only with quick troops. Now they assembled. – Victories had encouraged waverers always to follow victorious armies. Thus many men who were fit for military service and fled from the Huns' invasion into the forests on the Loire, emerged again little by little and reinforced the army of Aëtius.

The Huns came in open terrain now by Troyes. The Salian Franks, who didn't want to let escape Gundebaud with the Ripuarian Party, saw the chance to settle up with the enemy: Here the quarrel for the heritage between Salians (Salii) and Ripuarians (Ripuarii) had to be finally settled. When Attila turned onto northwest after crossing the Seine, the moment for the battle had come. Attila did not yet want to take on the battle, he wanted to reach before the Campus Mauriacus, that fortified camp by the village Mauriac (today: La Cheppe), which the bishop of Châlons-sur-Marne had showed him. There was not only the loot, but also the "tross" (rations' troop). This camp had besides the wide plain of the Champagne outside and met with it the best requirements for a battlefield: protection for the defenceless "tross" and free way for the cavalry.

Gepidi and Franks (Franconians) had to beat back the first flank's attack. Attila already got a foretaste of the battle by the vehemence of this attack and knew what he still had to expect. The result of the combat between Gepidi and Salian Franks: 15,000 dead warriors on both sides.

This combat seemed to have already caused one of the decisions which this encounter of the peoples involved. A Frank of royal blood was said to be killed in action. That could be Gundebaud, the head of the Ripuarian Franks. Merowech had achieved his goal with it. He was the victor of this battle and could lay the foundations of a new dynasty, the dynasty of the Merovingians, who ruled more than 300 years over Franconia.

The vehemence of this first encounter was caused by the Burgundi, who went for the first time in action and fought bravely all along the line. It is true that they didn't like Aëtius, therefore they fought at the side of the young Westgothic prince Thorismund too, but they still had an account to settle with the Huns. But their furious attack met the Gepidi who responded with the same courage, and not the Huns. This prelude to the big battle showed that it was a combat amongst Germanic tribes. The most veteran tribes of the great Germanic family slaughtered themselves mutually now, whilst the Huns and Romans could lead back considerable parts of their effective strength after the battle.

The Champagne covers three zones between Troyes and Châlons-sur-Marne giving some information by names, which many people have forgotten today. The first zone, the western Côte Champenoise, so the coast of the Champagne, is a hilly edge area between Reims and Sézanne. It was so unsuitable for the movement of larger military units like the third zone, which was the eastern zone, the so-called Champagne humide. This third zone, the zone between Troyes and Saint-Dizier, is namely interspersed with many little and bigger watercourses, with lakes and ponds. There also dense forests made military movements impossible.

So there was still the centre strip, the so-called Champagne pouilleuse. This Champagne pouilleuse was the corridor, which Attila got to know on the march to Orléans; it had been the well-spied out advancing way and had to be the way back too. For the Huns didn't want to be dispersed in the wide forests of Soissons or in the Forest of Argonne.

The Huns had already passed the Seine. The flank's attack of the Burgundi and Westgoths (Visigoths) should push the Huns away from the Marne and let start the battle in the Champagne pouilleuse. This landscape would have been the right area for a battle too. That still showed the large Camp de Mailly to the west of Vitry today. But the Gepidi had beaten off the attack, although they had many bereavements. The main army had conquered the bridges over the Marne, and behind the last crossing warriors these bridges were destroyed. All that showed that Attila was already hard pressed. He knew that he had to gain time for the concentration and formation of his units, which were dispersed on the long march.

Nobody could risk such a withdrawal under the constant flank's threat. Who knows whether there was time enough for digging trenches and for the right formation of the troops to the battle. Therefore the battle was bound to happen in spite of the bleak prospect. Thus began the great battle in the Catalaunian Fields (after Catalaunum, the name of Châlons-sur-Marne in those days). Crossing the Marne brought a tiny breather and the Camp d'Attila a certain backing. Here the "tross" at least was at a safe distance to the enemy and could be protected against a surprising attack by only some hundred warriors.

Aëtius and his allies had to cross the Marne more down the river, therefore they lost time and came across the west flank of the Huns. The allies protected in this way the towns Châlons-sur-Marne, Reims, Laon and the road to Paris. On this road thronged reinforcements from the Gallian provinces, which were spared the Huns. The Huns had again behind their back the escape route. With their left flank, here they had a west-north-west-directed front, they relied on the Camp d'Attila and the Roman road Reims-Toul-Basel. On the right side they had thrown up earthy ramparts in a hurry, which can still be seen today.

The unpaved road from Châlons-sur-Marne to Soppia (today the road Châlons-Suippes) ran from southwest to northwest, between Romans and Huns, between Westgoths/Visigoths and Eastgoths/Austrogoths. A flat hill was between the armies, but no mountain because we are in the Champagne here.

Now both sides tried to take the hill because a convenient place always presented a considerable advantage. The right (eastern) part of the hill was occupied by the Huns, the left (western) part was occupied by the Romans and Westgoths. The battle for the free top broke out first. The right (southern) wing was held by Theoderich with his Visigoths, the left wing by Aëtius with the Romans. In the middle was Sangibanus, the prince of the Alani. Since Theoderich and Aëtius didn't think Sangibanus capable of a success they surrounded him as a precaution with reliable troops' units.

On the other side, the side of the Huns, was Attila with his warriors as strongest troop in the centre of the formation. The king had arranged to be surrounded only with his troops. He felt at ease only amongst his warriors, only there he thought to be out of any danger. At the flanks fought the warriors of the many other ethnic groups. They belonged to the nations, which had been subdued by the Huns. Also the Eastgoths belonged to these nations. Their army under the command of Walamir, Theodemir and Widimir distinguished itself above all. Ardarich, the leader of the Gepidi, belonged with his huge army to Attila's allies too. He took part because of his great loyalty to Attila in all consultations. Attila thought highly of Ardarich because of his intelligence; therefore he was also of higher standing than the other princes with exception of Walamir. Walamir distinguished himself by discretion, cleverness and acumen whilst Ardarich was a reliable adviser. Attila could count implicitly on Walamir and Ardarich. He knew that both would combat the Westgoths, the brothers of Walamir. The other kings and leaders of the allies followed every sign of Attila like satellites. They hurried to carry out his orders without protest, when they took his command, their knees were shaking. Attila dominated them, he decided on their fate.

164

As already mentioned, at first they fought for the best starting point. Attila ordered his troops to take the top of the hill by storm, but Thorismund, the son of the Westgothic king Theoderich, and Aëtius forestalled him. They succeeded in taking the top and dispersed the advancing Huns by attacking them from above.

Thus the northern and southern wing of the Roman-Gothic army had turned to the centre (the middle of the hill) and united on the top. But that would be possible only if the Huns were completely encircled and then annihilated; therefore no historian believes in that. The historian Thompson wrote: "Each army succeeded in posting a force on part of the hill, but the summit was left unoccupied...of the precise course of the fighting we know nothing." The historian Altheim wrote: "There was a steep hill between both armies, from this hill one could control the battlefield. Both armies gained a foothold there, but the battle for the top ended in a draw." The historian Gordon said that the flank's attack only followed after the death of the Westgothic king as attack of the cavalry. He wrote: "At first, the Roman centre was pierced and the full weight of the Huns directed against the Visigoths on the right wing."

The contradiction of the reports on the battle among the historians is serious. Also other reports are very contradictory. Nobody knows who really held the top of the hill. Jordanes wrote: "Although the situation of the Huns was threatening, the presence of the king dispelled all doubts of the men, who were still undecided before. There was a fray, a terrible, inordinate and fierce struggle. We know no combat of the antiquity, which we can distantly equate with this battle.... The little stream that runs between the low banks through the plain (La Noblette) would have been coloured by the blood out of the wounds of the dead, if we can give credence to the old people. This stream had not, as it happens sometimes, swelled by heavy showers – no, it had swelled to a sweeping stream by blood. And those who were compelled to quench their burning thirst, which had been caused by the wounds, drank the bloody water."

Such facts particularly stick in people's minds. So the reporters especially remembered the words about the death of the Westgothic king too: "Theoderich was hurled down in this battle whilst he was riding through the army and spured on his warriors, and was trampled under the feet of his own warriors then. So he finished his life at the ripe old age."

Jordanes, the Gothic historian, wrote about the death of Theoderich: "Some people say Theoderich was killed by a projectile (javelin) of Andagis, an Eastgoth of the royal house of the Amals. The prophecy, which the fortune-tellers had heralded before, came so true. But Attila had related the words of the fortune-tellers to Aëtius and not to Theoderich. Now the Westgoths parted from the Alani, who formed the centre, and attacked the Huns. Attila would have been slaughtered if he hadn't fled in wise foresight before and hadn't retired behind the rampart of his camp with his warriors."

This rampart is the most significant rest of those bloody days in the Champagne, because the dead bodies of the warriors were swallowed up by the ground, the weapons found their way into the many museums, and monuments weren't erected by Attila or Aëtius.

The rampart, ten metres high, was surrounded by a water ditch with a depth of more than seven metres. Within this bulwark Attila's warriors who flocked back were protected from the enemy. This strong fortification illustrates why the Huns weren't annihilated during the battle too.

The following night was chaotic. Aëtius roamed about alone and Thorismund, the crown prince, had nearly bumped into Huns. Early in the morning the battle went on.

When the Romans saw the battlefield, which was studded with dead bodies, and the Huns didn't attack, they thought they had been victorious. But they also knew that Attila would flee if he had finally lost the battle. At the moment he didn't behave like a fugitive, on the contrary: He let ring out arms din and noise and threatened to attack again. He looked like a wounded lion, hit by hunting spears and walking up and down before a cave. Attila didn't risk an attack, but he frightened the environment by his noise.

The victors, the Westgoths and Romans, who were frightened of Attila, finally held a meeting in order to discuss the next line of action against the Huns. They decided to wear down Attila by a siege. They couldn't conquer Attila's camp because each attack was made impossible by a shower of arrows.

Attila had showed great strength of mind in this dangerous situation. He ordered to erect a stake. If the enemy conquered the camp he would have the possibility of plunging into the flames then. Also he wanted no one to say: "I have killed Attila by my own hand." He didn't want to be a prisoner of his enemies, either. The stake was erected by means of saddles, which were wooden or from bast in the early Middle Ages.

During the siege that dragged on, the people of the Westgoths began to search for their king and the sons to search for their fathers. They were surprised at the absence of their king, above all, since they were victorious. After they had searched for him for a long time, they found him in the middle of many dead bodies as was proper for a brave man.

Now they carried the dead body of the king away, that happened in full view of the enemy and with loud singing. Many Goths lamented loudly and paid their last respects to Theoderich, whilst the battle had not yet come to an end. Many tears were shed, true man's tears. The Westgoths had suffered a bereavement, but it was a glorious loss. The high spirits of the enemy were restrained, he had to see how the dead body of a great man was carried past on hostile shoulders. The Westgoths respected so their king Theoderich, also the brave Thorismund paid his last respects to his dead father as was proper.

The Westgoths had lost not only their last king with the death of Theoderich, but also the party of Aëtius had lost its second hand, the only man who could take steps against Roman interests and who could see through the intentions of Aëtius. Aëtius immediately took advantage of the situation; but that he did in his own favour. He quickly saw his chance by the death of Theoderich for the future European politics of Rome: Now the weak West Roman Empire could further tip the scales, now he (Aëtius) could further use an instrument for his power politics, the Huns. Also the Burgundi, his most fierce adversary, had sided with him in the fields of Catalaunum. So also Attila could be an ally tomorrow, an ally who fought with him against the victorious Westgoths or against the too strong emperor Marcianus in Byzantium. He had known Attila for many years, he would always be able to talk to him and reach an agreement, if the Westgoths didn't take by storm his camp by Châlons-sur-Marne. Thus Attila and his army had to survive, for his death was of no advantage to him.

The wish of Aëtius came true. When the battle was over, Thorismund asked Aëtius the question how it was to go on and how the death of Theoderich could be avenged. But Aëtius, who was older and wiser than Thorismund, advised the young Goth soon to go back with his warriors into the residential area of the Goths. That he should do in order to secure his claim to the throne, otherwise his brothers could seize the power and he had to fight for his inheritance.

Thorismund didn't see through Aëtius and took Aëtius' advice, perhaps, because he thought too much of his own advantage and the succession to the throne. Therefore he abandoned the plan to fight further against the Huns and went back to the interior of Gallia (Gaul).

So Aëtius had prevented the annihilation of the Huns and Attila. His army was strong enough to starve out the Huns, who were crowded together, and to decimate them. Also he had time to have led up reinforcements from the whole of Gaul. These reinforcements could replace the withdrawing troops of the Westgoths. The whole course of the short and fierce battle and the days after the battle showed that the Westgothic warriors had to get removed to save the life of Attila and to save the Huns for future plans. The Gallo-Roman veterans were really glad that they didn't have to storm Attila's camp; when Aëtius announced "the war is over" they gratefully retired into their garrisons, but before they had to stay up until the moment when the remainder of the Huns had crossed the Rhine.

The battle of Catalaunum, in the fields of Châlons-sur-Marne, was also without final combat very bloody. 165,000 warriors lost their lives on both sides. The fertile ground took them and changed their dead bodies into humus.

The people named the hill where most warriors were killed in action, Mont de Pitié or later le Piémont.

Attila didn't march on the same way back. He turned southwards and appeared soon in the northern part of Italy.

We write the year 452 AD

Aquileia was the first town in Italy, which stopped the march of Attila. The town was completely destroyed by the Huns now. The inhabitants who could escape fled into the lagoons by the sea, the Adriatic Sea. There they erected pile dwellings, which one could reach only by water. The town they founded later was called "Venice".

Aquileia had suffered a terrible fate, but the next towns on Attila's way, Verona and Vicenza, couldn't complain more of him than of other conquerors before. The inhabitants of Mediolanum (Milan) and Ticinum (Pavia) could pay to be set free by handing over of their precious objects. So they weren't harmed. Attila continued his horrible march southwards. His march to Rome was blocked up only by a small troop under the command of Aëtius now. Therefore he rejected to take Ravenna. These head-quarters of the emperor's were without use to him. Valentinianus III had fled from him and his huge army. He fled to Rome and hoped to be secure from the "flagellum Dei" (God's scourge) there.

Valentinianus III had hardly arrived in Rome when a delegation under the leadership of the pope, Leo I, left the Eternal City in order to go into the camp of the "flagellum Dei". There they had an important discussion with Attila, a talk important to world history, too. But what they discussed, nobody knows. The fact is that Attila agreed after the talk to do without any further advance. He turned, crossed the Alps and soon reached his capital on the Danube.

We write the year 453 AD

Attila threatened to return to Italy if the imperial princess Honoria wasn't fetched as his bride. But nobody knows whether he was serious about that, because he got married to Hildiko, a Germanic woman, after his return. Hildiko was Kriemhild from the German(ic) legend, the wife of Siegfried, who was murdered. In the legend Siegfried of Xanten was the famous hero of Germany of those days. Attila ate and drank too much during the wedding banquet. Early in the morning of the following day he was found in his bed. He was dead, at his side lay his young bride. A blood vessel is said to have burst in the night, and the blood in his throat had induced death from suffocation.

The huge empire of the Huns gradually dissolved after the death of Attila. The Huns were annihilated by other nations or merged into them. Thus the Awari later had blood of the Huns for the most part in their bodies.

Theoderich the Great and his Eastgothic Empire

We write the year 454 AD

The information about Attila's death encouraged Valentinianus III to take action himself. The "God's scourge" threatened the emperor no longer. Attila hadn't only threatened the Germanic kings, but also him with his scourge. Now he was sick and tired of being kept in leading strings of anyone. But that had done Aëtius, the "patricius". Aëtius had also kept his mother in leading strings, that should be over now too. He had his own friends, amongst them Petronius Maximus, who advised him against a dearest wish of Aëtius. The "patricius" wished that his son got married to the daughter of Valentinianus, Eudocia. The result of the rejection of the son of Aëtius was a violent argument now. Also Aëtius was sick and tired of a restriction of his power by the emperor whose throne he had saved by tricks and malice, by violence and cleverness from earliest childhood. He was prepared for the worst when the discussion began, but not for a murder. The mommy's darling, the peaceful and gentle emperor, Valentinianus, stabbed him to death. "What have you done?" shouted a man of the court at Valentinianus after the murder. "You have cut off all your rights by your left hand!"

We write the year 455 AD

The unhindered reign of Valentinianus took only some months. The senator Petronius Maximus, whose pretty wife he had violated, had him killed in Rome. After the murder Petronius Maximus compelled the widow of Valentinianus, Eudoxia, who didn't yet know about his incitement to the murder, to marry him, his own wife having died in the meantime. She died of grief. Eudocia, the daughter of Eudoxia, he gave to his son Palladius as wife. Short time after the wedding he confessed to the murder of Valentinianus. When Eudoxia heard his confession she was full of greediness for revenge and contacted the king of the Vandals, Geiserich. But a cry for help wasn't required to cause a king of the Vandals to put to sea a fleet full of veteran warriors. Up to now Geiserich was always involved with operations, which were from the start sure of his ground. So it was to be now too.

The ships of the Vandals, which were also loaded with many horses, didn't make a detour. Rome was Geiserich's goal, Ostia the harbour. The West Roman empire hadn't even a complete legion for the defence. On the way from Ostia to Rome he met only a little column of men who weren't even armed. At the head of this little column stepped the pope, Leo I, who was accompanied by his priests. Leo I courageously stepped up to the Vandals and began a discussion now.

Nobody exactly knows the subject matter of the discussion of the great pope with the Vandals. But the result was that all Christian churches of Rome were spared the plundering, which lasted fourteen days. Geiserich behaved like Alarich. But the plunder of the Vandals was more thorough than the plunder of the West Goths. All valuable things, which were still in the imperial palaces and the houses of the rich inhabitants were shipped by the Vandals now. The men and women of Rome were enslaved by the thousand. Amongst the women there were also the empress Eudoxia and her two daughters. Geiserich gave Eudocia to his son Hunerich as wife. He didn't care himself for Eudoxia. When now the new emperor of East Rome interceded for Eudoxia Geiserich sent her and her youngest daughter to Byzantium.

Geiserich didn't stay for a long time in Rome. He didn't like the ruins of a past great time there. He wanted to go back to Carthage, to his capital, and intended to develop this town by means of the stolen treasures. What happened with Rome was all the same to him. It would go to ruin like Carthage after the conquest of Rome. Would it ever revive again? It meant a lot to him to build up again the empire of Carthage. He conquered the Balearic Islands, Sardinia and Corsica and could reign by it without interference over the western part of the Mediterranean Sea. He was the mighty ruler over a huge empire. He and his Vandals lived so as was reported on them later: "They took a bath every day and had set the table with all the goods and deliciousness since they had seized Africa. They whiled away the time by going to the theatre, by watching horse racing or being amused by other occasions, which presented themselves, as hunting. They were also keen spectators of dances. In a few words, they enjoyed all sorts of art. Most of them were living in gardens with magnificent trees and excellent sanitary facilities."

The West Roman Empire existed by name only, in reality it went down already. Heruli, Skiri and Rugii, who were curbed under the control of Attila, had marched to Italy, there they took up residence where it suited them fine. That also happened by threatening the inhabitants with an occupation by force of arms. In the meantime one emperor after the other were proclaimed in the West Roman empire. The first successor of Petronius Maximus was Avitus, who was a West Gothic general. But the Roman senate, which had convened again during this general confusion, had refused him acknowledgement. He could nevertheless reign more or less over the remainder of the West Roman Empire till the end of the year 456 AD. During his reign the Franconians almost conquered all regions on the left side of the Rhine, which weren't under their control yet.

We write the year 457 AD

Now a Suebian, his name was Ricimir, reigned over the western part of the Roman Empire in Ravenna. He did it as "patricius", because Maioranus was emperor.

In Franconia Childerich became the new king. But Childerich I was only king of a tribe of the Salian Franks north of Gaul. His son was to found the Franconian Empire later.

We write the year 461 AD

Ricimir was dissatisfied with Maioranus therefore he deposed him simply. Now Severus became emperor. But he also was to be emperor for no long time.

173

We write the year 466 AD

This year Eurich became king of the West Goths. He was the son of Theoderich I and brother of Thorismund, whom he had murdered. The Visigothic Empire was to reach its biggest extension during his reign in Gallia (Gaul) and Spain. He could finally evade the Roman supremacy too. He had for the first time written down the Visigothic law, the "Codex Euricianus."

We write the year 467 AD

Ricimir, the real sovereign of the West Roman Empire, appointed again a new emperor. It was Athemius, who was a half-heathen philosopher and came from the eastern part of the Roman Empire.

We write the year 468 AD

This year West and East Rome commonly took action against the Vandals, what happened for the first time. Their united navy attacked the Vandals. By it they could win back Tripolis and Sardinia. But before the walls of Carthage they suffered a crushing defeat.

We write the year 470 AD

This year was to be an important year again for the Alemani (Alemanni). They warded off the attacks of other Germanic tribes and could consolidate their power in Forearlberg (Vorarlberg) and the northern part of Switzerland. Now they were never again expelled from there even though their empire was annexed by the Franconians and their name as Germanic tribe vanished forever many years later. But now their tribe was still existent by name. Only 300 years later parts of them appeared as Swabians (Swabi), their name was again traced to the Suebi (Swebians). Now these Suebi still formed a great part of the Alemani. Later the greater part of them fused into the Bajuwari/Bajuwarians (Bavarians/Bavarii).

We write the year 471 AD

The Romans had awarded Pannonia as permanent place of residence to the East Goths after the battle in the Catalaunian fields (fields of Catalaunum). So they settled between the towns Sirmium (Mitrowitz on the Save/Mitrovica on the Sava, Serbia) and Vindobona (Vienna, Austria) now. With it they were the neighbours of the Gepidi, who had marched and fought at their side a long time. But these Gepidi had already occupied the Hungarian lowlands under their king Ardarich before. Both nations had already been together at the mouth of the Vistula. There they had commonly settled after they had left Sweden.

The new settlements of the brothers of the royal family from the East Gothic dynasty of the Amals, Valamir (Walamir), Vidimir (Widimir) and Thiudimir, were so situated between Mitrowitz and Vienna. Thiudimir was more important in history than his two brothers because in his residence on the shore of Lake Neusiedel Theoderich was born in the year of 454 AD. Theoderich became the great king of the East Goths later and was called Theoderich the Great.

Theoderich was on his father's side a Goth of the royal family of the Amals, but his mother was a loot of those days when East Goths and Huns were shoulder to shoulder stealing and plundering on the way through the Balkans and Greek-Roman territories. Theoderich had gone to Byzantium at a young age. That he did just during the time when the imperial power gave rise to a fascinating late heyday.

There in Byzantium Theoderich as a little boy came to a world of manifold influences. The predominant religion was the Catholic faith, the faith of his mother, whilst he was a follower of the Arianism. Also later as king he was a supporter of the Arianian faith (Arianism). He also kept a certain distance from the teaching activities in Byzantium and seems to have received no usual education. But the sense of education dawned on him that year as well as the sense of the intellectual and cultural performance of the antique. With it he got the equipment for his reign over Italy later. But it had also a favourable effect on Theoderich that the inhabitants of Byzantium had a liking for Germanic people and Emperor Leo had taken a fancy to him. But there was also Aspar, a Goth, who held a high office during the reign of three emperors, exercised a great power and showed an interest in Theoderich now. There was moreover a Gothic clan in which the women played a part. Over and above there was Theoderich Strabo, who was descended from a noble Gothic family, but who was no Amal, so he didn't descend from the royal family. His pretty sister was on the other hand the mistress of Aspar. Many people called her "woman of sexual intercourse" as Theoderich's mother Eusebia.

The phase of Byzantium came to an end for Theoderich this year. He was seventeen years old and an educated Gothic prince and went back to Pannonia with his father now. If the emperor of Byzantium had thought that this young man would see to it that there would be a better understanding between East Goths and East Romans, then he was wrong about him.

Theoderich soon defeated Theoderich Strabo, who was older and had showed himself from time to time as adversary of Byzantium or as friend.

The emperor's effort to weaken the Gothic nation by agitating the two Gothic men against one another went wrong because the Gothic soldiers had rebelled against this kind of fratricidal war. They were also dissatisfied because their high leaders received by turns high military decorations and rewards whilst they came away empty-handed.

We write the year 472 AD

Anthemius, the emperor of West Rome, was executed by Ricimir this year. Olybrius became new emperor now. But after his coronation Olybrius lived for some months only, then he died a natural death.

We write the year 473 AD

The new emperor of West Rome was Glycerius. But soon he had to make way for another emperor. By it the West Roman Empire came near to the end.

We write the year 474 AD

The new emperor of West Rome was Julius Nepos. But he also reigned over the West Roman Empire some months only. In the following year there followed the last emperor of West Rome.

This year a new epoch for Europe was to begin. The East Goths, who settled in Pannonia, had to start any war because they suffered from hunger although this lowland was a fertile region. The only cause for their misery was their laziness, but also the continuous feuds amongst them. Now, in this situation, Thiudimir died of an illness in the County Görz area. But before that happened he could still assemble faithful men at the sickbed. He asked for the consent to elect Theoderich king and received it. All faithful men also swore to remain always loyal to Theoderich.

Theoderich had already won fame; he was acquainted with the other world of Romans and Greeks too. He knows that he couldn't blindly attack them, what had been done by the barbarians. So he was the best man to the East Goths, the best man who took power now.

The first questions of the East Goths Theoderich had to answer were: Where can we go and loot? Where can we find new land? Land that we haven't to cultivate, land that was cultivated by other people!? The East Goths had lost the virtue of a peaceful acquisition of land during their long migration, a virtue they still had in South Sweden, on the island Bornholm and at the mouth of the Vistula (Weichsel). Therefore Theoderich had a look at Italy now.

We write the year 475 AD

In Italy the inevitable integration of the Germanic people that had been going on steadily, reached its climax. That integration was an instructive example to Theoderich now. Two ministers of Attila had gained influence in Italy. One of them was Orestes. He didn't play an exceptional part at the court of the Huns. He was only a simple official, perhaps a little bit more than a chief of protocol, but less than a head of the interpreters. It may be that he was also a legal adviser of sorts, an adviser in foreign affairs. Orestes had gone to Ravenna after the death of Attila. There he could gain influence on Germanic troops. Thanks to this influence he could proclaim his son Romulus new emperor of West Rome.

The other minister at the court of the Huns was Edekon, a confidant of Attila, who had distinguished himself during his many political journeys to Byzantium and other important countries. He had also exposed a plot against Attila. Edekon had taken over the power over the Germanic tribe of the Scirians who had settled before their great migration in East Prussia. Edekon had married a Scirian princess who had given birth to a son whose name was Odoaker.

Odoaker became an inconsiderate warrior in the course of time, he entered the bodyguard of the West Roman Emperor and then rose in rank by becoming leader of the Germanic auxiliary troops. By it he was in charge of the only military power in Italy, which was worth mentioning.

We write the year 476 AD

There was a battle between Orestes, who was obsessed with power, and Odoaker, who strove for power, that year. This battle took place close to Pavia. Orestes was defeated and killed in action. His son Romulus (Augustus) was banished. The little boy Romulus, who was the last emperor of West Rome, could feel happy that he wasn't murdered. He was only deposed and sent to Campania (South Italy).

Odoaker didn't strive for the imperial crown, what the other Germanic men also did before. He paid homage to the East Roman emperor Zenon and let himself recognize as "patricius". Odoaker's sharing of possession now in the Germanic-Roman regions of Italy was a brilliant idea. Since Italy was closely settled and completely cultivated in contrast to Pannonia and Thrace he couldn't give his soldiers unoccupied estates as payment. – The soldiers belonged without exception to Germanic tribes as Sciri (Scirians), Heruli (they settled at the time in the region of the middle Danube and were a North Germanic tribe), Alani and Rugii (they settled at the time in the region of today's Lower Austria and came originally from South-West Norway). – Odoaker determined that each Roman landowner had to deliver a third of his harvest to the Germanic people. But the Roman law wasn't invalidated, the Roman administration remained intact and also the senate of Rome wasn't hindered in its function. The tax law wasn't changed, either. Also the Catholic church didn't suffer under Odoaker, who was a follower of the Arianism.

This situation in Italy was very tempting for Theoderich. He had namely the possibility after a victory over Odoaker to get a perfectly organized country. As for the rest he saw Odoaker only as parvenu. Now he was looking for a reason to invade Italy. But some years were to pass to realize that.

We write the year 482 AD

The Franconian king Childerich died this year and Chlodwig became king of the Salian (Salican) Franks. He was to found the great Franconian Empire of the Merovingians later.

We write the year 486 AD

This year Chlodwig finally got rid of the Roman supremacy by victory over the last Roman governor in Gaul. First he conquered the remainder of the West Roman empire between the rivers Somme and Loire, then he defeated the Roman general Syagrius in the battle

179

of Soissons and occupied the Roman part of northern Gaul. Now he also prevailed against all other minor kings, for that he stopped at nothing. He had made out as heathen that the local bishops were the authorities in the towns of Gaul, therefore he was looking for a good cooperation from the beginning. Later, after his baptism, he seized the opportunity to increase his influence as Christian-Catholic king. Chlodwig promoted the approximation and the relationship by marriages between Franconians and natives by taking over the Gallo-Roman administrative institutions. He legally put the original inhabitants of Gaul (Gallians) and Franconians (Franks) on equal footing too. That he did without violating the tradition of the tribes. He knew very well that he depended on the loyalty of the natives, because the Franconian settlements only formed an island within the occupied territory. But he had also ingratiated himself with the people when he made a patron to his house and the empire of the popular holy Martin (Saint Martin) and had given his ancestral church in Tours many valuable presents. Whilst economy and culture were thriving in the Roman south, Paris became the political centre of the empire of the Merowingians to the north of Franconia. Now the "Empire of Cologne", the empire of the Riquarii (Rhine-Moselle-Franks), was wrapped up in the empire of the Merowingians too.

We write the year 487 AD

Odoaker destroyed the empire of the Rugii, who had expanded into Noricum (former Roman province in the region of the East Alps). The remainder of this nation joined the East Goths now. But Odoaker didn't venture to set foot on East Roman area or to attack Byzantium (East Rome) even. He relied on the Heruli mainly and Sciri when he took action and didn't violate Roman interests. He also tried to be on good terms with the East Goths in spite of the extermination of a great part of the Rugii. That didn't make a campaign easy for Theoderich, who sought for a pretext to his intent to invade Italy. He and Odoaker were also on friendly terms, only the Germanic legend speaks against it. But he had also lived for a long time in Byzantium and was more than ten years king now, so he knew very well the tricks of the nations, which were his neighbours. Therefore he found enough pretexts together with Zenon, the emperor of East Rome, and a Rugian prince who was chased away by Odoaker, to invade Italy. Now he only had to wait for Zenon's order.

We write the year 488 AD

Odoaker wasn't Romulus or Honorius, he defended himself bravely. So Theoderich had a hard time to get access to Italy in spite of the constant training in arms of his warriors. In autumn of this year he succeeded at least in securing the needed provisions for the winter time. That happened after a long march via Mitrowitz (Mitrovica) towards west. During the combats on the little river Ulca the Gepidi were the adversaries of the East Goths. There they were threatened to get wiped out too. But Witiges (Wittlich of the German(ic) legend) performed real wonders by his battle's courage now.

Why didn't the East Goths interrupt the campaign in view of the problems? In addition to the problems they had still many casualties by the attacks of Odoaker's marauding hordes. The East Goths were in possession of the most fertile ground in the south-east of Europe after their victory over the sons of Attila. Why did they leave this friendly area in Pannonia (Hungary today!)? Theoderich still had the possibility to turn this area into profitable farmland because he was intelligent and well educated.

When the Goths weren't just on raid, they were on the move with their families and all their possessions like the other Germanic tribes. Theoderich had started his long march in this way too. He was on the way to Italy with thousands and thousands of carts and wagons, he was on the road with human beings who slowly and with difficulty moved forward. They could only return if there was a catastrophe or no other alternative.

We write the year 489 AD

The East Goths attacked over and over again. A vanguard even tried to cross the Adriatic Sea by ships to get out of the way of Odoaker's troops in the north of Italy. But this vanguard failed in its attempt, so Theoderich had to take on the powerful and equivalent adversary, had to expose himself and his people to the risk of a battle and with it to the danger of a complete annihilation of the "tross" (the whole of baggage wagons of the troops) and the non-combatants. That was the fate of the migratory people since the time of Moses: When they weren't victorious then they were wiped out.

Theoderich was victorious in some unknown battles. Then he left the Julian Alps as victor after he had broken every resistance by clever leadership and by sustained courage. In North Italy he met with a friendly reception as general of the East Roman emperor. The inhabitants hoped he would put an end to Odoaker's reign of terror now.

There was a great battle after countless minor fights against West Roman legionnaires. The East Goths appeared with all their possessions. Two thousand wagons they had lost by their first failures, were replaced by loot's property and each family had still enough grain for some battle's days. They also had meat, and that for quite a time because they had slaughtered all their livestock before. They knew that the province Venetia (Venice) was a rich region where they could get new flesh any time.

Behind their backs the hunger, before them the country of yearning, so fought Theoderich's East Goths like mad before the ruins of Aquleia. The cavalry had overcome the tiredness of the long march and the foot troops had conquered the field fortifications of Odoaker, which were thrown up in a hurry. Odoaker had to retreat, he hurried back to the walls of Verona and the banks of the torrential Etsch (Adige, a little river in the north of Italy). With it the East Goths had achieved a great success. They hadn't conquered Italy, but they could secure the feeding of their soldiers and families.

The Franks' Ford (Frankenfurt,
the city Frankfurt today)

Where King Chlodwig I (Clovis I) crossed the river
Main with his Merovingian army under bloody battles
was later built the city of Frankfurt (an der Furt der
Franken – at the Ford of the Franks / Frankford or Frankfurt on Main) – Clovis crossing was done in 496.

The battle of Verona was bloodier than the battle before. There Theoderich also was in a bad way for a time. Odoaker had set a trap for the Gothic cavalry. When also Theoderich's bodyguard was in danger and had to retreat, he tried to flee, but his mother and sister stepped up to him and said in hard words: "Do you want from us that we are the loot of Odoaker?" Now he turned and summoned in a hurry a small crowd of true warriors to start off with them the decisive counterattack.

This battle in autumn close to Verona made Theoderich ruler over the northern part of Italy. Odoaker retreated from the northern part and went to Rome. But there he didn't find the necessary support, therefore he made up his mind to go to Ravenna now.

183

We write the year 490 AD

This year Odoaker attacked, relying on the strong fortress Ravenna, with support of the Burgundians (Burgundi) of the Lake Geneva, who rushed to his aid, so energetically that a great part of Northern Italy came under his reign again. Theoderich had to retreat into Ticino. There he was waiting for help by the West Goths. When West Gothic contingents came to his aid now, he ventured to give a battle. This battle took place on the little Alpine river Addua. He defeated Odoaker who had to retreat and found his place of refuge in Ravenna.

The military development was marked by treason, hypocrisy and intrigues. Generals of Odoaker deserted to Theoderich. But then they abandoned him again at the decisive moment and betrayed with it a group of capable East Gothic officers. A prince of the Rugii, who had fought side by side with Theoderich, changed sides and went over to Odoaker. Theoderich's response to this was that he had all deserters from the camp of the adversary slaughtered like animals to protect himself from further treason.

Whilst Ravenna could defend itself heroically, Theoderich conquered all Italian territories from the Alps to Calabria in the following months. As real ruler over the whole of Italy the Vandals gave him the island Sicily as a present.

We write the year 493 AD

Ravenna couldn't be conquered by force of arms, how Alarich had realized already. Theoderich resorted to a ruse therefore after three years of unsuccessful siege and lasting attacks of Odoaker out of town. He sent Odoaker a very favourable peace offer by Johannes II, who was bishop of Ravenna. He offered Odoaker, who was completely encircled by Gothic troops, a common rule over Italy. That happened with the intent of keeping that only for a short time, perhaps even for no time because he held all the trumps and he knew the famine in Ravenna. But the peace treaty still comprised sworn statements on Odoaker's liberty and an unharmed life for him.

The gates of Ravenna were opened and Theoderich went marching in with some faithful men. Odoaker intended to celebrate the conclusion of the peace treaty with him now. They entered the festively decorated hall with their entourage. Odoaker expected a friendly handshake of Theoderich but got his sword in the breast instead. Before he dropped dead, he asked the question: "Where is God?"

Theoderich was awarded later the "honouring" epithet "the Great". He also became a legendary figure of the German (ic) saga, there he was Dietrich of Bern.

We write the year 507 AD

Theoderich got into serious trouble only with Chlodwig, the king of the Franconians. Chlodwig was that he already was when he was young: ambitious and addicted to conquests. He had started his career as heir's king of a Roman border area. There his family, the Merowingians, had settled during the time of imperial power and then extended this area to an impressive kingdom.

Chlodwig was thinking of a similar mixture of nations as it did Theoderich. But he hadn't Theoderich's patience and neither the support of Byzantium, therefore he executed the fusion of the nations by force. His compensating activity was confined to the use of the French language. He gave order that all Franconians (Franks) had to speak Latin, the preliminary stage of the French language of today (= the language of the Franconians) Also he compelled his new subjects to accept the Franconian people's law, the "lex Salica". The royal residence became Paris. There he made up his mind about the conversion to the Christian faith too.

Theoderich had tried by a legation that Chlodwig converted to the faith of his family, to Arianism. But Chlodwig's wife, who came from Burgundy, was a follower of the Catholic faith. She wished to convert

185

him to her faith. – The Catholic bishop of Tours advised the queen and won the confidence of Chlodwig. But Tours belonged to the West Gothic Empire and the West Gothic king was a follower of Arianism. Therefore Alarich II, the king of the West Goths, banished the bishop from Tours now.

Chlodwig invaded the West Gothic Empire on the pretext that he didn't want to leave his friend in the lurch. But now he was also attacked by the Alemani. That happened at the request of Alarich II. He swore now if he were victorious he would be baptized into Roman Catholic faith himself. And he defeated the Alemani and was then able to continue the campaign against the West Goths. He forged ahead to Bordeaux. But only when Theoderich went into action against him he was willing to make peace.

Chlodwig knew that he could only extend his borders in direction of the Mediterranean Sea by a life-and-death struggle with Theoderich. But for it he didn't yet feel strong enough. He turned to north and east against the Alemani and allied himself with the Burgundians who ousted the common enemy from their territories. Chlodwig extended his empire by these campaigns and laid the foundation of his determined position in Europe. Also by his conversion to the Catholic faith he could strengthen his power. By the standardization of faith and culture Franconia was on the way to become a super power too.

Theoderich was worried about the conquests of the Burgundians (Burgundi) on the ground of the Alemani. He could do nothing when the fleeing Alemani called for help. But he gave them permission to settle in West Roman provinces, which were under his reign. So they settled in the area between Danube, Lech and Iller. There they fused into the "Bajovari", the new Germanic tribe. These "Bajovari or Bavarii" (Bajowarians/Bajovarians, later Bavarians) came from the country Baia (= Bohemia), the country of the former Marcomanni. Therefore many historians suppose, at least, that they were related to them because the Marcomanni have disappeared forever. The Bajowarians, the today's Bavarians, formed an integrated nation with the greatest part of the Alemani now.

Theoderich had extended his sphere of influence in the east too, but that without force of arms. He supplied Rodulf, the king of the Heruli in today's Hungary, with the necessary equipment and gave him the title "Weapon's Son". The emperor of Byzantium, Anastasius I (491 – 518 AD), didn't like this enormous increase in power. But he didn't want to be at war against him either. Anastasius's only possibility to keep Theoderich in check was an alliance with Chlodwig. Theoderich allied himself as far as he was concerned. That he did with Alarich II. It should be a counterweight to the alliance of Anastasius with Chlodwig. Chlodwig seemed to have expected that. He again invaded the West Gothic Empire, whilst a fleet of Byzantium cruised before the eastern coast of Italy.

Theoderich was not intimidated. It is true that his Goths came too late to save Alarich's II life, but in the nick of time to defeat the united Burgundian-Franconian troops in Gallia.

The death of Alarich II meant a further extension of Theoderich's power. The West Goths offered him to be their king. He refused and was content with the rule as governor.

Now Theoderich tried to win Chlodwig to the foundation of a great Germanic nation of all Germanic tribes. That should happen on West Roman ground. But the title of a consul, offered by Byzantium, had a greater value to Chlodwig.

We write the year 511 AD

This year Chlodwig died and the empire was shared out amongst his four sons, whilst Theoderich couldn't realize his plan of life any more. The Langobardi could free themselves from the supremacy of his "Weapon's Son" and occupy the Herulian Empire on the Danube little by little.

We write the year 518 AD

The Langobardi founded a new Germanic empire under the leadership of Tato. This was made possible by help of the emperor in Byzantium, Justinus I. Justinus I, who was the successor of Anastasius, didn't want Theoderich was too powerful.

Junstinus I had a hard time. He knew he wasn't the right man for the succession of Anastasius who had been an important emperor. Anastasius had built a defence wall, more than 60 kilometres long, from the coast of the Marmara Sea to the Black Sea and had accumulated a huge state treasure. – Justinus was a parvenu from Illyria. He had seized the power after a national uprising and after the death of Anastasius. He was successful because no competitor was quicker. But he could only remain in power by the cleverness of his nephew Justinianus, whom he had educated.

We write the year 523 AD

Justinianus, the administrator by order of Justinus, had seen that all heathens and heretics had to leave the court, the administrative machinery and the army. Also the followers of the Arianism came under this order. Theoderich was worried therefore, in his kingdom the followers of the Catholic faith were at liberty to practise their faith. It was rumoured that his deposition as "rex" and "patricius" was approaching because of his faith, the Arianism. That should happen by the Roman senate, which he had even equipped with power, and not by the emperor of Byzantium. Theoderich investigated and could find out that there was an actual plot against him. On whom could he rely now? He was sure that he couldn't rely on his chancellor, the philosopher Boethius, who had drawn up an anti-Arianian paper about the Trinity. Also a friend of Boethius, the senator Albinus, was considered to be a plotter.

Boethius and Albinus were arrested. After that Theoderich wrote to the emperor of Byzantium. The text read as follows: "If anyone reasoned with a ruler, then it meant that he arrogates a privilege of God to himself. The power of a ruler is confined to the political leadership of the state. He has the right to punish persons who disturb the public peace. The most dangerous heresy is the heresy of a ruler who only breaks with a part of his subjects, because they have another faith."

Justinus answered that he had the right to withhold offices from people if he could not rely on their faithfulness and loyalty. The order in a state required the unity of the faith.

In prison Boethius wrote one of his important works of the early Middle Ages: "De consolatione philosophiae" (About the consolation of the philosophy). Fortune, said Boethius, one can find neither by riches or fame nor by desire or violence. There was no real and certain fortune except in the uniting with God: "Bliss is the deity itself."

We write the year 524 AD

Theoderich had executed Boethius, who had translated the works of Platon and Aristoteles into Latin. One of the greatest historians of Byzantium later wrote that Theoderich soon regretted the death of his chancellor.

We write the year 526 AD

Theoderich the Great dies in Ravenna, where a great tomb was built for him. This tomb is an object of interest today. The same historian, who was already mentioned above, reported on Theoderich too: "His powerful hand took care for justice all over. He was the patron to law and order. He was a tyrant by name only, he was in reality a true emperor, not a hair's breadth less than persons who had held this dignity before."

The end of the East Gothic Empire

We write the year 527 AD

Justinus, the emperor of Byzantium, didn't survive Theoderich for a long time. He died this year. His death didn't leave a gap behind him, because Justinianus took over the power, which he had already held during the life-time of his uncle. He didn't like to do that to all appearances. He would rather continue acting in secret and give his undivided attention to his personal diversion. This diversion was contrary to the diversion of his swinging teacher. Justinianus didn't like risqué and slippery amusements. He had better become a poet, lawyer, philosopher, musician or architect. The splendid housekeeping at the court with all its wasteful dishes on the table of the emperor and the grossly exaggerated diversion were a molestation for this abstemious man who only ate vegetable foodstuffs and worked from daybreak till late in the night.

He even wanted to abdicate short time after his coronation to calm down some troublemakers in the empire, but his wife insisted on the title empress. She was the daughter of a man who tamed bears. Theodora, as she was called, grew up in a circus and became an actress. But she was more in action with rich men who loved the pleasure of life, than on the stage. She became known as dancer in slippery performances. Prokop (Procopius of Caesarea, 490 – 562 AD, history writer of Byzantium) reported in his "anecdota" on Theodora that she had interrupted some pregnancies. Nobody would know the fathers. But she had given birth to one child of an unknown father. Prokop didn't report whether the Syrian Hekebolos was the father of this child. But it is known that Theodora had been in Alexandria (Egypt) during this pregnancy. Also Hekebolos was there at the time and saw Theodora every day. Therefore he was supposed to be the father.

But soon Theodora was in Byzantium again and earned money as poor and respectable spinner. - Prokop wrote about a statue of Theodora: "The statue is uncommonly pretty. But it doesn't do justice to the looks of the empress. No human being can reproduce her charm in words, no human being can chisel her charm in stone."

That Justinianus, who was a bookworm, fell in love with Theodora in view of her beauty, wasn't surprising. But there was astonishment at the court of Byzantium that he was married to a woman who had a so scandalous former life like Theodora.

Justinianus was sure of this ground: This young woman who had met all the depths of life, would never long to be back in the gutter. He was right in the end. Theodora became so good a wife that also the malicious slanderers couldn't say anything against her. She also became the best adviser of Justinianus whose vital inexperience was complemented by her experience. That she was greedy for money and power was of advantage to him. It was also irrelevant to him that she ate and drank well whilst he fasted. He didn't even prevent her from putting on luxurious dresses whilst he wore simple clothes.

The way of life in Byzantium, which outdid itself in its overdone exhibitionism of exquisite costumes and valuable jewels was to express the richness and power of the East Roman Empire. This way of life wasn't only expressed by opulent banquets, which even surpassed the Roman festivities during the heydays of Rome, but also by magnificent buildings, palaces and churches. The "Hagia Sophia" (Holy Wisdom), the former cathedral of Byzantium built by Justinianus, is today an impressive monument of the splendour of this city. Now the "Hagia Sophia" is a museum in Istanbul, the Turkish city with some million inhabitants.

Whilst Theodora was the empress of the great fashion and luxurious life, Justinianus was a simple man but also a henpecked husband, who exactly knew to what extent he had to give in and when he had to show who was the boss in his own house. He sometimes gave Theodora permission to be cruel to her adversaries. So he could avoid the cruelty ascribed to him. But he also accepted merciful acts of Theodora, so that he hadn't to show mercy himself and was eventually regarded as weakling by it. Justinianus and Theodora worked together although it often seemed not to be the case. If they weren't working together then it happened in mutual consent.

The aim of the imperial married couple was the reunification of the former great Roman Empire. For it they had to liberate Africa from the Vandals, Italy from the East Goths, the Iberian peninsula from the West Goths, Gaul from the Franks/Franconians and Britannia/ Britain from the Anglo-Saxons. Also they had to restore the unity in faith again, the condition for a standardization of the empire.

Justinianus didn't recoil from huge tasks. He thought to have all prerequisite for it – money and excellent generals. So there was Belisar, who descended from a farmer's family of Illyria and was an ambitious man. He was also a man devoted to his emperor only.

We write the year 529 AD

This year the Bajuwari/Bajuvari (Bavarii/Bavarians) conquered the town Regensburg/Ratisbon. This town developed from the Celtic settlement Radasbona and the later Roman border fortress Regina Castra. Now it became the capital of the Bajuwarian invaders and by it also the capital of the first counts of the Bavarian tribe. The first count of the Bavarians who could be proved, resided in Ratisbon (Regensburg), it was Garibald (560 – 590 AD). He was the founder of the dynasty of the Agilolfingers.

We write the year 530 AD

This year Justinianus started with the attempt to extend his empire towards east. He was interested in the control of the trade routes towards central Asia and India. Because the kings of Persia disputed his right to these routes, Belisar marched out with some troops. The two super powers had been at peace for more than a hundred years, but the East Roman Empire broke this peace now. In some battles the Persian king was defeated by Belisar's troops, which were actually outnumbered by the Persians.

We write the year 531 AD

Justinianus had made use of the glorious absence of Belisar in the meantime, had gathered a hundred warships and five hundred escorting ships in the Bosporus and was keen to have this big navy set sail. First he made peace with the king of Persia. The Persians could stab him in the back no longer and he could start his great enterprise which was very important to him.

Justinianus called Belisar back after the signing of the peace treaty with Persia and gave him the order to conquer Africa.

This year another great event took place in the middle of Europe. The Bajuwari/Bavarians conquered the country Thuringia. But later they got into dependence of the Franconians themselves.

We write the year 533 AD

The great extermination war against the Vandals had begun in Africa. The Vandals had lived as fully saturated Roman citizens after the death of their king Geiserich. They weren't any more the warriors ready for a battle, but they were people of a nation who were weakened by their former allies, the Moorish nation (Mauritanians), in the meantime.

Now Belisar could take them by surprise. When he put ashore five hundred riders, the Vandals didn't offer stubborn resistance. So Belisar could take Carthage by a coup de main.

Gelimer, the last king of the Vandals, who was on the verge of death from starvation, surrendered. Whilst he was brought to Belisar, he roared with laughter. The persons present understood him to have gone mad by the excess of suffering and his laughing to be the laughing of a lunatic. But his friends contradicted this opinion. They explained the reaction of Gelimer by saying that he had very well a clear head, but he had come to the conclusion as prisoner that the whole life was worth only a great laugh. The empire of the Vandals came to an end with Gelimer, never again there was a new empire of this nation.

We write the year 534 AD

Whilst Belisar celebrated his triumph in Byzantium, Moorish warriors, who had already attacked the Vandals, attacked the troops of Belisar in Africa. Now Belisar had to leave as quickly as possible the ceremony of victory to return to his troops there. Back in Africa, he immediately took the offensive. The Moorish troops suffered a crushing defeat and Belisar could consolidate the power over North Africa, the former West Roman province. Now in Africa he also prepared for carrying out of the new great order, which Justinianus had already given him.

The prerequisite for a significant campaign of conquest was always the local and by events caused opportunities. The successor of Theoderich, the great king of the East Goths, was his grandson Athalarich. Because he was still a child, his mother Amalaswintha ruled for him. Her teacher was her own father. She had to be Goth and Roman according to the will of him. Her liking for the Roman way of life predominated so much that she wanted the young king of the Goths educated as Roman. But the noble Goths at the court were opposed to that. They forced the king's mother to have her son educated by Gothic teachers. The endeavours of the Gothic noblemen to make a real Gothic man of Athalarich, who shouldn't be a Roman weakling, brought matters to the stage where he proved too much his virility. His excesses also caused his death. He reached just an age of eighteen years. His successor was the cousin of Amalaswintha, Theodahad, on whom she imposed the condition to share the throne with her. He accepted, but arrested her. Now she turned to Byzantium and asked for help. That happened by support of confidants in prison.

Justinianus had formed an alliance with Amalaswintha before Belisar had started off for the campaign in North Africa. That he did to avoid the East Goths are suspicious if he defeated the Vandals.

Now he sent a courier to Paris, to the successors of Chlodwig, the four kings with equal rights in Franconia, to prevent them by friendly protestations from meddling in the forthcoming fighting. Justinianus had chosen the right moment for his courier, because the kings of Franconia didn't want to be disturbed in their own intentions of expansion. They had conquered the greater part of Thuringia, which was occupied by the Bajuwari, and settled the region by the river Main. They also wanted to get the northern part of Thuringia, which was occupied by the Saxons. They moreover wanted to occupy Burgundy and the Bavarian (Bajuwarian) regions, in which the Alemani were settled by Theoderich. Nothing was farther from the mind of the Franconian kings than a support of the East Goths, who could dispute the right to their new possession.

The Franconian kings Chlothar I, Childerich I and Theudebert I actually defeated the Burgundi (Burgundians) this year. Their empire was occupied after that by the Franconian kings. The Bajuwari still had a reprieve.

We write the year 535 AD

The East Goths didn't get aid from any side when Belisar left North Africa to conquer Sicily. East Goths were at variance with the claim to power of both opposite camps, the camp of Amalaswintha and the camp of Theodahad. On which side Justinianus and Belisar would be? Since the East Gothic Empire was weakened by quarrels for the succession to the throne and didn't dispose of enough troops, it was easy for Belisar to invade Italy. The inhabitants of the Italian towns welcomed Belisar as liberator. He also could win over the clergy of Italy to his side because he was a true follower of the Trinity and no East Roman heretic who was fond of the Arianian faith. So he could march into Rome without meeting resistance.

195

We write the year 536 AD

Belisar had again reached what was normally impossible. He had conquered an empire for his emperor with only five thousand men. For he knew that the emperor wanted to keep the conquered countries to himself. He may take care of Amalaswintha, but only as needy woman and not as queen. But before Belisar could send her an invitation to come to Byzantium, she was murdered by her cousin. Justinianus couldn't wish for anything better. He could take revenge for the insidious murder, demand the deposition of Theodahad. But the East Goths anticipated him, they elected Wittigis (Witichis) new king.

We write the year 537 AD

Wittigis marched with a hundred and fifty thousand warriors, the whole of the Gothic armed forces, towards Rome and besieged the Eternal City. In the city there was soon a lack of foodstuffs and water. But Belisar didn't risk reinforcing his little army with Roman men to attack the Goths out of the city, because the senators could lay the blame on him that they couldn't have their daily bath because of absent staff then. Also they would miss the remainder of the well-being, which they still had after the plunders of the West Goths and Vandals, if Roman men had to go into the army. – Belisar stayed in the Eternal City and hoped to get reinforcements from Byzantium soon.

Whilst Belisar was stuck in Rome, the Franconians got the remainder of the country of the Aleman(n)i, which had belonged to the East Gothic Empire up to now, and the Provence (a region in the southern part of France). By it the Franconians had access to the Mediterranean Sea now.

We write the year 538 AD

One year was over. But the hoped for reinforcements from Byzantium hadn't come for Belisar. That also did not happen when Wittigis stopped the siege of Rome and retreated again. For he saw no sense in a longer siege and was also weary of that, therefore he went back to Ravenna with his complete army now. Wittigis had just set off, when East Roman ships landed on the coast of Italy and some legions went ashore. Now Belisar could start his great attack and besieged Ravenna. But there he fought a losing battle. The lagoons and the sandy ground before Ravenna made it impossible to take this town by storm. But Belisar trusted in his own ability and toughness. In Rome he had to supply with rations only five thousand legionnaires of his own but in Ravenna considerably more Goths went hungry. So time worked for him. Then was coming the hoped-for moment, the East Goths offered the surrender of the town. But they also made the condition that he should become their king then.

This year the Franconians under the leadership of Theudebert had begun to extend their empire up to the Danube. So they also occupied Bajuwarian/Bavarian territory and became the leading super power in the middle of Europe.

We write the year 539 AD

Belisar agreed to become king of the East Goths, because there was no better and quicker way for a victory over this nation. He marched into Ravenna and arrested Wittigis. Now he gave to his emperor Ravenna and the conquered East Gothic Empire as a present. That was a great gesture, but Justinianus didn't highly rate it even though Belisar hadn't taken the crown ultimately.

Back in Byzantium, Belisar celebrated his success in a great measure. He was a good-looking and tall man. His face radiated an exceptional kindness. He was always friendly and affable to everyone, rich or poor.

The army stood by Belisar, the people loved him. What could prevent him from chasing away Justinianus and Theodora? Justinianus and Theodora were really afraid of losing the crown and of having to leave the imperial palace. They had to guard against that absolutely. They withdrew the leadership of the army from Belisar, but not forever.

We write the year 547 AD

The generals Justinianus had sent to Italy instead of Belisar weren't up to the "furor teutonicus" of the East Goths, which was aroused again. Totila, since 541 AD king of the East Goths, had joined them into an army, which was fit for new actions. With this army he besieged Rome now.

When Belisar, who was sent once more by Justinianus, appeared before the walls of Rome, Totila had already conquered this city. He had moved into the Eternal City with ten thousand warriors and plundered it. The loot of the East Goths was all the inhabitants of this former rich city possessed after the earlier plunders. But the inhabitants were spared the murder of defenceless men and violation of women.

We write the year 548 AD

Totila had left Rome and occupied Ravenna in the meantime. Belisar could recapture Rome because there was only a small part of the Gothic troops. Thus it was finished for the time being the campaign of Byzantium in Italy.

Could Justinianus think of a conquest in the East after Belisar's success in the West now? He did, and declared war on Persia. But for a success there he needed Belisar too. Belisar had proved his worth during the last campaign against the Persians, so he was to lead the East Roman troops again.

We write the year 549 AD

Belisar left Italy. No sooner had he gone back to Byzantium, as Totila took the offensive again. He recaptured the Eternal City, but also Sicily, Corsica and Sardinia. It seemed as if the East Gothic Empire would rise in splendour again.

We write the year 551 AD

Whilst Belisar drove the Persians out of Syria Narses, who was an eunuch, took command of new troops who were to wipe out the East Goths forever. He crossed the sea with an army, which was head and shoulders above the East Goths, and immediately started his campaign on Italian ground.

We write the year 552 AD

Narses made a thorough job of the campaign. Totila was defeated in the battle of Tadinae. He was killed in action. His successor became Teja, who was killed during the battle of Vesuvius close to Naples. That was the last great battle of the East Goths, who got a free withdrawal now. But some Gothic castellos (castells) still offered resistance till 555 AD, then they were conquered too. Now the last Gothic warriors left Italy forever.

The Goths who had survived put to sea. They sailed for the north of Europe. In Scandinavia, their original home, they found a place of stay now. Some East Goths found perhaps whereabouts in Spain where their brothers, the West Goths, were living.

We write the year 558 AD

Chlothar I became king of Franconia. He could once more unite Franconia into one empire till his death in the year of 561 AD.

Whilst Chlothar I was king of the Franconians (Franks), the forcible attempt of Justinianus to restore the Roman Empire in its former greatness accelerated, the final ruin of Rome. The Apennines Peninsula was no longer a valuable part of the Roman Empire after the bloody wars against the East Goths, which had depopulated all of Italy. It didn't pay to protect the impoverished and devastated regions by armed forces. There it was enough to appoint someone governor. This so-called "exarch" had to save that what he could still save on the spot. Also he had to maintain all estates in certain condition, which he could make possible by available personnel. The conquered regions in Africa, which Belisar had conquered for his emperor, lost in political and economical value by the incessant unrest of the people. Also there was no holding in a long run of the bases, which his generals had occupied at the West Gothic coast of the Iberian Peninsula. The East Roman garrisons in Syria and Egypt moreover didn't withstand the new attacks of the Persians who couldn't keep quiet any more.

But more dangerous than the campaigns of the Persians were the invasions of warlike nations. They invaded regions settled by Huns, East Goths and other Germanic tribes. New nations, which went down in history, appeared in Europe and the Near East.

Nomadic tribes of Asia formed the first Turkish Empire now. They had united with wild mountain people of Central Asia and other marauding tribes into one nation and were called Oghusi. These Oghusi threatened the Persian Empire now.

Also China felt threatened in those days. The wild tribes of Asia hadn't formed boundaries, but they constantly bore arms and looked for new living space. A large part of these tribes were neighbours of the Chinese, therefore they often found themselves compelled to repulse their attacks. They had already anxiously noticed the invasion of the so-called "White Huns", who invaded India. There, in the regions of the rivers Indus and Ganges, the storm of the wild hordes had led to the decay of a great empire. The Chinese emperors were friends with this empire, therefore they were prepared for the worst to their own empire now. This former Indian Empire was

200

the country of origin of Buddhism moreover, which was the religion of China now.

China couldn't escape the unrest in the world in spite of its Great Wall and its deeply rooted culture. The Chinese Empire was split into a northern and a southern part. That was caused by the interruption in the succession of the imperial family. Now the sovereign of the northern part as well as the sovereign in the south of the empire strove for the former unification. But first both sovereigns had to combat and to chase the untamed attackers away to reach this goal and to make a great nation of China again, as it had once been.

The defence of the Great Wall began. Also the Turks were at a crossroads of their great migration like the Huns some hundred years ago. Also now predominated the desire for a migration in the direction of Europe and riders, who were greedy for loot and for land, drove forward the fleeing people.

The Turkish-Mongolian steppe's people, who were called in the Persian language "Avari" (Awari), crossed the Caucasus Mountains and reached the region of the Danube soon. There they subdued the Slav tribes.

The Awari weren't the wild riders like the Huns before. They had perhaps a certain order in their region of origin or they had the order of the Huns, who went back eastwards again after the death of Attila, and learnt their way of making war.

Since the Slavs and also the Awari didn't have history writers during their time of migration, nobody exactly knew where they were coming from and who they really were. They were named according to the regions where they appeared, so for example Serbians, Sorbians (Sorbi), Wendians (Wendi) or Wilzians (Wilzi). Later there were more Slav tribes in the middle and south-east of Europe.

Slav people had flooded the northern part of the Balkan Peninsula. They had settled there and had advanced to the coast of Dalmatia then, as did the Croats. Other Slav tribes worked their way through to the south-east Alpine regions, as the Slovenians.

We write the year 561 AD

Chlothar I, the king of the Franconians, dies and his empire was shared again. Now there were three independent parts: Austrasia with the capital Reims, Neustria with the capital Paris and Burgundy with the capital Orléans. The head of the government of each independent part of Franconia was the house-meier (Maior domus). This highest official at the court seized the power later and was the real ruler over Franconia then.

We write the year 565 AD

There were combats over and over again between the Langobardi and Gepidi, who settled in the regions of today's Austria and Hungary. But neither of the two nations could make a success of these combats. Also the great battle of this year didn't bring the wished for decision.

This year the Awari also invaded the lowlands of Pannonia and threatened their new neighbours there, the Langobardi and the Gepidi. The Langobardi were once supported by Justinus and Justinianus when they had erected their empire on the Danube against the possible extension of the East Gothic Empire of Theoderich. Now they should keep away other people of the Far East who wanted to invade regions of the East Roman Empire. But the Langobardi were weakened by the constant fights with the Gepidi.

We write the year 567 AD

The Langobardi had to pay a high price for the peace with the Awari. They had to hand over a tenth of their livestock to them. But they didn't have any other possibility. The war against the Gepidi was still lasting, therefore an additional war against the Awari was impossible. Now their king Alboin called the Awari for help after the signing of the peace treaty. The Awari willingly followed the call of Alboin. They invaded the Gepidian territory from all directions and wiped out, sitting on small and quick horses like the Huns, this nation. Thus the Gepidian nation vanished into thin air for ever. – Now the Langobardi were also threatened by the Awari in spite of the peace treaty.

We write the year 568 AD

The power of the Awari became too strong for the Langobardi, therefore they abandoned the lowlands of Pannonia and set off for the long march to Italy, which was weakened and without protection. They knew the route very well because Narses, the former commander of the East Roman troops in Italy, had made use of them during the fights against the East Goths there. Twenty thousand Saxons and people of other Germanic tribes followed the Langobardi. This mixture of Germanic tribes invaded North Italy under the leadership of Alboin. There in the north of the Apennines Peninsula, they founded a new Langobardian empire.

There were combats with the occupying forces of Byzantium. Also the Franconians, who wanted to extend their empire, pressed the Langobardi hard. But that were only occasional disturbances for the new kingdom, which had begun to consolidate its power in the north and middle of Italy. Whilst parts in the middle of Italy were subordinated for the time being to independent dukes, Byzantium could hold some forts for some time, so Ravenna, Rome, Liguria and Naples.

The capital of the new Langobardian empire in Italy became Pavia.

How did the Langobardi (Long Beards) get their name? There was reported that one day a delegation of them appeared at the court of Byzantium. Justinianus, who didn't know these people, asked his wife the question: "What is the name of these men with the long beards?" Theodora answered the question: "You have just called their name!"

We write the year 572 AD

Alboin, conqueror of North Italy and founder of the Langobardian Empire there, since 560 king of this nation, was murdered on 28 June in Verona. Whilst the horror of the Gothic wars and the devastation caused by invading Germanic tribes had messed up more and more the order in Italy, a new epoch had begun under the reign of Alboin, the epoch of the economic rise. The job of his successors was, to guarantee that also for the future. They made it possible, North Italy and so Langobardia (Lombardia) became a flourishing country, the country of the profiteers. So many economic designations came from Lombardia, for example a term of the bankers, "Lombardsatz" (rate for loans on securities). But also the first paper money came from Lombardia/Langobardia.

The Franconian Empire

We write the year 580 AD

This year Magnus Cassiodorus (Cassiodor) died, the famous West Roman scholar and historian, who was employed by Theoderich the Great. He was born in 485 AD. So he was a very old man when he died now. His old age was unusual in those days. He tried to reach a reconciliation between East Goths and the Romans during the East Gothic reign. The history of the East Goths (Historia Gothorum), which he had written in 12 volumes in the years between 526 and 533 AD, unfortunately survived by extracts of Jordanes only.

We write the year 586 AD

Leowigild, the king of the West Goths, died this year. He had conquered Cordoba and the empire of the Suebi in Spain. By it his empire comprised almost the whole Iberian Peninsula.

We write the year 587 AD

The successor of Leowigild, who was a supporter of the Arianian faith, converted together with his people to the Catholic faith. Rekkared, as was his name, was considered to be the symbol of the unity of Spain.

We write the year 600 AD

The Slavs expanded their territory in the east of Europe. They had pushed ahead even up to the river Elbe and the area of North Bavaria. Now they were the neighbours of the Saxons and Bajuwarians (Bavarians/Bavarii).

The Sears, the today's Swedes, expanded their territory on the whole of Sweden and ruled by it over the entire space of the Baltic Sea.

We write the year 613 AD

There was only chaos in the three parts of the Franconian empire in the years before. The inconsiderate competition for the superiority, the open and secret fights amongst the kings and queens of the Merovingians, had resulted in continuous unrest and moral degeneration in the whole of their empire. Murder and sexual offence in the royal family were the order of the day. But the term "king" was so strengthened in Franconia, that the kings of the dynasty of the Merovingians didn't lose their crown in spite of the opposition of the great national men. Under Chlothar II the three Franconian kingdoms could even unite into one kingdom this year.

The new king of all Franconians shortly after his elevation issued the "edictum Chlotarii", a decree by which the proportions of power shifted. The counts, the "comites", who had administered the separated parts of the empire as royal commissioners and were responsible for the jurisdiction, the army and the economy, were appointed by the kings at their discretion. The both king's makers of Chlothar, who had struggled for the crown to him, were members of the most wealthy families of Austrasia: bishop Arnulf of Metz and Pippin. They had secured the power in those territories, in which they had possessions.

The heads of the royal household, who also were leaders of the mounted royal attendants and managers of the royal estates, bore the name "Maior domus" (house-mayor/house-meier). They set themselves up as mediators between the kings and the nobility. Although they were subjects of the kings according to their name and had to pay homage to them, they were the real rulers in the empire by the accumulation of estates and privileges. Only the bishops were equal in power to them. They had extended their church estates by royal donations, which became by it real power areas.

The bishops martly held office in former Roman towns in the province. The looks of these towns had so extremely changed in the last decades that there were only ruins and place names, which had been linguistically modified in the meantime. The houses were adjusted to the new habit of life of the occupants. These occupants wore different clothes from the Romans before. The Romans wore the light shirt-like tunica and cape-like toga, but the Franconians wore heavy capes, long pants, long skirts and coats now, all that was unusual during the Roman period. The fashion was plump. Also the meals had changed. There were eaten simple, nutritious dishes instead of the refined and tasty dishes of the Romans, who had spiced all they ate. Since theatre and circus were frowned upon, the only allowed diversion was churchgoing. So the sermons had more and more influence on the minds, and the bishops, who determined the content of a sermon, more and more power.

The noble landowners, mostly living in mansions, which were situated on hills near the towns, endeavoured to make bishops of their members of the family. During the first time of the forcible immigration to the Roman provinces the priests had met the educated Roman middle classes to try to get back with help of the church what they once had lost. But also the new lords of the manors, who had learned nothing but the war trade, now knew that it would be wise to educate themselves mentally and spiritually. Priests became teachers at the noble courts and the pupils became priests. But it went without saying that young men, who were designated by their families to become bishop, also trained the application of a weapon. Those bishops were often war lords, who exchanged the robe of the mass, if it was necessary, for the armour and so reinforced the military forces of their families.

This was done by the bishop of Metz, when he and Pippin the Older had helped Chlothar II to get the crown. Reims had been the original capital of Austrasia. Soon it was changed to Metz. Pippin the Older became house-meier/house-mayor and controlled the administration and the army of Austrasia.

We write the year 629 AD

Chlothar II died and his successor was Dagobert I. He thought to bring back the former glamour of the royal house. In contemporary papers it is reported on him: "He did equal justice to poor and rich people. He didn't sleep and eat much. He always tried to behave so that nobody went away from him without being full of joy and admiration." That Dagobert had three queens and an army of concubines and a 'slave of the non-abstinence' was a fact one could also find in his family. But he also was a personality, a man who could limit the power of the house-meiers and the great counts.

We write the year 632 AD

An important year, which was to change the world and so also Europe. Mohammed, the founder of the Islam, dies in Medina. The great prophet was born in 570 AD as son of Abdallah, a member of the impoverished family of the Hashimides, in Mecca. Medina and Mecca were the two most important cities of Arabia in the years of the early Middle Ages. – "Arab" means "barren". So Arabia is by name a barren country, a country of desert and without vegetation. There were only in some areas plants, which throve on the barren ground. In the oasis throve dates and other fruits, but also fragrant plants whose delicious oil was a much sought-after commodity. There were market-places and ports on the western seaside. There were also trade routes in the interior, connecting the east with the west. But the caravan routes nobody could use as wagon's track. Therefore the most important means of transportation of the nomadic pastoral people, who were restlessly living on the ground of the dry Arabian peninsula, were the camels. Their udders donated milk, their hair and hide were basic material for clothes and tents, when they died after a strenuous life. Also the flesh of their dead body was still delicate enough to be eaten as meat.

The best friends of the herdsmen in the desert were the horses. On their backs the Arabs could at least venture to ride for a short distance into the desert. There they looked out for areas of grass for their livestock, which they drove from pastureland to pastureland.

The Arabs of the last years of the sixth century only differed from the original state of the early-roaming nomads by their experience and knowledge, which they had gathered in the course of generations as trading travellers all over the peninsula. It is true that what they absorbed also stimulated their imagination, but didn't excite the wish to change their free way of life. Was there a better living space for an Arab when he could live in the open air of the desert, which was his property? Whoever disputed his right to freedom of movement, was his enemy. And he combated an enemy not only out of principle, but also out of love of adventure and bellicose habit. The armed robberies onto persons who got into the desert, his property, he took for granted. These robberies he exercised in cold blood to ensure the success.

A clever circumspection, which he needed to survive, belonged to his special character, but also the merciless cruelty, taught him by the inhospitable nature of his environment, and the blind-furious courage with which he pursued each goal that he could reach.

The Arabs believed in the threatening and conciliatory forces of nature like the ancient Egyptians. The moon was a frightening goddess in its form of appearance, but more terrible were the unpredictable ghosts, the "Dshinns", who could make a courageous man defenceless by their mysterious appeal. This paralyzing ghost belief might be caused by the odd and inexplicable natural phenomenon of the desert. No earthy power seemed to be a match for the diverse, disturbing "Dshinns". A prayer was sometimes helping, but who wasn't up to these powers with their vitality couldn't hope to placate them in the death.

Was there a life after death? Like all people, also the Arabs yearned for eternal life. The descendants of a deceased often fastened a camel on the tomb and left it without food to the last breath. So it could be prompt to serve the deceased on the uncertain other side of life, as well as it had done when its master was still alive.

In the Holy City of Mecca, the most important meeting place of the trade caravans, which continuously passed through the Arabian peninsula, rose a quadrangular building like a tower, the "kaaba". Within the "kaaba" is adored the "Black Stone". This stone, which is actually dark red, came from heaven according to the faith of the Moslems. This stone is also said to be symbol of the tribe of Ismael, the descendants of Abraham, that didn't recognize Israel. The religious admirers of the "Black Stone" referred to the words of the 118th psalm: "The stone, which the workmen of the building had rejected, has turned into a corner stone. That happened by the Lord and is a miracle before our eyes."

There also were idols in the "kaaba". The Arabian tribe of the Quraish worshipped one of these stones as highest god and called him: Allah.

From the noble people of the Quraish, who traced their origin back to Abraham or Ismael and held one of the leading ranks in Mecca, also maternally descended a son of the trader Abdallah. He got the name Mohammed, meaning "Who is praised". Five camels, one herd of goats and one female slave, that was all he inherited from his father. His mother, Amina, died when he was six years old. Now his grandfather and his uncle took care of him.

Mohammed learnt neither to read nor to write. He was twelve years old when he accompanied his uncle Abu Talib for Syria. There, after the arrival with a caravan, he was initiated into the business methods of the merchants of Mecca.

Mohammed was already self-employed when he was twenty-five years old. He was agent of the rich widow Chadidsha, who was forty years old and mother of several children. Mohammed got married to Chadidsha a little time later. Chadidsha made Mohammed an affluent man. She gave birth to two sons for him and some daughters. But the sons died in infancy.

The most famous daughter of Mohammed was Fatima, who got married to Mohammed's cousin Ali, the son of Abu Talib.

Mohammed led an exemplary family life in this life he also included a relative of his wife. It was Waraqha, who knew the scriptures of the Hebrews and the Christians. He gave Mohammed food for thoughts of the real faith. The discussions culminated in the question: Had the Messiah, who the Jews were expecting, already come? Was there Jesus Christ, who was nailed to the cross and died to put mankind out of its misery, godlike but also of human nature according to the opinion of the Arianians (Arianism) in the west or only of divine nature, what most Christians believed in the east? But was a godlike being able to submit to the disgrace of the crucifixion and die like a human being?

Mohammed, who had a very likeable face according to what Ali said and therefore nobody could tear himself away from his presence, tried to find out the answer by opinion polls. He had himself informed of the revelations of the Holy Scriptures. These scriptures were a confirmation to him that there was only one God: Allah.

Mohammed wanted to reach the intellectual elevation, which would be clearing up all secrets, by absorbing of spiritual impressions, by thinking and religious feeling, as the Christian hermits did. Each year he retired and went with his family into a cave quite near to Mecca. Here he devoted himself to a passionate thinking about the meaning of life. That he always did for one month only, because he couldn't neglect his business.

In the year of 610 AD he was alone in the cave, when the archangel Gabriel appeared to him. At home he told Chadidsha then: "Whilst I was sleeping, Gabriel appeared. The archangel showed me a blanket of silk brocade. On it something was written. He said: 'Read!' I answered: 'I can't read'. He pressed the blanket so tight on my body that I thought my death was coming. Then he relaxed the pressure and said again: 'Read!' And I read aloud, and he went away. Then I woke up and felt how the words got into my heart. I set off up to the half way to the mountain peak. There I heard a voice from heaven: 'Oh Mohammed, you are the envoy of Allah and I'm Gabriel!'

I raised my eyes to the sky, there where is heaven, and saw Gabriel as human figure with his feet at the rim of heaven."

The saying of Jesus: "A prophet is accepted least of all in his native country and in his house", had Mohammed strengthened during the first years of his obsessed eagerness of faith. In Mecca he was considered to be an insignificant person, even though Chadidsha, who was already growing an old woman, didn't prevent him from keeping an open house and from inviting all human natures for turning an ear to him. Many pilgrims came to Mecca and the "kaaba", but nobody was convinced by the excited businessman that he was to be the prophet of Allah, the almighty God. Therefore they doubted that he had a clear head. It became known that Mohammed often suffered from spasm, got into a sweat and collapsed. Then he lost consciousness too. His narration about the archangel Gabriel appearing to him to herald the divine revelations, whilst a bell-clear tone accompanied the words, fell flat. But Mohammed could convince Ali finally. He also achieveded that his servant Said, who was his released slave, converted. Also Abu Bekr, a relative, converted. He was a rich man, who paid for slaves' release to win them over to Mohammed's new faith. Abu Bekr could also win five other influential businessmen of Mecca over. They became with him the "comrades of Mohammed". Their reminiscences of the prophet were rated as sanctified tradition.

Many people didn't kindly behave to Mohammed. Most people were rude to him. Well-meaning people advised him to go to a doctor, who would cure him of his tomfoolery. If there had not followed him a certain Omar, who had an enormous strength and was highly esteemed, the first Moslems would have had a bad time. There were ultimately at stake the earnings, which the inhabitants of Mecca fetched by the pilgrims. That was taken more seriously than the imagined apparitions of the merchant, whose followers paid for slaves' release and molested the pilgrims with their new faith.

Mohammed had to retire first. He went into a separated district of Mecca to avoid bloody clashes with his adversaries. Then, after the death of Chadidsha and Abu Talib, he tried to settle in the little town Taif, which was situated to the east of Mecca. But there he was driven out again. When the inhabitants threw stones at him, he had to leave this town hastily. Now he only saw one possibility, to go back to Mecca.

Mohammed was already fifty years old and didn't lose courage. He compensated himself for the bad blows, which he had to take very hard. He got married to a young and charming widow and at the same time got engaged to Aisha, who was just seven years old. Aisha was the daughter of his best friend Abu Bekr.

The world of the supernatural appearances indemnified Mohammed for his failed change of place too. He had a dream about the fate of thousands and thousands of human beings. In this dream he mounted a horse with wings at the wall of lamentation in Jerusalem and flew to heaven. His waking up in his bed in Mecca in the morning didn't affect the real effect of his dream, because he proclaimed now: Jerusalem is like Mecca a Holy City of all Moslems.

A short time later, after an excited sermon, by which he could win important merchants of the town of Jathrib over, new persecutions of Mohammed's followers began. The beneficiaries of the "kaaba" feared that Mohammed would instigate his followers and the inhabitants of Jathrib, where many Jews were living, to a combat against Mecca and the supporters of the "kaaba". Therefore they wanted to arrest and murder him. Mohammed went to Jathrib. Since then this town was called Medina, the city of the prophet. Now the first day of his flight, the "Hedshra", the 16 July 622 after Christ, became the first day of the Moslem chronology.

In Medina joined together the followers of Mohammed. There Mohammed threw himself on the ground and called out before his followers: "Allah is great!". He brought about by this humiliating subjection the symbol of taking to the will of God, to make peace with God, what is called in his language "Islam". The faithful were called "Muslims (Moslems)". Those are persons who have made up with Allah, who have devoted themselves to him. These "Muslims" entrusted the commanding power to Mohammed, and that not only in questions of faith.

First there weren't many followers of Mohammed, because most inhabitants of Medina, Arabs and Jews, feared the presence of Mohammed would involve their town in a war with Mecca. He tried to win the Jews over by the promise of religious freedom. They were to form an only and common nation with the "Muslims (Moslems)" according to his opinion and have equal rights for help and services like his people. When two hundred Arabian families migrated from Mecca to Medina Mohammed got into trouble, because there weren't enough foodstuffs for these families, who were lured by Mohammed's promises to go to Medina.

Mohammed knew the habits of the desert occupants from experience. He also knew the many tribes, that moved around freely. He reached an agreement with their chieftains. It was intended to give them four fifths of the loot of their raids on caravans in the desert, the remainder they had to give him then. For this he would also see to it that the share of the loot of a looter who was killed during the raid, was received by his widow, but he himself would be sent to paradise.

Soon there were men enough volunteering to risk a raid for Mohammed. The prophet prepared the raids so factually and professionally that they were mostly successful. When he succeeded in defeating a protecting troop of nine hundred men of the merchants of Mecca, he rose in esteem of the people. Now he was also the army commander whom God had sent. From now on he could show his warlike talent in more than 65 raids, which he had planned and also mostly led in person.

The number of his followers, but also the number of his adversaries, was growing. The fight between the supporters of the "kaaba" (=cube) of Mecca and the followers of Mohammed spread. When Jewish settlers supported the Quraishes, who were related to Mohammed but also enemies of him, he attacked them. There were executions of heroic Jews because they refused to become Moslems and subjugation of people, who faced the facts that they had to hand over all their possessions but could keep for that their faith. Also the bride of a Jewish attendant, his name was Kinana, was simply added to Mohammed's household.

After a long war Mohammed made an armistice treaty with his relatives of a different faith in Mecca. By this treaty he provided that he and his followers could carry out the usual pilgrimage every year. Now he moved ceremoniously, coming from Medina, into the town Mecca and touched the "Black Stone" with his pilgrim stick in an awe-inspiring way. "There is only one God – Allah", he called out now. That was a warlike provocation, but it was well-meant. His attitude seemed to be friendly to the inhabitants of Mecca, therefore he could be certain of a return to this town forever. He was the prophet, who was also highly esteemed in his native town now.

In the following year Mohammed came into Mecca with ten thousand men and proclaimed: "This town is the Holy place of the Islam, no person of a different faith is allowed to set foot on the ground of Mecca." Now he subdued the whole of the Arabian peninsula in a short time, which amazed many people. But nobody upset Mohammed's plans when he conquered the whole of Arabia. The east Roman Empire was at war with Persia. Neither the emperor of Byzantium nor the Persian king took the messengers seriously who asked them to convert to the new faith in the name of Mohammed.

Mohammed had time enough. The doctrine he had created allowed him to have ten wives and many concubines. He didn't have bedrooms. He spent every night with another woman. There were jealousy and quarrels, which were caused by the dirt-obsessed housewives of Mohammed. But he could look after himself. If a woman asked for precious presents, he promised paradise instead of giving her a present. Mohammed seldom took advantage of the godlike revelation, on which he relied in the execution of his reign's power, for personal purposes. He only changed his behaviour if there was no other possibility. So he desired one day to marry the wife of his adopted son Said. He explained his intent simply with the words now: "Allah has given the order, and Allah is great!".

215

Now the kalifs, the highest fellow believers of his faith, disseminated the "Islam" by the war cry: "Allah is great!" Their holy book was the Koran, the lecture. It was the book about Mohammed's sayings, the law, which was revealed by God and promulgated by him. The Arabs of those days only knew fragments of the Koran. The prerequisite of their unquestioning following was the belief that God had confided in the prophet. What Mohammed demanded of them and what he promised them, that essentially met their habits and wishes too. He was neither against the commercial greed for profit nor against sensual pleasure if it was sealed by marriage. He also obliged his compatriots by permitting them to marry several women. But he didn't allow the compatriots to make his example their own. He thought four wives were enough for a man. Mohammed also gave the wives permission to leave the house, but only if they needed something badly. They should amuse their husbands in the harem where there was no entry for strangers. What was badly needed was only decided by the head of the household.

It took many years to reach the regulated words of the Moslem doctrine, which finally determined the public and domestic way of life of the Islam. Also a certain time passed to the first call of the "muezzin", who summoned the faithful five times every day for prayer. Then he heralded always: "Allahu Akbar – God is the Greatest. I testify that Mohammed is Allah's envoy. Come to the prayer, come to the salvation. Allahu Akbar – there is no God except Allah." When this call was heard, then the Moslems had to wash their face, feet and hands, to kneel down with the face towards Mecca and the "kaaba" and to join with Allah in a short prayer.

Mohammed had adopted the idea of hell and eternal life in heaven from the Old and New Testament. He had conjured up the last Judgement too. He didn't deny neither the godlike revelation of Moses nor the psalms of David. Also he didn't reject the "good message" of Jesus Christ. He accepted the biblical history. But he rectified certain passages, which doubted the honour of God too. So the Christians were of the holy persuasion that God had his son Jesus die on the cross. In Mohammed's opinion also Jesus was a prophet. Neither he was also in no doubt about miracle activity of Jesus. But that he was the son of God, he couldn't acknowledge: "God is verily the single God. He is too grand to have a son."

Mohammed condemned neither the Jews nor the Christians when they observed the rules of their faith. But he also did not prevent them to do that. He conjured them to submit themselves to the Koran, because God had replaced all preceded revelations by his prophet. The Old and New Testament were the words of God, but now Allah wished the whole of mankind to be reformed and united into the Islam.

The dissemination of the Islam was turning to the holy war now. What words didn't reach, should be gained by the sword. The kalifs would have failed in the attempt to disseminate their faith in the world in spite of the belligerent love of adventure of the Arabs, which was supported by their fatalism and longing for the promised paradise, if the revelations of Mohammed hadn't obliged the Christians, who were confused by their own religious quarrels. There was much splitting hairs in the interpretation of the eastern Christianity, so it wasn't astonishing that faith-willing Christians didn't turn a deaf ear to the Moslems, who advanced with good words but also with brutal force. Also the legislation of Justinianus, which put all Christians who didn't profess to be of Catholic faith at a disadvantage, caused many followers of other Christian sects to seek refuge with the tolerant kalifs.

The bloody armed conflict between the East Roman Empire and the Persian kings had weakened both super powers so much that it wasn't difficult for Omar, who was successor to the first kalif Abu Bekr, to conquer the garrisons of Byzantium with his belligerent riders. Also Damascus and Jerusalem he could conquer. The Arabian shadows invaded Armenia. They conquered the two-river-land (Iraq) and became successors of the kings of the Sasanids in Persia.

The world power Islam, which had developed by unrestrained conquests in some decades only, already comprised under the reign of the kalif Othman already the Arabian native country, Syria, Palestine, Persia, Egypt and a big part of North Africa. Soon also the Iberian pe-

217

ninsula (Spain, Portugal) was to become part of the Moslem Empire. Also a part of today's France belonged to the Moslems for a (very) short time. Later Sicily and South Italy were conquered by the Moslems.

There wasn't always a homogeneous denomination of the Moslems. There came into being schisms, which led to acts of violence within the Islam. But the Arabian language was dominating in all territories, which were conquered by the Arabs, because it wasn't allowed to translate the Koran into any other language. Besides, the faithful had to know the Koran by learning by heart.

The European sovereigns of the Germanic empires could not deal with the rapid extension of the Islam, because they had to pay their full attention to the rearrangement and consolidation of their conditions of life. Also the repulse of the attacks of the Awarians and Slavs kept them busy. But Byzantium, the only power, which had survived as part of the former gigantic Roman world empire its ruin, had to defend itself against the dangerous assault of the Arabs, who didn't recoil from conquering Byzantium. So appeared the kalif Muawija with a huge navy before Byzantium. Byzantium didn't have the disposal of enough troops and wasn't in possession of many ships, which it could set against the Arabs. But Byzantium was the inventor of a disastrous fire: the so-called Greek Fire.

In a summer night of those days rode at anchor the Arabian navy in the harbour of Byzantium. At the moment when the Arabs intended to disembark, the water turned into fire. All Arabian ships, which couldn't escape from the mysterious fire, burnt and with it were burnt to death the crews of these ships too.

Was that the rescue from the Arabian assault for Europe? But the annihilation of the greater part of their navy didn't discourage the holy warriors of Islam. They changed their way and advanced under the command of the kalifs of the dynasty of the Omaijads (661 – 675 AD) in North Africa. In the years between 695 and 698 AD they conquered Carthage, the last bulwark of Byzantium there. Now the next mark was Europe.

The end of the West Gothic Empire in Spain

We write the year 639 AD

Dagobert I is dead and the Franconian Empire shared again. His successors, the so-called "loafer kings" of the shared Franconian Empire, were his sons Chlodwig II in Neustria/Burgundy (639 – 657 AD) and Sigibert III in Austrasia (639 – 656 AD). They found themselves compelled to entrust the house-meiers with the power they had once owned.

We write the year 656 AD

In Austrasia Dagobert II, the son of Sigibert III, became king after the death of his father. But he was banished by the house-meier Grimoald in the year of 660 AD and had to go into an Irish monastery.

We write the year 657 AD

In Neustria and Burgundy Chlothar II (657 – 673 AD) became the new king after the death of Chlodwig II. He united the whole of Franconia for a short time (661/662 AD)

We write the year 662 AD

In Neustria still another man was made king apart from Chlothar II. It was Childerich II (662 – 675 AD). Also Childerich II could unite the Franconian Empire again (673 – 675 AD). In 675 he was murdered by the nobility of Neustria. Later his son, Chilperich II, was king of Franconia till 721 AD and his grandson till 751 AD. Then in 751 AD the grandson Childerich III, the last king of the dynasty of the Merovingians, was deposed.

We write the year 675 AD

In Neustria the new king was Theuderich III after the murder of Childerich II. After his death in 691 AD his son Childibert III became king (till 711 AD).

We write the year 676 AD

Dagobert II leaves the Irish monastery, the place of his exile, and becomes king of Austrasia again. But three years later he was murdered.

We write the year 687 AD

All previous kings were kings without power. The power was in the hands of the house-meiers. So Pippin II (the Middle), who was house-meier since 679 AD in Austrasia, could completely seize the power. He was the son of the daughter of Pippin I (the Older, house-meier in Austrasia, 623 – 640 AD, together with bishop Arnulf of Metz) and Bishop Arnulf of Metz. This year he defeated his rivals in the bloody battle of Tertry and adopted the title "dux et princeps Francorum". Now he absolutely ruled over the whole Franconian Empire, which belonged according to the name to the kings of the dynasty of the Merovingians. But Pippin II was having a rough time with his power. In the south the dukedom Aquitania proclaimed its independence and the dukes of Alsace, Bavaria and Thuringia weren't willing to submit themselves without resistance. But Pippin II had also achieved that after his death (714 AD) nobody inquired his successor of the kings of the dynasty of the Merovingians. There was no doubt that one of his sons would become house-meier.

We write the year 689 AD

Pippin II defeated the Frisians under their leader Radbod. Now the western part of Friesland became part of the Franconian Empire by the peace treaty with this Germanic tribe.

We write the year 698 AD

In the Eifel is founded the abbey Echternach (Luxembourg), an abbey of the order of the Benedictines. In this abbey is buried Willibrord, a holy man of the Goths. The crypt there still dates from the time of the Merovingians. The city of Echternach became famous by its jumping procession of today.

We write the year 701 AD

Egika, the last of the great West-Gothic (Visigothic) kings, dies. The Gothic Empire was still mighty during his life. The Goths of Spain were excellent people for combats, distinguished in the skill to use the arms. They combated not only with thrust-lances on foot but also with javelins on horseback; they relied upon the impetuous run of their horses, they liked to practise the throwing of javelins and the sham attacks and warlike games they arranged every day. But all this was of no use, destiny took its course. Nowhere in Europe the history of Judaism is joined so manifold with the history of the country like in Spain. For the first time the Jews are the destiny of a nation here. The first communities of Jews we have in the late first century and early second century on the peninsula Iberica. The first documents about big Jewish communities in Spain we find from the year 306 AD. The council of Elvira in Andalusia appointed that Catholic girls were allowed to marry neither heretics, like the Arianians later, nor Jews. Married Catholics, who had intercourse with Jews or Arianians later, were menaced by excommunication. During the blessing of fields and other religious customs in connection with the agricultural labour it was no longer allowed to take into consultation the rabbis. In the presence of this early anti-jewish behaviour of the Catholics the Arianian conquerors, the West-Goths, appeared for the Jews as a safe retreat. Especially in the region of Narbonne Judaism took a clear pro-Gothic bearing because the oppressors of this region were the Catholic Franks/Franconians.

The fortunate phase of a quiet development with quick economic prosperity of many Jewish families was suddenly at an end at the moment when the discord of both Christian creeds was no longer existent and the collected power of the Catholicism, since Rekkared I, could turn against the Jews now. For the Jews it was coming hard rights now. This happened in the name of the Catholic church. For all Jews it was the beginning of hard times. Rekkeswind and Egika with their "Jews' Rights" even aimed at the expulsion of the Jewish minority.

The attack of the Christians was primarily directed against Jewish families, who had Christian slaves. It was unthinkable for the bishops and Christian communities that Christians should serve the Jews and should be exposed to their humours and concupiscence.

If the Jews didn't feel the rights by full hardness there were reasons. Once the rulers were quickly following in a certain time, so that it was impossible to apply the "Jews' Rights", then the Jews had something while many West-Gothic kings lacked something, namely money. So many Jews understood it by plenty of rates to escape a hard oppression.

But in the course of time hate of Jews was arising so that many Jews didn't see another chance but the getaway. The Jews mostly owned more than the rest of the population, which led to jealousy and hate at the end. So many Jews crossed the Channel of Gibraltar to North Africa, where they were taken as friends of the Moslem Arabs, especially because they brought along much money.

But in some towns of the West-Gothic Empire Jewish communities remained; here they didn't have to be afraid of pursuits. The towns were enjoying a certain independence and the Jews were the main financiers of the town-economy.

In North Africa the emigrated Jews already mobilized for an invasion to the Peninsula Iberica together with the victory-accustomed Arabs. In the year 698 AD, king Egika already perceived the danger. Therefore the bishops concluded the complete subjugation of the remaining Jews in Spain. The Jews became serfs of state, their kids were taken away with attainment of an age of 6 years and then educated in the Christian faith.

The Jews had clever leaders, who knew at once, which destiny was waiting for them in a Christian-West Gothic Spain and on which weak foundation rested it after the death of Egika.

We write the year 709 AD

In the autumn-time of the year 709 AD the Arabs started the first command-undertakings to reconnoitre the best time for the invasion. Based on the help of the Jews in Spain these undertakings were so successful that the Arabs could think of an invasion in the next months.

We write the year 710 AD

This year there was a decision in July, because the Arabs were now convinced that they couldn't have big difficulties with the invasion. The necessary information they had from Jews who had fled, they informed the Arabs of rebellions of the Basques in the north of the peninsula. Thus Arabs and Jews mobilized for the great invasion.

Roderic, the king of the West Goths, fought against the Basques in the north of Spain when he heard that an Arabian army under the commander Tarik ibn Ziyad had crossed the Channel of Gibraltar. This army constituted the first bridge-head on European ground. It was following a Jewish army under Kaulan al Jahudi, which was reinforced by Berbers. Both armies assembled in the south of Spain and marched together towards Cordoba.

We write the year 711 AD

When Roderic heard that the enemy was marching towards Cordoba, he approached in a hurry with some true combatants only to organize the defence of this town. When Tarik heard that Roderic was already in Cordoba, he had the onward march stopped to wait for reinforcements. A short time later many ships with Berber and Jewish troops landed who strengthened the front. However Roderic had a bad time, because he could only remove a part of this troops from north, the rest had to keep fighting against the Basques in Spain. Therefore he was very inferior to the invaders. On 19 July there was the decisive battle at the mouth of the Rio Salado.

This battle was one of the most important battles on European ground. Arabs and Jews had together 20,000 combatants, the Goths only 8,000, because the greatest part of their troops was still fighting in the north. Furthermore, Roderic had traitors in his army. Entire lines deserted and were then fighting on the Arabian side. After hard actions and many casualties for the Gothic side the battle came to an end on 25th of July. The battle was lost for the Goths, Roderic himself was killed in action. Gothic lances, throw-spears (javelins), drill and military exercises were for nothing and couldn't bring victory for the Goths. Under clouds of arrows from the Arabs the rest of the Gothic army turned to flight. This victory of the Arabs opened the gates to Europe for the Islam.

Andalusia, the Vandals called it Vandalusia, is called Al Andalus now. In Granada, Cordoba and other towns in the south of Spain the Arabs strike up their songs of victory. But the combats were continued against the rest of the Goths for more than one year; then the last Gothic towns in the north of Spain fell. In the end the Arabs were helped by the Basques to defeat the last Goths.

But in the year of 721 AD some regions in the north of Spain rose up against the invaders. These regions had the first success in the year of 725 AD, they could beat the Arabs in a fierce battle. This is the beginning of the "reconquista", the reconquest of the peninsula Iberica by Christian sovereigns of the north; but the Goths didn't matter in this case. The remainder of the Goths mingled with the native population. Thus came into being new kingdoms, as for example Castilia and Arragon, which united more than 750 years later and constituted the base of a new empire, the Spanish Empire, and the last Arabs were chased away from Andalusia.

But were there really the last Goths, who were fighting in Spain in the years 711 and 712 AD? No!!! On the peninsula Crimea in the Black Sea was a little Gothic principality still existent more than 800 years later. This principality went to ruins only when the Turks conquered it. 100 years after the conquest travellers were still reporting that people on Crimea were speaking Gothic.

The years before Charles the Great

We write the year 712 AD

Luitprand is the new king of the Langobardi. During his time of rule till 744 AD the Langobardian Empire reached once more a culmination. It was mighty and militarily powerful. The generals of Luitprand pressed him to conquer the cities Ravenna and Rome, which were still East Roman garrisons. But especially compared with Rome he had scruples; here is the pope and the Langobardi are Catholic. A war would be turning against the Catholic head, therefore he refrained from a war of conquest.

We write the year 714 AD

Charles/Karl Martell (martell = hammer), son of Pippin II, takes over the rule of the Frankish (Franconian) Empire as housemeier. He immediately began with the reorganization of the Frankish Empire and intensified the contacts to the pope in Rome without getting into his dependence. He was the first great ruler of the great power Franconia.

We write the year 722 AD

Pope Gregor II appoints Bonifatius – who does missionary work in those days in the Frankish Empire – to be bishop, this took place with benevolence of Charles Martell. After that Charles Martell vested the adherents of Bonifatius with benefits in order to secure their following.

This year also the wars of the Frankish Empire began against the Frisians, Saxons, Bavarians and Alemani, which were lasting some years. All these wars finished with the victory of the Frankish Empire.

We write the year 724 AD

One of the last West Gothic wandering bishops with name Pirmin founded the abbey Reichenau (island Reichenau in Lake Constance) in the south of Germany and some years later monasteries in Alsace, the Palatinate (Pfalz) and Bavaria.

We write the year 730 AD

The Arabs conquered some of the North Spanish principalities, which just came into being, and reached the border of the Frankish Empire.

We write the year 732 AD

The Arabs passed over the Pyrenees with a big army and invaded Franconia. In a short time they conquered a great part of West France. The house-meier Charles Martell thereupon concentrated his troops in Middle France and marched from here against the enemy. Between the towns Tours and Poitiers the decisive battle was fought. In an exasperated slaughter over some days the Arabs were beaten and had to retreat in a hurry to avoid the complete extermination of their troops.

We write the year 737 AD

In Franconia, Charles Martell has become so powerful by his victory over the Arabs that he could rule without the Merovingian king. But he didn't strive for the king's crown himself.

We write the year 739 AD

Bishop Bonifatius founded numerous bishoprics in his last years of life till 754 AD, so Freising, Passau and Würzburg. All these bishoprics are in regions where he did missionary work.

We write the year 741 AD

Charles Martell died. A short time before his death he had divided the Frankish Empire amongst his sons Charlesman and Pippin the Little (or the Younger).

We write the year 743 AD

Pippin the Little, the last house-meier, appointed (himself) once more a king, it's Childerich III, the last member of the family of the Merovingians. But because the real rule was in the hands of Pippin, Childerich III was only a sham king.

We write the year 744 AD

The dukedom Swabia (Suebia) within the Frankish Empire, was annulled. With it was to be blotted out the last recollection of a proud nation. But this only succeeded for the rest time of the Frankish Empire; later on, in Germany, a new Swabian dukedom will be founded.

We write the year 747 AD

The brother of Pippin the Little, Charlesman/Karlmann, joined a monastery. So Pippin the Little was absolute ruler in Franconia and the father of the Carolingian dynasty.

We write the year 748 AD

Bonifatius became bishop of Mainz (Mayence). In the same year Tassilo III became duke of Bavaria. Bavaria was only a dukedom now.

In the region of the south-eastern Alps, the Slovenian dukedom was threatened by the Awari. The Slovenians, Slav people, had immigrated there a century before. Now they took shelter of the Bavarians because they feared an Awarian invasion. Later, from the Slovenian region arose the countries Carinthia and Slovenia of today.

We write the year 751 AD

The last Merovingian king, Childerich III, was deposed by Pippin the Little. He had himself elected King of Franconia by the Frankish nobility in Soissons when he sent Childerich into a monastery. Bonifatius, the legate of the pope, anointed Pippin with the sacred oil. That was important for Pippin, because he was lacking the charisma, the blood sanctity, which was conferred him and he could found his own kingdom now. The coronation followed three years later.

The Langobardi conquered Ravenna and threatened Rome this year. But the pope could still hold his ground against this threat although the pressure was growing more and more.

We write the year 753 AD

The pressure of the Franks on the Bavarian dukedom was so hard that Tassilo III had to do homage to Pippin the Little as vassal.

We write the year 754 AD

Bonifatius was on mission tour in Friesland. There he was killed.

The peril of a Langobardian invasion for Rome was growing from day to day. As a result the pope was looking for a protector. After Stephan II, the pope, had fruitlessly entreated for help the emperor of the East Roman Empire (Byzantium), he put in an appearance in the residence of Pippin the Little to ask him for protection against the intended invasion of the Langobardi. Pippin promised protection, more so, he assured the pope by document of the warranty of the returning to the Romans of all former regions of Byzantium in Italy. For equivalent the pope crowned Pippin the Little. Now Pippin was the official king of the Frankish Empire. Furthermore the pope bestowed on Pippin and his sons, with agreement of the emperor of Byzantium, the title "Patricius Romanorum" = patron of the Romans. Thereupon Pippin the Little subdued in two campaigns the Langobardi and obtained from them the delivery of all conquered regions of the last years. This was the hour of birth of the Church State. Now the pope was a secular ruler and finally absolved himself of the dependence on the East Roman Emperor. In the papal chancellery this "Present of Pippin" was immediately transformed into a far extending claim to possession. For this was forged another document, the so-called "Present of Constantin", after which the emperor Constantin the Great is reported to have transferred to the then pope Sylvester the imperial rank and all provinces in Italy. This event should be a hard burden to European politics over some centuries.

We write the year 757 AD

Duke Tassilo got his dukedom Bavaria as fief from Pippin the Little (the Younger) now. By it he had bound himself in case of war to compulsory military service. He was friendly with the Langobardi, who were beaten by the Franks, as you know. So he had wisely acted in this moment and could save himself from the complete subjection by the engagement for military service. Although he was only a holder of a Frankish fief now, soon he had refused the obedience and bound to the Langobardian royal family by his marriage with the Langobardian princess Luitbarc. There again begins, the conflict with the Frankish Empire.

Charles the Great

An interesting book about the life of Charles the Great is the German novel by Thomas R.P. Mielke (Karl der Grosse). Here you can read up the real life of Charles the Great between the years 767 and 814 AD, the year of his death. It was exactly written the situation of the great Franconian Empire during this time, but also the life of Charles. It was the great time before the foundation of the Holy Roman Empire of German Nation. – Here an example with supplements to the text of Mielke, sorted out according to the years of the events.

We write the year 767 AD

The October-feast approaches. Charles, a son of Pippin the Little, just wants to celebrate his 25th birthday, when news were coming from Rome. Pope Paul I is dead – under his pontificate Desiderius had taken the place of the Langobardian king. He isn't martial like the Langobardian king but not less dangerous. – The name of the new pope is Constantin II.

Pippin the Little was informed of the changes in Rome by Irish monks. Constantin II isn't sitting on a safe chair, because one was speaking about other popes, who could replace him. Pippin is angry at this information, because according to his opinion he cannot rely on the Catholic Church furthermore.

Charles didn't envy his father, because quick-successive popes are a signal for unrest and insecurity in the whole of Franconia. The people need constant and reliable values to give them support. For the rest the summer was quiet. When the autumn was coming, nothing much happened. In the last weeks the members of the court were wandering with a small army from palatinate to palatinate, because the Frankish Empire didn't have a capital but only palatinates for temporary places of government. Now the winter was approaching and the Frankish noblemen left the court to spend the winter time with their families in their villages.

We write the year 768 AD

One year later, Charles was celebrating his 26th birthday. "What's happened in Rome?" asked the Irish monk, whilst there was drinking, eating and singing around him. But this question was amusing, the monks thought and laughed. "What do you laugh?", was Charles' strict question. "We thought you know what's happened and …" Charles turned round and went to his father. Pippin was drinking with enjoyment his burgundy when Charles came to him. "Do you know what's happened in Rome?" he asked his father. "No", he said. "Did Pope Constantin II marry ?" Now the noblemen around father and son laughed loudly. Charles pressed his lips, turned round and went back to the monks. "What's happened in Rome?" "Nothing, Charles, nothing", said the monks. "Constantin was only a counterpope", said another monk "A good pope!" "And further?" "Philippus was intended for being new pope". "Is he the new pope now?" "No, not either, he was also a counterpope!" "But who is the pope now, please, please say it!" "Stephan III!" it sounded like a choir. "Stephan III!?", Charles repeated. "Does my father know that?" The monks shook their heads. For the first moment Charles knew enough; or didn't he? Perhaps he liked to know more about the occurrences in Rome?

The first days of May were cold and rainy. But now there was warm weather and the "assembly of the empire", the meeting of all noblemen, conferred on the next military plans because it rumbled all over the empire, so in Bavaria, Thuringia and Saxia (Saxony), even in the Bretonic boundary mark (mark or march = conquered territories, mostly on the boundary line, often also on the other side of the border as satellite state) – During the 3rd day the "assembly of the empire" decided that Pippin's eldest son should command an expedition. Charles accepted this order with uneasy feelings. On the one hand he was proud of this first military action and on the other hand he felt humbled because he knew he wouldn't find a real adversary. Nevertheless he carefully prepared this expedition. Man after man had to show the harness, shield and arms. He gave exact instructions how everybody had to arm. Never a Frankish warrior was mustered so; he even renounced counts who didn't have an adequate number of arms-servants. In the evening he had got together a hundred people of the Scara Francisca, a hundred armed riders and three hundred foot-warriors. He decided that no women and children were permitted attendance of this expedition. In return he took armour-makers, shield-makers and turners, furthermore masons and experienced administrators. When Pippin came into the army camp, Charles explained to him what he intended. "I'll quickly go to Aquitania and want to be mobile". "And for what craftsmen and administrators?" "I think of the time after the victory. What is the use of an overcome Aquitania if it keeps to what we have now. No, I want to know, which equivalent has Aquitania for us, how we can complete the settlements and increase the outputs". "That is what you mean!" Pippin said shortly. "Do you want to know my mind nevertheless?" Charles looked at his father. "If I can decide whether I can accept it!"

"Yes, but I'm talking with you as father and not as the king." Charles didn't want to take advice, but his father entreated and didn't command. Now Charles saw how old his father already looked at his 54 years. "What do you fear?" Charles asked a question. "First I must tell you that you took a good selection; but 500 warriors don't make any impression on the Aquitanians". "Perhaps you are right!" At this moment Charles saw his brother Charlesman maliciously grinning and suddenly he had an idea. "I could imagine Charlesman to escort me with his own contingent of warriors because two sons of the king certainly leave more impression on the Aquitanians than one". "That's rational", said Pippin. Charlesman got angry. "I'm not willing to go with him!" "You aren't willing to go with Charles?" asked Pippin with astonishment. "No, because he is to have no might over me" "And if I order that you have to do it?" was the question of Pippin for this answer. "Then I'll ask the noblemen the question whether you can give this order to a son of the king". "Charles is your brother" "Charles is against me and I am against him!" Pippin, who was otherwise mighty, wasn't able to put Charlesman's foot down. "Well, Charles, then go without your brother;

but take the way via the bishop's town Angoulemere, there you can reinforce your troops with additional warriors and arms."

Charles had a good march with his small army. They rode quickly, harnesses, helmets and arms flashed in the sunlight. It was summer and warm and the resting places were dry. But danger could be everywhere, as Charles knew, therefore he observed carefully the surrounding of each resting place. "Are you suspicious?" asked Count Cancor, his most important attendant. "No, only cautious!"

This caution just saved the small army of Charles from a catastrophe three days later. They made the rest in front of the village Perigeux. In the morning of the next day they rode to the source of the stream Isle. Charles and Cancor ridded themselves of their dresses and sprang into the cool water of the pond of source. They swam some rounds, climbed over the levee and let themselves dry by the sun. "I want to visit the monastery here", said Charles. "The monastery?" asked Count Cancor. "Yes, because I'm surprised that no monks have come to meet us! Get you ready for the march; in the meantime I'll see what's happened in the monastery, therefore I take twenty horsemen who have to follow me!"

Not more than half an hour and all horsemen were ready to follow Charles. Reposed well and refreshed, so Charles went off on horseback. He took a short look at the old maps, which partially originated partially from his grandfather Charles Martell. He chose a forest's way, which directly guided to the monastery.

"Keep your eyes open, my lords", commanded Charles, because he didn't know what they had to expect. Some minutes later they reached the monastery. Although one had perceived them, the gates of the monastery kept shut. One of the armed riders, his cuirass glittering in the sunshine, knocked at the door with his sword. "Open the door!" called another one; but it didn't move anything. "Open!" Now the abbot appeared in a small aperture of a window. "Forgive us not opening the door, but we were just saying the mass for the dead!" "For whom?" asked Charles. "For Waifar, the Duke of Aquitania. He was killed whilst he was sleeping, by his own people!"

"When?" "Three days ago!" "And why do you keep the gates and doors shut?" "Because we fear Hunold, the father of Waifar, will come to punish us!" "Why?" "Because we kept him imprisoned by order of Waifar until this morning, and when we were praying he could flee".

"So, mh, Hunold is the man! Nobody could count upon that", said Charles to his men. "And we even form the guarantee that the parties within his 'political camp' don't dispute and have to acknowledge him. Where did he ride to?" "I don't know", said the abbot. "Five men ride back to Count Cancor to tell him he has to follow us whilst we trail Hunold. Go, we don't have time!"

In the morning of the next day Count Cancor met the troops of Charles in a small forest. "Hunold is slipped away", said Charles, "but nevertheless we have good luck, because we found one of his servants here who has sprained his ankle!"

In the following weeks the architects were on full-time with the ground plans for the new Frankish bastion in middle Aquitania. Peasants and day-labourers of the surroundings were additionally engaged and the works for the bastion made a good headway.

At the end of July Pippin arrived. Charles was shaken at the bad looks of this father. "Dad, what's happened ?" "Oh, my son, I'm very sick. It's the high temperature I caught in the swamps of this cursed land some years ago". "You have sent me away!" "Yes, I didn't want you to see how I die". "Dad, you shall not die!" "My son, I have still a short time of my life and within this time I want to have arranged all that is necessary; so I have decided that you will share the empire with Charlesman. Therefore I ask you that you get along with him".

During this time Hunold's own people handed him over, the last sovereign of Aquitania, to the Franks (Franconians). The Aquitanian resistance was broken down, Aquitania a Frankish province. – From day to day during this time the physical condition of Pippin went from bad to worse. For all that he made the journey back to Tours again together with the complete court.

235

"I'm feeling that my end is near", said Pippin to Charles in the first week of September. "But I'm not willing to die here; I want to die in the monastery St. Denis". And the members of the court began with the last march for Pippin. Ten days later they reached St. Denis close to Paris. In the morning of the following day Pippin called his sons. "My sons, I want, that you both inherit the Frankish Empire by equal parts. Charles, you get Austry (Austrasia), Bavaria, Hollanda and the Frisian country. Charlesman, you shall be the king over Neustry (Neustria), Alsace and the region from Augsburg to the Champagne. Now swear that you both will live in peace". Both of them swore. Whacked by exertion, Pippin let himself fall back in his cushions.

Three days later, it was the 24th of September of the year of 768 AD, Pippin the Little died. The last house-meier and the first king of a new Frankish dynasty was dead.

Charles I, king of Franconia

We write the year 769 AD

Charles had gone to the palatinate (Pfalz) of Aquis Grana (Aachen) with the beginning of the winter the year before. Now the year 769 AD had begun and terrible news were coming. Irish monks had again reported alarming information. "In the empire things are going from bad to worse. A terrible famine has burst out in Burgundy and many people are already dead". "Burgundy? Why ever there, in this rich and sunny country?" "The Lord has given, the Lord has taken away", said the monk.

From all provinces of the empire more and more bad information was coming. Charles had to do something, so he gave the following order: All monasteries, abbeys and royal estates of his part of the empire should give so much of their provisions that nobody had the necessity to eat in fever of hunger the meat of dead persons. Then an event happened, which directly and unprepared fell on him. Himiltrud, his friedel-wife (friedel = not officially married) told him as he was coming back into the palatinate from the hunting: "I'm pregnant" "What did you say?" "We'll have a child!" Charles was laughing loudly. "A child. You and me! Are you sure?" She looked at him and didn't know whether to laugh loudly too. Ten years Charles had been living together with her now. She was a quiet and humble companion and always present for him and his pleasurable sensations and desires. And now, after ten years, she was pregnant. "We have to inform Rome immediately", said Charles. "The pope is to confirm our friedel-marriage officially. I don't want my first kid to be born in obscure relations". But the pope didn't answer and the noblemen of the empire were contrary to the marriage with this friedel-woman. – The day of birth approached and the mother in law took all in hands what was necessary, whilst Charles walked for many hours, shaded by forebodings, through all rooms of the palatinate.

237

In the meantime spring had come and in the western part of Aquitania, the part of this province belonging to the empire of Charles, people rebelled again. Waifar was dead, but Hunold, his father, wanted to seize the might again. Not only the territory of Charles but also the whole of the empire being threatened, Charles asked his brother to take part with his own contingent in an intended war. But Charlesman didn't want to speak with Charles about the matter "Aquitania". That was the beginning of an open hostility amongst the royal brothers.

Some weeks later Himiltrud was in labour. Charles was hunting again when he was informed. Charles kicked his horse in the flanks with the heels of his boots, which were without spurs, and hurried back as quickly as possible to the palatinate. "Well, how are things?", he called loudly when he arrived there. "You have got a son!", said his mother. Charles was radiant with joy. "And why do you make a face?" His mother didn't answer. "What's going on here? Tell me the truth!" "I can't. Please forget all what's going on here and ride back to your hunting friends" "What's the idea?" "What's the idea!? She has born a humpback for you, this woman! A disgrace to the empire!" Charles stared at his mother. He was already king, but nobody of the greats and noblemen in the whole of the empire would accept a humpback as heir to the throne. "Why that,why, why, why?" Charles was disappointed. "As soon as Himiltrud can travel, she is to go with the baby to St. Denis, to abbot Fulrad. He'll help her. I don't want to see this baby for the first time".

However, against his intention Charles several times went to Himiltrud and his son, who was christened Pippin in the meantime and almost recognized. – Charles' mother had already the intention to marry him to a Langobardian princess. When the pope heard of that, he wrote a letter to the Frankish court and pointed out that Charles could not marry a second time, because he was still married to Himiltrud in spite of "her offence".

For by the birth of the hunchbacked Pippin the marriage was proved to be consummated.

But the pope let himself be convinced some months later, so that short time before Christmas in Mainz the archbishop Lullus brought together the Frankish king of Austry and the Gaus on the Rhine (gau = small province) with the daughter of the Langobardian king, Desiderius. Charles had talked with his prospective wife no more than three words before the swap of rings.

The wedding ceremony took place without the king of the Langobardi, who had only sent his highest dignitaries to Mainz. They brought big cases with gold and silver, in addition to it barrels of exquisite wine of the empire of the Langobardi, as well as spice, cloths, cheese and the famous bacon of Parma. The dowry wasn't half bad. Nevertheless, it was a deplorable wedding, neither the newlyweds nor the guests enjoyed it.

We write the year 771 AD

In the course of the year Charles dissolved the marriage to the Langobardian princess and sent her back to Pavia. A few weeks later he married the fourteen-year-old Hildegard, daughter of a nobleman of Alemania. The wedding took place without great extravagance. – Some time after that, we write the 4th of December, his brother Charlsman died. He caught sudden nosebleeding and no medicine could stop it. When Charles heard that, he was shocked. He didn't like his brother, but however, it was his brother. He decided that his brother was to be buried according to his last wish in the sacred church Remigus in Reims. Some days later all noblemen of the empire had a meeting in St. Denis, near Paris, and decided that Charles was to be the king of both Frankish empires. So the Christmas days were celebrated with a great feast. Charles was the winner and now he was king of the whole empire. In spite of that, he didn't stay at St. Denis. In the same year he even went on the old Roman road via Soissons and Reims up to the palatinate Attigny, where he stayed for the rest of the winter.

We write the year 772 AD

It was March and good weather, so that the complete court left for the north. Hildegard was pregnant in the meantime and should spend the time till her confinement in the palatinate Diedenhofen.

It was a long way to Düren, the place between Aquis Grana (Aachen) and Colonia (Cologne). The royal household had hardly arrived when there was an incident. Saxons had arrived, who demanded to speak to Charles, which was allowed them.

"Salute, sublime and pious Frank!" "Who are you?", questioned Charles. "My name is Wido and I'm lord of big forests and fields on the river Diemel and I visit you with my most noble people here!" "And what do you want?" "I ask no more than to retain my villages, servants and women." "You are afraid I might exterminate people" "It's a question of time, when you enter our country and I'm a Christian, christened by Bonifatius". Charles snorted softly. He grinned as he fancied that he was sitting in a heavenly clearing together with the princes of the Westphalians, Engerians, Eastpahalians, Thuringians and Northalbringerians, talking about the new salvator from the Orient. "Well, what exactly do you want or can you betray something?" "I take you to the castle Eres" "We know where this castle is" "But I know how you can enter without difficulties!" "Is it all or something more?" "Noble Charles, you are a Germanic man as I'm too, and I assume that you know what the Roman named Tacitus has written about us in his book 'Germania' long ago!" "You are trying to say that you can read it?" "No, King Charles, only that we Germanic people are of divine blood. Our ancestral father was Tuisto. From his descendants are derived the "Ger-men", the warriors with the 'Ger', the holy spear". "What's the idea? Historical teaching?" "No, only that later from the descendants of Tuisto also the three kings Ingvo, Istvo and Irmin are descended!" "Of course, I know that!" "The Ingv(ae)onians settled in the north, where now are living the Nor(th)men (Vikings), the Istv(ae)onians in the western part of Germania and the Irminians there where we, the Saxons, defend ourselves against you and the Roman faith. Do you understand now why a christened Saxon is a

240

Germanic man, who has to revere his ancestors up to the deities?"
"Do you want me to be a heathen?" "No, no, on the contrary, I want
to say only, that the god of the Saxons, like in many other Germanic
nations, is still called Irmingot and Irminsul, the column or the tree
is the bridge to eternity!" "Stop it!" "Just as I said, I'm christened,
but we Saxons don't need a Son of God, we have had him always, he
is in nature, in every leaf, every blade of grass!" Charles pressed his
hands against the thighs and watched the Saxon with a sharp look.
He felt the anxiety and the desperate pluck of this man, who exactly
knew that there would never be peace for him again and his nation
and the freedom would be over.

"I want to protect the place where Irminsul is and therefore to de-
scribe to you this place exactly!" "You want to protect this place by
betraying it?" "Yes, to protect it from the Franks, who would use it as
triumph and to protect it from those who could try to forge the myth
of a new empire by our downfall" "What do you talk about downfall?" "You want to destroy our world!" "Stop it!" screamed Charles.
So martyrs had to die surely, it flashed through the mind of Charles.
Wido suddenly broke down and dying, he betrayed name after name.
The last name Charles could hear sounded like Widu-kind, son of
the forest.

The army band of Charles moved through the Eifel (-mountains)
towards Cologne. Here he stopped, even though he didn't like this
old town with the Roman name Colonia Claudia Ara Agrippinensis.
Therefore he stayed there only some days to pay a visit to the bishop.
The day after, the army crossed the Rhine and marched in direction to
the Bergish Land. Here he was already in the country of the Saxons.
Here in the mountains he visited a monastery and learnt from the abbot, who friendly welcomed the Franks, something about the habits of
the Saxons. Because his warriors also needed a breather, he stayed for
some days before beginning the long march towards east.

After some weeks they arrived in the valley of the Diemel. Here
was the Saxon castle Eres; it was more a fortress than a castle. The
Frankish army came unnoticed to the castle up to some kilometres
only. Charles selected fifty warriors who approached with him to the

241

ramparts of stone of the castle Eres in the night. The Saxons didn't notice that and trusted in the peace of the night, which was suddenly broken. The army of Charles had divided into small groups and surrounded the fortress at long range, where they were waiting for the order of attack. Now this order happened by loud shouts, which was more and more compressed by the noise of the Franks, who pressed forward with all their strength. For the first time a Frankish army didn't attack in broad phalanx and in the daytime but under the cover of night, in a kind of nippers and divided in small groups. The Saxons hadn't expected that even though it was their tactics.

When the first flames blazed out of the roofs of the fortress, the gates were opened as if by magic moved and the "scaras" pressed forward to these gates now. The nocturnal noise of the battle turned to a cruel mixture of clank of swords, screaming of triumph and terrible death shouting of men, women and children. All buildings of the fortress eventually went up in flames. Flames and smoke drove the Saxons up to the outer ramparts and bulwarks. Here they were killed by the arrows, spears, lances and swords of the Franks, who massacred all as if intoxicated. On all sides the dirty Frankish warriors, covered with blood, carried off cases of jewellery, tumblers, tinned drinking horns and valuable arms. These were the riches of the killed defenders from Engern, Westphalia and Eastphalia. The jubilation of the Franks, who were drunk with joy by the victory, drowned out the last screams of pain of the dying Saxons. In their intoxication the eyes of the Frankish warriors were radiant with blood and loot. They were mad at all the Saxons, and their rage had been too great, because Saxons had too often destroyed boundary villages and killed the inhabitants by attacks like a flash.

Except for twelve hostages no Saxon was left alive, because all women and children were killed too.

The Frankish army set out again early in the morning of the next day. On the mouth of the Diemel (river) into the Weser (river) the main camp was pitched for the rest of the year. From here the next campaigns followed through the land of the Saxons then; but now it were the Saxons who often attacked the Frankish army under cover of the dark forests and inflicted this army many casualties.

During the following winter time Charles was in the palatinate Diedenhofen. Here his son Charles was born; he was very proud of him. But he also received bad messages here. Monks came into the palatinate and reported that the pope had fled from Rome to Marseille by ship. All country roads were blocked by the Langobardi. – This message moved Charles deeply whilst it did not other bad messages. So he heard about the victory of Tassilo III of Bavaria over the Slavs, who had invaded the Alps.

The conquest of the Langobardian Empire and more

We write the year 774 AD

Charles set out with a small army to conquer the empire of the Langobardi. It was a hard way through the Alps. Not far from the North Italian town Avigliana on the little stream Dora, the Frankish army met with the Langobardi. By a flash attack the Langobardi were put to the flight. The Langobardian army was divided into two parts in order to be quick on their run on both sides of the river towards east. Desiderius, the king of the Langobardi (or also called the Long Beards), reached Pavia with his part of the whole Langobardian army some hours before the other part, which had taken the southern escape route. But at the mouth of the stream Ticino into the Po (the big Italian river in the north), Charles blocked the escape route to this part of the Langobardian army. Thus just before Pavia a part of the Langobardi was forced to withdraw to the fortress Verona, because they couldn't reach Pavia any more. Short time later a delegation came from Verona to Charles to inform him that the fortress Verona put itself to the command of Charles. Charles triumphed, because other Langobardian towns did the same one by one. Pavia finally stood alone. Charles besieged the town and ultimately forced Desiderius to capitulate. Desiderius left the town with his family and surrendered to Charles, who banished him to the imperial cloister of Corbie. When Charles held the iron crown of the Langobardi in his hands now, he didn't know what to do with this comic thing; but in this moment all his warriors screamed: "Put it on, put it on, put it on!" He was persuaded to do that and lowered the Langobardian crown on his head slowly. "Carolus, Dei gratia rex Francorum et Langobardum et Patricius Romanorum", called several Frankish warriors. Charles was the new king of the Langobardians. A short time before the campaign against the empire of the Langobardi, Charles had confirmed once more the "Present of Pippin" (the present of his father for the pope, to have an independent church state).

The church state, the "Present of Pippin", wasn't accepted by Byzantium up to now, because East Rome (Byzantium) considered this country part of the East Roman Empire. That always led to conflicts between Franconia and Byzantium, because (West) Rome was under Frankish protection.

We write the year 775 AD

Charles made war against the Saxons again. His army marched in some weeks to the Harz mountains and didn't meet with much resistance. After some little victorious battles, many Saxons had themselves christened. Now Charles set up Frankish administrations in all Saxon regions, which were controlled by him, and marched back with a part of his army again.

We write the year 776 AD

Couriers informed Charles that the count of Friaul (North Italy) intended a rebellion against the Frankish occupying forces. Aquileia was already extended to a Langobardian centre of resistance against the Franks. Charles knew that he had to take action quickly. With a small army he set out immediately, crossed the Alps and reached Verona, when rushed couriers arrived at this town too. "Killed!" the first courier gasped for breath. "All Franks were killed in the whole of the march!" (march or mark = boundary region). "It happened in only one night!" gasped for breath another courier. – "We take a rest here", ordered Charles. "Tomorrow, early in the morning, we hurry to Padua where we'll pass the following night to go to Treviso then." "Directly to the March Friaul?" "Yes, directly to the March Friaul", answered Charles with a sneer.

It was a hard way. The small Franconian army met the troops of the rebels just before Treviso. Charles gave immediate order: "Attack and kill them". It was Good Friday and Charles yelled to this warriors: "This good friday these bastards never will forget!"

The noise of battle and the cry of dying warriors let Charles cold. He put the iron crown of the Langobardi on his blonde hair, but he didn't take part in the extermination of the enemy. It went on for just one hour, it was already all over. In the evening the Frankish (Franconian) army marched into Treviso. Here the count of the March Friaul was brought to trial. The text of judgement read as follows: "Death by rope!" All the estates of the rebels were awarded to Frankish noblemen and the rebels were killed by sword. Their families were sent into cloisters, the farmhands became serfs at the Frankish court.

We write the year 777 AD

For the first time a king of the Franks called upon to come to an Imperial Diet on Saxon territory. Thereupon all noblemen of the empire had come to the palatinate of Paderborn. Also Arabs had come and reported that the Umayyad intended to assail the Frankish Empire. The Arabs who appeared in Paderborn suggested to Charles to make an expedition against the Umayyad, who would be their enemy too. After the successful expedition Charles was to establish a boundary march of the Umayyad borderland in North Spain and the Frankish Empire. Charles promised to think it over; then other important news rushed to Charles too. So Widukind, the Saxon, was said to have allied with Danes and Frisians, and Tassilo the Bavarian was reported to have built monasteries one by one in East Bavaria, bigger than the Frankish monasteries in Fulda, Echternach (Eifel), Prüm (Eifel) and Lorsch (Hessen). – In the palatinate of Paderborn Charles was informed in detail about all, but didn't make further decision.

We write the year 778 AD

Charles began the campaign against the Arabs in Spain. His army consisted of Main(-river)-Franks, Austrasians (Austrasi), Alemani (Alemen), Aquitanians, Provencalians, Burgundi (Burgundians),

246

Bavarians, Langobardi, Frisians and Saxons. It was a big army that started to move in two marching columns and marched over the Pyrenees. The part of the army in command of Charles, moved above the pass of Rocevalles and invaded the province Navarra. Navarra belonged to the Emirate of Cordoba. The other part of the army took the way via Narbonne, Perpignan and Gerona and immediately occupied Barcelona.

Charles's part of the army camped one day in front of the walls of the town Pamplona whose ruler had surrendered to the huge army of the Franks. On the further march through the dusty sierra towards Saragossa in the province Aragon one town after the other surrendered. The situation was not clear yet.

When Charles took rest on a creek, there came a small riding troop through the valley towards him. The riders were warriors from the second army column and reported about a combat of Arabs against Arabs in front of the town Saragossa and that the emir of Cordoba was beaten. They proposed to him to move to Cordoba to pitch headquarters there.

But that didn't come about. Both Frankish armies joined together in the plain of the Ebro river. Here Charles heard that the ex-governor of Barcelona was wali of Saragossa now. Charles took this information with a shake of his head.

The Arabs shut the gates of Saragossa completely unexpected and filled all walls with armed men. Annoyed at this, Charles sent a delegation with scara-escort to Saragossa the next day. This delegation wasn't heard, but the Franks have already been received by arrows on the riverbanks.

"We refuse you!" called one of the Arabs to the Franks. "Beat it and let us settle the matter ourselves!" "Have you just beaten the emir of Cordoba or not? We are only coming to help you", said one of the Frankish delegation. "You err! We want rather to be vassals of the emir than vassals of the Franks". The Franks didn't understand this sudden change of mind. "We hope you know what you are doing", answered the Frankish delegate; thereupon the Franks rode back.

When Charles came to know how it had gone with his delegation, he said: "They have told us a lie and taken advantage of us; but no Frankish king will swallow that!"

"The town is strongly fortified", one of the delegation said. "Also with our two armies we can't conquer this town!" "I don't have a great mind to be encamped like before Pavia and to wait till they die of hunger. Moreover, the Arabs are strong enough to draw up a big army whilst we are inactively sitting around here. Perhaps they even get reinforcement by their hostile brothers, the Abbasid. We'll construct catapults and attack the town! How long do we need up to the time that we can use the tools of siege?" One of his designers of the retinue answered: "Four weeks to construct such tools of siege which are necessary for the assault on the strong walls." "Two weeks", ordered Charles.

Two weeks later the needed tools of siege were ready for an attack. Charles could see from a hill how the wooden monsters were set in position. By a signal from Charles some warriors weighed heavy big stones in the leather litter aprons of the first catapults. Charles signalled by hands, whereupon the warriors at the catapults beat through the blocking ropes. The strutting beams jerked up and heavy rock-pieces flew against the walls of Saragossa. More than ten times the catapult-volleys beat off big pieces from the top of the town walls. The Arabian defenders fell crying downward; then the Franks assaulted with ram-blocks the big gates of the town. But gates and walls held these attacks. "In this way we'll never conquer this town", said Charles to one of this officers, who were standing by his side. "We stop the assault and construct some more catapults. In two weeks we'll attack the town again".

The second assault on Saragossa destroyed the walls at two sides completely. Also three gates were broken down by the ram blocks. The Franks entered the town by force. A combat began in the streets and houses; but after a short time it was already over.

Charles razed the fortification of the town and took preparation for the return home.

With the return via Pamplona, Charles felt hostility blowing towards him all over. Pamplona denied Charles the wanted food-stuffs for his army and even shut the gates. Charles had ladders constructed and the town was immediately taken by assault. Pamplona already fell with the first attack. The town was destroyed, the treasures were distributed and the inhabitants taken along as slaves, provided that they weren't killed by the Franks before.

On 15 August the return began. The army of the Franks moved more and more asunder in the following days. Charles, with some cuirass-riders and the top of the Frankish army reached the Pyrenees passage, whilst the rearguard of his army under the leadership of his friend Roland, the count of the Bretagne (Brittany), toiled through narrow ravines some miles back. Suddenly big rock pieces were thrown on the Franks. "Go, go away!", cried Roland. He exactly knew what attacks from ambush were like. "Blow the horn for Charles to come and help us!" he cried to one of his companions when already armed Basque warriors fell upon the Franks. Roland drew forth his sword and cut off the head of the first assailant. But the Basque warriors were in forces, there were some hundreds, whilst the Frankish rearguard hadn't more than 60 horsemen. Roland and his warriors offered resistance with all their might. When Roland saw the shadow of a sword, he ducked and struck in a wall of dust. The outcry pointed out that he had hit. Three or four shadows leaped against him. He couldn't keep on his horse, slipped down and fell on a rock. He pulled himself up and went on fighting with bitterness. Man after man lost their lives. In the end Roland with some warriors of his troop was only fighting back to back against a bloodthirsty pack of hounds. Over and over smeared with blood on his body, he raised his sword once more for a beat, then he was hit by a lance in the abdomen. He fell on the bloody way and was still alive when a sword of an enemy penetrated his heart.

When Charles reached the place of the tragedy, he spoke no word. Roland (later his death is theme of the famous Roland-Hymn in the German(ic) myth) and some other noblemen of the Frankish Empire were killed in action, which was inconceivable for Charles. He raised his hands and wiped the tears out of his eyes, when one of the Frankish noblemen went up to him and said in a loud voice: "My king, friends were taken from you and sons were given to you. Your wife has born two sons for you". Sadness and gladness lay on the face of Charles. "They are to have Main(-river)-frankish names, Ludwig (Louis) and Lothar".

Some days later the Frankish army continued the march home. Back on Frankish ground, the army disbanded and everybody went back to their home region separately.

The slaughter of the Saxons

We write the year 782 AD

Imperial Diet in Saxon territory again. At the headwaters of the Lippe Charles held court and prepared himself again for the next war against the Saxons. During this preparation there appeared at court a dirty Irish monk, smeared with blood, to inform Charles that his imperial court on the Hase (little river in the north of Germany) close to Osenbrugga (Osnabrück) was burnt down by the Saxons and all men, women and children were killed. The leader of the Saxons had been Widukind.

The next day Charles set out with a part of his army. He made good headway. Each day armed messengers rode to and fro to keep in touch with the main part of the army. Nobody could foresee what would happen a short time later.

Charles had proposed the northern way to the Wesel (river), whilst a second part of the army moved through the dense-wooded valley of the Kalle (river). At the mouth of the Kalle into the Weser this group of the army was divided into two parts. One part moved in the direction to Vlothouwe (Vlotho), the other part in direction to Rinteln (town on the river Weser). That part ran into a pitfall of the Saxons at Süntel (little mountain land close to Rinteln) some days later. As it seemed, there were to be the same events as those of Rocevalles in the Pyrenees. The army-group, which was marching in direction to Rinteln, wasn't subordinate to unitary leading, but three noblemen shared in the orders. But they couldn't agree who was to give the effective orders, which the Saxons utilized. In the dense forest, in the jumble clanking of the swords and whirring arrows, which mostly reached their aim, no Frankish horseman and foot-warrior knew whom he was to obey, whom he was to follow within this chaos. Thus all men of this army-group were killed.

The third part of the Frankish army had reached the region between Harz (-Mountains) and Elbe (river). Here Charles got to know that a daughter was born to him, who was christened the name Hildegard. But this was no joy to him, because he got to know of the annihilation of one part of his army. "I ought to have known that the division of the army must be a catastrophe, because Rocevalles had shown us what can happen to an army, which isn't marching closed", said Charles to his selected adviser. – After a short halt on the banks of the Elbe the army moved now close to the Weser (river) near to Minden (town). Charles wanted to take vengeance for the disaster at Süntel: "Many of my best warriors are killed in action at Süntel. It's the blood of brave men, for their death many Saxons have to die", said Charles full of grief and rage. But only Charles allowed his warriors the well-merited pause for rest. He himself rode with some scaras on the right side of the Weser around the incision of the river into the hilly country, the Porta Westphalica. From a hill he could see the dense-wooded hills of Vlotho and further southward up to the town Rinteln. Also he could perceive the smoke of the ancestral castle of Widukind on the other side of the range of Porta Westphalica. "There they are!", said Charles. "There are the Saxon cowards who have killed from the ambush more than 2,000 of my warriors". – Back in the army camp, Charles ordered to set out to north next day. On the Aller (river) he pitched his next camp. "Here I'll take vengeance on this Saxon mob. But Saxons who went with me are to be guarded; therefore I give order that all Saxons of my retinue, who were always fair with me, have to go south immediately; perhaps it will be too late for them in two days."

Two days later, the Frankish warriors started a big movement in a kind of clamp. They advanced like a battue, step by step. By sunset the Franks had encircled many Saxons at the mouth of the Aller into the Weser. These were Saxons who had fled from the Franks when they advanced. All these Saxons surrendered without fight and resistance and had to deliver their arms. Then their hands were bound together on the back.

It was right, when Charles, on horseback, measured the captured Saxons in the light of torches. "How many?", he asked the officer keeping guard. "Five or six thousand", was the answer. "Identify all persons less than 14 years old. They are to leave this country and have to go with escort to Alemania. My friend, Count Cancor, is to settle them there". "And what shall be coming of the other Saxons?" "Give each one a tumbler of mead, we'll see tomorrow!", said Charles.

In the morning of the next day he called his noblemen. "I want revenge. Make an end with the Saxons! I can't stand them!" he shouted. "Do you want them killed?" asked one of the noblemen. "Yes, and I want that it happens immediately". "Within one day? That is impossible!", answered the nobleman. "You have got three days to do it, then every officer is to lay before me no less than a hundred Saxon heads!" "Do you want to watch us doing it?" "Yes", said Charles. "I want to see each head when it is bloody falling in the grass!"

In the evening of the third day more than 4,500 Saxons had been beheaded. Many Frankish warriors were full of blood, the river had been red for three days.

After two more days of rest, Charles ordered death penalty for all Saxons who didn't want to be christened, "Capitulatio de partibus Saxoniae".

After that the Frankish army marched off. On leaving, Charles gave the possessions of the beheaded Saxons to the monks, who had approved his action. Then the Franks marched up to the palatinate Diedenhofen, where the army was disbanded again.

We write the year 783 AD

The year had just begun when Hildegard, the beloved wife of Charles, seriously fell ill. From day to day she was more impaired by her illness. But best nursing and her will of life were a reason for recovery. – On 28th of April her condition went from bad to worse. The next day her condition was so bad that she didn't wake up on

30th of April, the day before Ascension Day. She had silently died. When Charles got to know that his wife was dead, one could see his other feelings than hatred and cruelty. He was sitting all day long at the deathbed of his beloved wife and didn't want to see any other person.

When a short time later also his youngest daughter died, he needed distraction and tried to find it by a war against his worst enemy. He called his advisers and said: "I want to march again against the Saxons." "Didn't you kill enough?", asked one of his advisers. "As long as Widukind isn't broken, the Saxons don't have time for rest. I want Widukind to die or to be christened."

The campaign against the Saxons soon began. The Frankish army made fast headway and that without resistance. The Franks marched along the sources of the Pader (river) towards Osning, the old Germanic Mount Asen. Close to Theotmalli, Charles stopped and occupied the destroyed but up to now strategic still important point of all region. There were the ruins of the castles Goth and Teuto(n). They were constructed as ring-walls, being a commemorative place for all Saxons since the defeat of the Romans under the command of Quintilius Varus. "Here Varus was with his legions; that was a long long time ago", said Charles. "And Hermann", repeated one of his advisers. "Yeeee, Arminius, he was a man of the Germanic tribe of the Cherusci but for us the first real Frankish hero, too!" – The Franks had hardly pitched the camp when a man of guard called: "Saxons! Saxons! They are coming!" "Alert! Alert! A big army of Saxons is coming!" shouted some men of guard a short time later. The Franks could see more and more Saxons coming out from the forest with naked upper parts of the body, swords and hump-shields. "How could the Saxons concentrate so many warriors?" the noblemen asked Charles. "Yes, Widukind, he is making the greatest mistake of his life, because he is struck blind!"

The Saxons wound like madmen, beat on drums and shouted, so that the valley at the lower end of the castles was only a hollow of noise. Then they forced an open fight against the best army of Europe. Swords and long-axes beat each other. The air was full of the noise of these arms, of flying arrows and the roaring of wooden and iron shields.

Nobody counted the Saxons who had already lost their lives after some minutes. Scaras (= cuirass riders and thus the first knights) and light-armed horsemen stormed forward and killed more and more Saxons. A small number of Saxons still offered resistance by courage of death against the very strong enemy in the afternoon.

At the twilight the scaras still pursued the last Saxon warriors far into the forests. The battle was won and the Franks marched in direction to north-west the next day.

Some days later, the Franks reached the river Hase in western Lower Saxia (Saxony) and prepared themselves for the next battle. – Kettledrums and bugles introduced the new encounter of Franks and Saxons. The Franks didn't understand where the Saxons had got so many warriors and arms again. Half-naked Saxon riders courageously attacked the heavy armed riders of the "Scara Francisca". The Saxons applied a new suicidal tactic. Some Saxon horsemen rode with burning torches towards the phalanx of the scaras. Just before the lances of the Franks they turned round their horses and threw nets over the Frankish warriors who were bursting with arms. Then the Saxon riders rode deep-stooped further and threw their torches against the Frankish enemy. Many defenceless Franks, pierced under the nets by Saxon lances or hit by throwing axes, perforated by arrows, fell down from their horses.

Charles was shocked to see how his best men, still sitting on their horses, hadn't to lift up their swords and shields against enemies but against burning nets; how their horses broke out in wild panic and ran up to the swamps of the river Hase, where horse and rider sank in.

The battle rocked to and fro; it was a fight of life and death till far into the night and thus into the second and third day too. But now the battle's fortune turned. After all it was a great victory of the Franks again.

In the autumn time of the same year Charles married for the third time. His new wife was Fastrada, the daughter of the count of Thuringia.

The name Deutschland is mentioned for the first time

We write the year 784 AD

In the spring time of this year it was decided to march against the Saxons once more, because the most important Saxon, Widukind, was still at liberty. Charles had sworn this would be the last campaign against the Saxons. Charles marched to Eastphalia, his son Charles to Westphalia. Battle after battle were won by both parts of the Frankish army and that till autumn. "Where are we going to be in the winter time?", asked Alkuin, who was a church-teacher from the English province York. "Anywhere in the land of the Saxons", answered Charles. "There we'll be also when Fastrada will give birth to her first child". "It's to be hoped not in Lügde", said Alkuin. "In the Easter time in this district the heathens let roll down gigantic fire wheels from the tops of the hills to the Weser. These fire wheels are wrapped around with straw and then set on fire before they roll down. So there isn't a good place for kings."

Whilst Charles was in the land of the Saxons his wife Fastrada bore a daughter who was christened in the name of Theodrada.

We write the year 785 AD

The year had just begun when in Lügde messengers arrived informing Charles that the Bretons had risen in arms. "They have held up monasteries and have killed monks", reported a messenger. "Nothing to shout about. These incidents aren't special events", said Charles. "Do you want to do nothing against that?" asked Alkuin. "I feel angry, neither the descendants of the Celts nor the Nor(th)-men, Wasgonians or Awarians (Awari) but only betrayal ..." "But Aquitania is simmering!", shouted one of the messengers. Thereupon Charles ordered an expedition to set out against Aquitania. No sooner had he given the order than messengers brought information about Tassilo. "It seems that Tassilo riots again", said

Charles when he got the information. "Perhaps he sees possibilities for a rebellion and means to have support by the Awarians (Awari) in the east and by his brother-in-law, the duke of Benevent", answered Alkuin. "Benevent is the seam of the Frankish-Byzantinian relations. East Rome has always sponsored the trouble region on the northern border of the Italian colonies. But now Byzantium has problems on the Persian border and cannot help Benevent. Therefore we can't have trouble from this region", said Charles. "Tassilo riots nevertheless", answered Alkuin, and was right. One week later Bavarian troops and Frankish (Franconian) contingents came to blows in Carinthia.

The news from the empire didn't disquiet Charles. He again held Imperial Diet in Paderborn, where the river Pader is born. Charles was implacable as never before. He decided new laws and nobody opposed.

"Henceforth is valid the death penalty for everybody who is opposed to the order of Charles", proclaimed the royal messengers a short time later in the empire. "And for all heathens there are only two possibilities, either christening or death".

And now came about what Alkuin had told before, Widukind gave up. No Frankish army could subjugate him, but these laws did it now. Widukind appeared in Paderborn. "It is over", said Charles to Widukind. "Yes, it's true, over for ever", answered Widukind. "I would like to be your godfather", said Charles after a while. "In order to take me down a peg ?" asked Widukind. "No, no, only to join my hands with yours, because you are the greatest of all Saxon counts", said Charles.

During the following days Charles and Widukind were talking for a long time. "Do you want to go back to Porta Westphalica where your Eastphalians are living?" Charles asked. But Widukind shook his head. "I should never be able to sleep quietly. With the rushing of the wind in the trees, with each blast of wind the army of the killed Saxon warriors would be agony for me. Never again I could go to Vlotho, Theotmalli, Paderborn or the castle Eres." "What do you want to do?" asked Charles. "I'm the last Saxon leader who offered resistance and therefore I'll write the history of this last resistance. And where is the blessed place for me? I think it will be the monastery on the island Reichenau within the Lake Constance". Charles agreed to that. And when the pope heard of the christening, he ordered a three days bell ringing and thank-divine service to be celebrated.

Whilst it had been quiet in the Saxon land, other regions were not quiet; so already the year before in the south east, where the Awari were living, who grew to be a problem more and more. The Awari were a rest-population of the mighty nation of the Huns. Because this new nation was very warlike, Charles had to observe the region in the south-east of Bavaria for the future.

That same year Charles still decided to raise Cologne to an archbishopric, based on the recommendation of the pope.

We write the year 786 AD

Irish monks reported on the christening of the last heathens in the Saxon region. "Charles, we are delighted to inform you of the construction work of many churches in the Saxon territories, which happens in your name. But the sermons are in the Latin language for the most part there, which most people don't understand. In some regions of the Saxon land we have also priests who preach in the language of the people, in Diutisc." "Diutisc?" asked Charles. "Yes, Diutisc, the language of all Germanic nations in the middle of Europe", answered a monk. "No, no, here in the western part of Franconia we don't speak this language. Here our people are speaking the New-Latin language, that is our Francish." "Francish or French, what some people say, this language the people are only speaking in the west of your empire, but in East Franconia, Bavaria, Alemania and Frisia people are speaking Diutisc or 'La Lingua Theodisca', as some scholars say. Also consider that your wife speaks Diutisc and your children, too." "Yes, that is all right, but I wasn't conscious of this common language of all Germanic tribes!" "But that's so, 'Glorious Ruler of the Franks'. Also you are descended from a Germanic

259

family!" "Okay, okay. Thus the land where the people are speaking Diutisc, bears the name Diutiscland?" "Yes, my king, some people say Diutchland or Dutchland (= Germany today and not the Netherlands), too. In our churches where the preachers are speaking Latin, there one speaks of an empire teutonicum, in memory of the Teutones, who had frightened the former Roman Empire." "For me Franconia is only one empire and what the people are speaking isn't important to me", answered Charles. "That is all right, but for all that you have already an empire of two different parts, West Frankland (West Franconia) or what some people simply call France and the other part, East Frankland (East Franconia), what is the old Teutonic land or the Teutish Land now or put into simple words Teutschland (Deutschland/Germany)." "Or Dutchland, Diutiscland and so on, but I'm the king of one nation where people are speaking New-Latin or French and Diustisc or Teutsch. It's very interesting but not important to me", answered Charles and the discussion was finished.

We write the year 787 AD

Charles stayed in the palatinate Diedenhofen for the year 787 AD. Now he had time enough for new edicts. So he issued exact instructions for the management of his estates in all regions of the empire.

We write the year 788 AD

Duke Tassilo III made trouble again in Bavaria. – Charles held court in the palatinate of Ingelheim (Bavaria). Here he intended to set right Tassilo. "Do you mean Tassilo will be Duke of Bavaria in future, too?" was the question of one of the advisers of Charles. "He has been in power too long. Nobody could make bold to do so much as Tassilo, neither Widukind nor another duke", answered Charles.

It was Maundy Thursday when Charles ordered his scaras to ride to Ratisbon (Regensburg), the capital of Bavaria, to fetch Tassilo to Ingelheim.

The show trial left Tassilo III no chance. Charles demanded that Tassilo were presented the consequences for this obstinate behaviour. Although Tassilo had advocates for his obstinate behaviour, he was condemned. He was banished into the monastery St. Goar on the river Rhine. With that had been put out the ancient Bavarian dynasty of the Agilolfingers, too.

Charles decided that the brother of his deceased wife Hildegard, Gerold, became 'Praefectus' in the Bavarian residence Ratisbon, which was the strongest palatinate of the Frankish kings henceforth.

In Ingelheim Charles was informed that in the Emirate of Cordoba the last Omaijade, Abd al-Rahman, was superseded by Hisham I.

We write the year 789 AD

For this time the Imperial Diet took place in Aquis Grana (Aachen). Most of the noblemen would rather be in Worms, Mainz or Ratisbon (Regensburg) than in this plain valley with the bad smelling hot fountains. But Charles had decided to hold his Imperial Diet here; he wanted to make Aquis Grana capital of the Frankish Empire and that was to be decided here now. Many friends of Charles proposed to raise Worms on the river Rhine to be capital, that would be better than this little village on the edge of the Eifel. But Charles had already decided. Aquis Grana will be the capital of the Frankish Empire.

Because the Slavic tribes made the eastern borders unquiet again, it was decided at this Imperial Diet to send an expedition against the Slavic nation of the Wilzians (Wilzi), which was realized some weeks later. At this expedition the Franks advanced deep into the Slavic territory and could beat a troop of the Wilzians. After that, the Wilzians made peace with the Franks and Frankish warriors stayed in the villages of the Wilzians to keep peace also in future.

Charles is emperor of a new Roman Empire

Frightful news from the north of the empire attained to Charles. Wild Germanic tribes from Scandinavia plundered and murdered in the northern territories of the Frankish Empire. These Nor(th)men, also called Normans or Vikings, were coming by their dragon boats from sea, trespassed upon the mouths of the rivers, held up villages here, ravished and retired again with loot. Before Frankish scaras could interfere, they were at sea again. The Frankish Empire was powerless against this tactics. This will be continuing for decades and nobody could do anything.

We write the year 791 AD

Charles commissions his son, Pippin the Hunchback, to take action against the Awari, who had advanced up to the eastern Alps and so had reached the Frankish Empire.

Pippin marched with his army from Regensburg (Ratisbon) south-wards along the Danube (Donau). After leaving the region of the Wachau (part of Lower Austria today) they reached the plain of the Danube. "We have been in the region of the Awarians (Awari) for some days already", said one of Pippin's officers. "Soon we shall see the first ring villages". "Is it possible to take these villages quickly and easily?", Pippin asked. "No!" said another officer, who knew this region. "We have only one possibility to advance through close-guarded passages, because the walls are surrounded by brambles and thorn-hedges. But most villages are abandoned here". "Abandoned? I think the inhabitants saw our army and fled", answered Pippin. "Yes, and they took along all the provisions. Perhaps we'll have nothing to feed our army with only one day and the way for supply is getting longer and longer from day to day." "You are all right", said Pippin, "to continue this expedition doesn't make sense and a defeat my father would never forgive me." The Frankish army retired, but the war against the Awari was not over.

We write the year 793 AD

Charles decided to make war against the Moors, what was the name of the Arabs in Spain now (the Moorish population). It should be a short expedition. The Frankish army crossed the Pyrenees and beat an Arabic troop within the first days. The northern territory of Spain was rapidly occupied. The Arabs were prepared to make peace and ceded the northern region. Here Charles established the Spanish March now, a Frankish frontier province that was to be getting the centre of the Spanish reconquista (reconquest) – After that Charles had time enough to turn towards east.

We write the year 794 AD

Riots in the country of the Saxons again. Charles decided not to make an expedition against the rebels, but he let reinforce the Frankish garrisons in Saxia/Saxony. From here he fought against the rebels, but nobody could foresee that this fight would take a time of 5 years. But then there was peace for a long time in Saxia.

We write the year 795 AD

In Rome a new pope was elected, his name was Leo III. – This year Pippin, king of Italy and son of Hildegard, started war against the Awari, who advanced again and again into the eastern Alps and threatened Bavaria. After unsuccessful fight against the Awari, Charles decided to beat the Awari with a big army once and for all. He planned the campaign for the following year.

We write the year 796 AD

It was Pippin again who made war against the Awari. South of the Alps it was warm enough for a fast march to north-east. Some Bavarian contingents joined company with the Frankish-Langobardian army on the river Drau. In a short time Pippin advanced up to the mouth of the

263

river Raab then. The first resistance followed by Slavs, but they surrendered after short actions. – Captives reported that the Awari had set up their biggest plant of defence close to Györ (today town in Hungary).

Two days later followed the attack against the plant of defence close to Györ. Ring rampart after ring rampart was conquered by the Frankish, Langobardian and Bavarian troops. But the resistance of the Awari increased. Clouds of arrows hailed down on the assailants before the ring ramparts. Now they knew why they could conquer the weak outer ramparts. But here in the heart of the Awarian defence were the best archers and throwers.

"It is useless", gasped the Langobardian warriors and began to fall back. Also the Bavarians had problems and weren't willing to advance furthermore. "Tortoise like Roman legionaries!", screamed the Frankish officers. "Do tortoise and smash the barricades on the ramparts!"

A miracle now. The arrows and spears of the Awari hailed down on the shields of the attackers without effect. The last defenders on the ramparts were overrun. Surge after surge of warriors forced its way inwards to the bulwark of defence and a dreadful massacre began. The sunset hadn't yet begun when the last resistance of the Awari was broken down.

The loot of the Frankish army was immense. Charles was content with the loot of his son when he came back to Regensburg.

After this expedition the Awari had admitted the rule of the Franks. Their empire was part of the Frankish Empire now and Charles established the Awarian March (or Mark)

We write the year 797 AD

Charles friendly received an Arabic legation from Bagdad. Harun al Rashid, the ruler of Bagdad, handed over great presents by his legation;

so he gave Charles an elephant as a present, too. It was the first time that the Franks saw a 'terrible animal' like this.

Charles was pleased about this honour and decided to establish diplomatic relations with the empire of Harun al Rashid.

We write the year 798 AD

Charles raised the settlement Salzburg (Salt's Castle) on the edge of the northern Alps to an archbishopric and with it to the heart of the Bavarian church province.

We write the year 799 AD

Charles spent Easter in Aquis Grana (Aachen). The palatine chapel was still under construction but shortly before completion. The last work to be finished was indoors.

Charles welcomed delegations from many countries; so monks from Jerusalem, too. "The patriarch of Jerusalem sends to you his benediction and relics from the tomb of the Lord", said one of the monks. That was the most valuable present for Charles, more important than the statue of Theoderich the Great, which was brought from Ravenna to the new palatinate of Aachen.

"With the victory over the Awarians we have finished the extension of our empire", Charles told his advisers in the course of the ceremonies.

"I have annexed to the Frankish Empire the kingdom of the Langobardians, all the territories of the Saxons and Frisians, the dukedom of Bavaria, the Awarian Empire and the Spanish March. I don't have the intention to annex the whole of Spain." "And Asturia, this Christian enclave in the north west of Spain? You don't have the intention?", asked one of the advisers. "No, not Asturia, this Christian country, or any other part of Spain; neither West Goths nor

Moors, what is the name of the Arabs in Spain now, fit our empire." "But, my king, the Christians of Asturia are the descendants of the Suebians (Suebi)." "Anyway, I don't want to provoke the Moorish people in Spain. At the frontier of our empire we must have peace", said Charles.

The world for Charles was changing four weeks later. Irish monks reported to him alarming news. "Something dreadful happened in Rome! Pope Leo led the procession of riders from St. Peter to the church St. Laurentius, when the people of Rome thronged on the road-side receive the benediction from him. But they didn't get him round to give benediction, because from bushes some armed men felled him, pulled him from his horse, clobbered and took a kick at him, tore the clothes off his body, cut off his tongue and tried to cut out his eyes, too", reported a monk. "Terrible! Is he still alive?", Charles asked. "Yes, he was immediately taken to the monastery St. Erasmus. But there he wasn't safe; therefore Frankish scaras took him away from this place the same night. Now he is on the way over the Alps with an escort."

In August the pope arrived at the monastery of Lorsch. From here he travelled to Mainz and then to Fulda. In Fulda he spoke his benediction in spite of the cut tongue; it bordered on the miraculous that Leo III could speak and see again, with problems but fully conscious of godlike grace. From Fulda he travelled to Paderborn, where Charles held court again. Charles' son Pippin, king of Italy, was likewise present but no other son. Pippin the Hunchback was expelled from the family and Louis the Pious Man didn't come, because he had trouble in the palatinates of Diedenhofen and Ponthion.

Charles was happy; his wife who had been ill for some weeks, was on the way of recovery. It was Luitgard. Charles had married Luitgard after the death of Fastrada in the year of 795 AD. – In Paderborn Pippin had also arrived with his children. Presence of the pope, son and grandchildren, that were good days to Charles. His intention was to take the pope in power again, although he wasn't favourite of the townsmen and townswomen of Rome because of this bad behaviour.

266

Charles the Great

From Paderborn Charles went with the pope to Prüm (little town in the mountains of the Eifel) After the consecration of the rich 'Golden Church' by Leo III there, their ways separated. Leo went towards south and the Frankish court moved in direction to north. Charles wanted to be in Aachen during the winter time.

We write the year 800 AD

The pope had problems with his neighbour again, the duke of Benevent. Therefore Charles decided to go to Rome with a small selected army in the summer time.

It was a hot summer; the Frankish army made nevertheless good headway. The Franks moved on old Roman roads southwards. In Pavia Pippin, king of Italy, met the Frankish army and reported to his father that he had problems with the duke of Benevent, too. "What do you intend?", Charles asked his son. "A penal expedition against this rebellious Benevent", answered Pippin. "Penal expedition or raid?", was the following question. "Benevent must be quiet again", was the short answer of Pippin now, "and also the pope we have to check in his performance and excesses." "No more of that; if you are talking like this, you are never the right man for Italy and I would have to take back the king's crown and to give this crown to another one then, my son", said Charles, because he was angry at the way Pippin was talking. "Never I take myself this crown, you gave me this thing", was the new answer of Pippin. "Do you want to keep this thing, my son?" "Yes, I want to! Because never I'll have the crown of the empire. The owner of the crown of the Frankish Empire will be my brother Charles in the future. I'm only king of a part of the Franish Empire!" "No more for today", said Charles, because this discussion was enough for him now. At this moment he thought of his wife Liutgard, who died shortly before his march southwards.

In Rome Charles met the pope the day after his arrival there. "Welcome to Rome", said the pope to Charles. "Thanks. I hope that you know what we have to discuss", answered Charles. "Yes, step after step we have to take action. I assume you know that you are in a fix", was the answer of Leo. This answer startled Charles. – Charles took the pope to a prepared dining-table. Both were sitting side by side. "Before you tell me more you are to know that every word is noted by my writers and notarii", said Charles after a while. "By my writers too", was the answer of Leo. – Charles did not eat much, but the pope did. "Why is he eating so much?" Charles asked one of his advisers. "The Romans are daft!" was the answer. "I don't like this", said Charles, got up from the table and left the room. – In the afternoon he had a meeting with the pope in the palace Lateran.

Charles stayed in Rome for a long time. At Christmas a great mass was celebrated in the basilica St. Peter and many Romans and Frankish noblemen took part. When Charles was deep in devotion, Leo grasped the crown of the Frankish king, which he had placed beside himself, and pressed this crown upon Charles' head. At this moment a loudly speaking chorus resounded through the church: "Carolo Augusto a Deo coronate et pacifico Imperatori Romanorum Vita et Victoria". – Charles was crowned as emperor of the Romans. He intended to jump up, but his own Franks kept down him. "Leo, you condemned hog", were the only words Charles could say, because he was carried out the church under the jubilation of the Romans now. – In the evening Charles still conferred with his advisers. "Charles, calm down; West Rome has an emperor again who has power like the emperor of East Rome (Byzantium). Now we have a new Roman Empire under the leadership of a Frankish king and you are the emperor of all nations in the middle of Europe".

This was the beginning of a new Roman Empire at the end of the year of 800 AD. This empire was to finish more than 1.000 years later.

The last years of Charles the Great

We write the year 801 AD

Charles, the new Roman emperor, was still lingering in Rome. Here two mistresses sweetened his life and presented him successively with two daughters. Madelgard gave birth to Ruothild and Gerswind to Adalthrud. At the same time Charles's daughter Berta gave birth to her second illegitimate son who was named Hartnid.

On Easter Monday some boys of the Frankish noblemen were running through the streets of Rome shouting in Diutisc: "Karl is the Greatest, Karl the emperor of Rome is father! Drago! Drago is his son!"

"Drago?" the pope asked when he heard these news. "Who is the mother?" he furthermore asked his advisers. "Her name is Regina." "That must be a sluttish person Charles took to his bed after Gerswind. It would be better for him to marry again, for example a personality like Irene of Byzantium", said the pope. – When Charles heard that, he laughed and only said: "Leo is crazy and talking nonsense! Byzantium and its daughters, never! We had better drive away Byzantium from its last territories in North Italy and Dalmatia."

We write the year 802 AD

Charles was lingering in Rome in the first months of this year, too. He was happy when his mistress Regina bore a second son to him, named Hugo. But Charles longed back for Aachen. He liked the fresh air of the Eifel, the forests and his hunting-ground there, instead of these narrow streets in Rome and the heat in the summer time in Italy. Also the sweetening of his life by Regina could not hold him, so he decided to go back to Aachen before the year finished. – In the same year the monastery in Münster/Westphalia was founded.

We write the year 803 AD

„The Saxons are to get back the old rights of their nation", said Charles shortly before Easter. "If they are willing to receive Christendom, I shall relieve them from the payment of tribute. Only the district's counts I'll appoint furthermore. But they are to have the same rights as Frankish district's counts." – "Your son Louis accomplishes his job as king of Aquitania better from year to year", was reported to Charles, "and Barcelona is conquered, so that your Spanish March is larger now." "I would like to have had taken part in this campaign", was Charles's short answer to this information. The opportunity for a campaign came to Charles the following year.

We write the year 804 AD

The Saxons rebelled again. High in the north there was a revolt against the Franks. Therefore Charles marched with his army into the region of Osenbrugga (Osnabrück). The warriors of Charles were resolute to demonstrate no pardon. Saxons opposing the army, were falling under the beats of the swords like rotten boughs. The Saxons rather went to death than let displace themselves and Charles didn't take an interest in the tears of so many women and children. Thus whole families were killed. "Resettle the remainder", ordered Charles. And the warriors went and fetched tens of thousands of Saxons from their own farms, out from burning shanties and earthy hiding-places in the forests. So many treks of expellees moved southwards. Most people were women and children of killed husbands and fathers. The long trek was accompanied by priests, who christened by compulsion. "The whole of Germania is free of gentiles now", were the last words of Charles after this expedition.

We write the year 805 AD

Charles regulated the succession to the throne in this year. His son Charles was officially determined to be his successor. He was to be ruler of the Roman Empire of Frankish Nation in future, because he successfully carried through some expeditions like his brother Pippin. If Charles died before his father, his brother Pippin would be emperor. The third in the series was Louis; his name in Diutisc = Ludwig. (Diutisc = Deutsch = German)

This year some castles were built on the border of the Slavic neighbours, who passed over the borders by warlike intention again and again.

We write the year 806 AD

The Franks had conflicts with the empire of Byzantium again, which they could only decide on the diplomatic parquet. This possibility they hadn't in Spain, where they had war again and again.

"In Spain the Basque Navarrese and the town Pamplona have placed themselves under our protection. Also Tarragona is Frankish in the meantime. The counter-attacks of the Moors failed", said Charles the Great highly delighted to his noblemen, "what more do we want!"

In Saxia (Saxony) was established the bishopric Paderborn and some expeditions against the Slavic Bohemians took place, who had made insecure the borders in the year before.

We write the year 807 AD

Charles felt the years were running away. He already perceived certain senile decay, therefore he was happy to have a very young maid with long brown hair in his bed during the nights. Her name was Adelinde, a real sweetheart for Charles, just what he needed in the long winter nights in the Eifel. And then he was more than happy when she gave birth to a son during this year, his name was Theoderic.

We write the year 810 AD

Charles established the North March as defence-line against the Danish nation in the north. The castle Hamma (Hammaburg) was built as bulwark between the rivers Elbe and Alster and formed the centre of the North March. Later the place of this castle became one of the biggest seaports of Germany. Today its name is Hamburg, the second-biggest city of the Federal Republic of Germany.

Charles reformed the monetary unit. He knew it was hardly possible to raise gold for coins furthermore, therefore he introduced the silver currency. One pound was 20 shillings or 240 denares or pfennigs (pennies).

Charles suffered some heavy blows this year. First, his favourite daughter Rotrud died and then his son Pippin, king of Italy.

We write the year 811 AD

Charles didn't feel strong enough to lead himself the necessary expeditions against the rebellious Moors and Britons. He charged his commanders with that. Now Charles had a foreboding: if it should be past, something, what is bad, could take place within his family.

Charles went to church in the middle of the night, prayed loudly and spoke with his chancellor, who was the archchaplain and archbishop of Cologne, about the state of God often. It was a rainy day in November, when Charles learnt that his son and successor Charles was dead. For Charles the Great the world had broken down, all his hopes had come to nothing. "Now I have only Louis of Aquitania", he shouted through the room. "Louis is my most religious son, but not hard enough for the leadership of an empire and even a weakling to stand against you, the churchmen", he told his chancellor in the course of the conversation. It was no important point to him that his son Pippin the Hunchback also died this year, he had forgotten this son.

We write the year 812 AD

Charles had tried to remove the differences with Byzantium in a diplomatic way. One day he asked the bishop of Basle, Haito, who had started discussions with Byzantium by order of him. "What's the matter with Byzantium, with the discussion about my empire?" "Well, East Rome accepted all conditions." "What's your exact opinion?" "We can reach an agreement with Byzantium on the following basis: you get the title 'Carolus, serenissimus, Augustus, a Deo coronatus, magnus, pacificus Imperator, Romanum Imperium gubernans, qui et misericordia Dei Rex Francorum et Langobardum'". "One moment, please, moment, please, you are saying, if I correctly translate your Latin, who rules the Roman empire. Or I'm not the Patricius Romanorum? Then I can be the emperor of the Roman Empire, too!" "No, Charles, you think in error now, but this isn't an error of Michael, the new emperor of Byzantium, because he is the real and legitimate ruler of West Rome and so our emperor, too!" "But, who rules is another than who it is – only I was crowned as emperor by the pope." "You can't confuse the problem with what your father has conceded to the pope. Today might isn't at stake, but legitimacy according to older rights, and that is clear, that has the emperor of Byzantium." "And not me?" "Of course! You have rights too! But the pope, Leo, gave you something what didn't belong to him. That is the problem that could be resolved now." "What do you think?" "Retire from some towns at the seaside of the kingdom Italy and give them to Byzantium, so Venice for example. For this Byzantium will admit the empire of the Franks. Coexistence between Aachen, Byzantium and Rome. It's simply so!" "What is the title of the emperor in Byzantium?" "Imperator Romanorum." "And what is my title?" "Imperator, too!" And how is the empire of Michael called?" "Imperium Orientale." "And mine?" "Imperium Occidentale!" "Thus two empires!" "Yes, but having equal rights, Charles." "I agree. Write to the emperor, write to Byzantium that I agree. I'm willing to sign this pact." Charles was feeling better after that.

We write the year 813 AD

An Imperial Diet is held in Aachen again. Charles had to inform the assembly of the Imperial Diet about two important points. "I have raised Bernhard, the son of Pippin, to king of Italy", he loudly said to the assembled noblemen of the empire. "Furthermore, my wish is that Ludwig, as Louis is called in the Diutisc part of my empire, will be emperor at my side and after my death will bear the imperial crown." The approval was following with loud cheers. "Then it is to happen," said Charles, turned round and went the way to the chapel of the palatinate. His son Louis and all noblemen of the empire followed him. In the chapel he prayed very long together with his son Ludwig/Louis. Then both turned round, and looked one another into the eyes. "And so I admonish you, my son and king of Aquitania, as emperor to protect the church, your brothers and sisters, nephews and nieces and all relatives, like I did. I ask you to be charitable against monasteries and the poor and to live so that one will call you always 'Louis or Ludwig the Pious'. Are you willing to promise this before the assembly here?" "Yes, my father, that I do!" Charles turned round to the assembly "Do you still want my son Louis to get the crown of emperor?" There followed loud applause. "Take the crown, which is on the altar here, and put it on your head!" Louis carried out the order of his father, took the crown and put it on his head. Now the Frankish Empire had two emperors.

We write the year 814 AD

On the 21st of January Charles had a high temperature after a bath in the thermal springs of Aquis Grana. He went to bed and never got up again. – The third day Charles had pain in the upper stomach, the fifth day one couldn't talk to him. The sixths day he received the Holy Communion. On Saturday, 28th of January, Charles gasped for breath in the morning. Some minutes later he was dead. All over in the palatinate men were weeping, women and children. The imperial corpse was laid out, but nobody knew where the corpse was to be buried. Some noblemen proposed the palatinate Diedenhofen, other the palatinate Ponthion or the monasteries Fulda, Lorsch or

Prüm. Most of the noblemen wanted to bury him in the Diutisc part of the empire. So it was decided to bury him there, where he had died, in Aquis Grana or Aachen, what is the name in the Diutisc language.

The noblemen didn't wait for the arrival of the new ruler Louis I. The dead body of Charles was sitting up buried in a pit of the palatinate late in the evening of the same day. When Louis arrived, the stonemasons had already driven in stone the epitaph (in Diutisc):

"Hier unten liegt der Leib Karls,
des großen und rechtgläubigen Kaisers,
der das Reich der Franken herrlich vergrößerte
und 47 Jahre hindurch regiert hat.
Er starb, ein Siebziger, im Jahre des Herrn 814,
in der siebten Indikation, am 28. Januar"

"Below lies the body of Charles,
the great and orthodox emperor,
who the empire of the Franks wonderfully enlarged
and has reigned 47 years.
He died, a septuagenarian, in the year of our Lord 814,
in the seventh indication, on 28 January"

Louis/Ludwig and his sons

We write the year 815 AD

Louis the Pious had been in possession of the power just one year when he already began to purge the imperial court of all that was contrary to his severe interpretation of morals.

Charles the Great liked the social life whose focus he was himself. But the new ruler drove away the easy-going riffraff, banished his sisters from court and displaced the former companions of his father. All the illegitimate sons of Charles the Great disappeared into dungeons. Now only the ethics of the church was asserted.

We write the year 816 AD

Louis' striving for the unity of the empire led to his second coronation that year, which was done by Pope Stephen IV in Reims. That was a political success to the papacy, of course!

Amongst the church's advisers at the court was the abbot Benedict from Aniane, too. Louis supported the hard reform of the life in monasteries but also the life of the worldly clergy. Because of this reform the intellectual life in the monasteries was also promoted as we can see with the literary achievements of church's school of the Fulda monastery.

The harmony between emperor and clergy was important for the unity of the empire after the death of Louis, too. The unity of the Christendom within the Frankish Empire was to be realized: One God, one church, one empire.

We write the year 817 AD

In Aachen at the Imperial Diet the new order of the empire was proclaimed: Ordinatio imperii. It was a compromise according to which the former Frankish principle of the partition of the empire was not given up. The emperor Louis the Pious had three sons by his first marriage: Lothar, Pippin and Louis/Ludwig. According to the first order of the empire Lothar became co-emperor and successor of his father, whilst the younger brothers Pippin and Ludwig/Louis got the title king and smaller part empires: Pippin got the country Aquitania and Ludwig the German (that was his name later) the country Bavaria. After the death of Louis the Pious both sub-empires were under the sovereignty of Lothar.

We write the year 819 AD

Irmingard, the first wife of Louis/Ludwig, had died the year before. Because Louis the Pious, he was forty years old now, wanted to marry again, he let present to himself the daughters of the nobility according to the report in the "Reichsannalen" (Annals of the Empire) and had finally selected Judith from among the noble beauties of the empire. She was the daughter of the influential and mighty count Welf. Judith wasn't only beautiful but also intelligent and more energetic than Louis.

We write the year 823 AD

That year Judith gave birth to a son, Karl/Charles, who was also to bear the epithet "the Bald", which pointed to the fact that he wasn't yet provided with an inheritance but didn't allude to a possibly bald-headed person. Judith, who was also a very ambitious woman, aimed at a big share of the inheritance for "Baldie". That was a legitimate aspiration, but the "Reichsordnung" (Rules of the Empire) of the year of 817 AD had to say something against that. Also the rules of the year of 821 AD, which were especially certified by the high nobility of

278

the empire stood in the way of Judith's efforts. But the emperor gave in later. He couldn't resist the incessant urging of Judith.

Whilst Judith gave birth to "Baldie", Lothar was crowned emperor by the pope in Rome. Lothar was a son of Louis by his first marriage, as you could read before.

We write the year 827 AD

The Arabs who were sitting down for a long time in the north of Africa, crossed the sea from there and conquered the island Sicily. There the occupying forces of Byzantium offered resistance, but they couldn't prevent the Arabs from conquering the island. The Christendom lost Sicily for more than 250 years. Then the Nor(th)men (Normans or Vikings) could win back this island for the Christians again.

We write the year 829 AD

At the Imperial Diet of Worms it was announced that Louis the Pious had made over an own territory to his son "Baldie". It was the core of Lothar's landed property in Swabia, Alsace and Burgundy.

When Lothar voiced his anger at the expropriation, he was banished and had to go into exile. Whilst he lived in Italy, to the place of his exile also other men who had rejected Judith's politics and the new sharing of the empire disappeared from the court. There weren't missing bitter accusations and suspicions on both sides what finally led to the rebellion against Louis in the following year.

We write the year 830 AD

An open rebellion broke out against Louis. The emperor was arrested, and his wife Judith disappeared into a convent. There already came up the subject of a deposition of Louis. After hard humiliations he succeeded in separating his rebelling sons once more. But that only happened by mutual interest. – The fear of Judith and her party, which was growing stronger, brought Lothar, Pippin and Louis together to take action against their father again a short time later.

We write the year 833 AD

In summer the armies of Louis the Pious and his rebelling sons were facing each other close to Colmar (town in Alsace). But there was no battle because the sons succeeded in winning over to their side most of the warriors of Louis. Therefore Louis I gave the order for the remainder of his army: "Go to my sons, I'm not willing that someone of my warriors should lose his life or limbs." Today people call the place of the betrayal "the field of lie".

Now Judith was banished to Italy where she was taken into a dungeon, whilst Louis was taken to Reims by his sons. Here he was stripped of his dignity, titles and expelled from the church. Nobody was allowed to speak with him. Short time later he was taken to Soissons, where he had to make public his guilt for perjury, murder, sacrilege and misreign. He confessed in tears his guilt and begged for public atonement, in order to give the church satisfaction. With that the emperor was to have never more the possibility to take over the power.

We write the year 834 AD

The case how Louis was deposed caused a lot of sympathy, especially amongst the nobility in the Diutisc part of the empire. Once more Louis I succeeded in separating the rivals and winning the younger sons over to his side. But it was the attempt to re-engage Charles, the son of Judith, in a part of the inheritance at the expense of his brothers. With that the empire didn't have peace for a long time.

We write the year 838 AD

Pippin died unexpectedly and after that Louis I divided the empire again. Lothar and Charles were to share the empire, only his son Louis (Ludwig the German) was to receive Bavaria. That was a motive for Louis/Ludwig the German to revolt against his father. But there was no armed conflict amongst father and son, mutual threats merely.

We write the year 840 AD

Emperor Louis I the Pious died on 20 June in Ingelheim and was buried in Metz. The question referring to an integrated whole of the empire or the partition respectively was unsolved. The decision had to bring about a brothers' war.

The right of Charles to receive a part of the empire wasn't cast doubt; therefore nobody did that. With his mother's energy and self-assertion he had inherited, he could consolidate his position in the West of the empire. Lothar, the elder brother of Charles and Ludwig, tried to carry through his claim to the supremacy of the empire owing to the rules of the empire. But he only achieved that his brothers, Ludwig the German and Charles the Bald, narrowly joined forces.

We write the year 841 AD

Now there was a war amongst Ludwig the German, Charles the Bald and Lothar, since a consensus was not obtained. The battle took place by Fontenoy close to Auxerre/France. The army of Lothar was entirely wiped out. After that Lothar fled to Italy.

We write the year 842 AD

The victorious brothers, Ludwig the German and Charles the Bald, met close to Strasbourg (Straßburg) and confirmed their alliance by oath. Both swore their brotherly faithfulness to the common repulse against the claim of Lothar. Ludwig/Louis the German took his oath in Old-French and Charles the Bald in Diutisc (Old-German). After that both armies swore each in their own language. Thus the oaths of Strasbourg are an early testimony of the development of both languages, for the Deutsch/German and the French language, but no proof of a renunciation of the unity of the Frankish Empire.

We write the year 843 AD

In view of the superiority of the partial kings and out of consideration for the tiredness of war of the nobility Lothar was willing to renounce previous claims. In August all three sons of Louis the Pious met in Verdun and made a new treaty of partition, but the unity of the empire was to survive. Charles got the western part of the empire with the eastern borders on Shelde, Maas and Rhône (rivers), Ludwig the German the part in the east of the Rhine. Lothar kept the title "emperor" and got the narrow stripe of land between the western and eastern parts of the empire (plus the northern part of Italy). Thus that treaty was the basis for the coming into being of the future empires France and Deutschland/Germany.

The East Frankish Empire of Ludwig the German was inferior in politics and economy to the other imperial parts. It was sparsely populated, hardly developed and organization and legislation not so much advanced as it was in the western empire. But the population was more homogeneous by common language and Germanic extraction. Ludwig II the German also had a stronger position to nobility and church than his brothers.

The intellectual and literary life of that time we can see at the court and in the cloisters of the eastern empire. It showed the feeling of solidarity of the East Frankish tribes in which the Saxons had a considerable part too. The Saxon monk Gottschalla already wrote about the Teutsch/Deutsch (German) Nation, even though most of the tribes on the right side of the Rhine were Franks (Franconians).

We write the year 845 AD

The Nor(th)men, also called Normans or Vikings, the name of
Danes, Swedes and Norwegians, invaded the West Frankish Empire,
which was richer than the eastern part, very often in the last years.
But this year that also happened in the eastern part. The Vikings
destroyed the place Hammaburg (Hamburg). As a result the bishop
of Hamburg moved his residence to Bremen.

Chronology

Important years of the history

200 BC – 100 BC,	the beginning of the migration of Germanic tribes and the great time of the Teutones and Cimbri
90 – 50 BC,	the great time of the Suebi

The time after Christ

In the year(s)

5	Tiberius fights against the Langobardi on the Elbe
9	Varus' Battle
14 – 16	Germanicus in Germania
17 – 21	Arminius' argument with Marbod, the leader of the Marcomanni
28 – 89	Germanic tribes rebelled against Rome
100 – 251	he great time of the Romans in Germany
257	The Franks (Franconians) for the first time put themselves in the picture of the history
259 – 261	The Alemani devastate Helvetia and North Italy (Germani ante portas)
265	Franks and Alemani on the left side of the Rhine
276	Franks and Alemani plunder in Gallia (Gaul)
277	Vandals and Burgundi invade Raetia
286	Franks and Saxons invade Gallia (Gaul)
289	Alemani, Burgundi and Heruli crossed the Rhine
298	Chlorus, Roman emperor, fights against the Alemani
300	The beginning of the great time of the Langobardi

800	Charles the Great becomes emperor of a new Roman Empire
816	Louis the Pious emperor of Rome
843	Treaty of Verdun, partition of the Franconian Empire

Some important persons

(Roman emperors on the pages 119 – 121)

Aëtius (about 390 – 454), Roman general and statesman

Agrippina (15 – 59), empress of Rome in 50 and murdered in order of
emperor Nero in 59

Alarich (370 – 410), king of the Visigoths, he was the first Germanic
conqueror of Rome

Alboin, king of the Langobardi 560 – 572 and founder of the
Langobardian empire in Italy

Amaslawintha, she was the mother of Athalarich

Arminius (Hermann), leader of the Cheruski (Cheruskers), he defeated
Varus in 9

Ariovist, he was the great leader of the Suebi who fought against Caesar

Arius (260 – 336), religious founder of the Arianism

Athalarich, king of Eastgoths 526 – 534

Athanarich, count of the Visigoths, he died in January of the year of 381
in Constantinopel

Athaulf, king of the Visigoths 410 – 415 and husband of Galla Placidia

Attila, king of the Huns 434 – 453, he was the last founder (togehter with
his brother Bleda) of a great empire of the Huns

Ausonius, Decimus Magnus (310 –393), he was poet and teacher of the
princes at the Roman court in Treverorum (Trier)

Belisar (about 500 – 565), general of Byzantium, he destroyed the empire
of the Vandals in Africa

Boethius (about 480 – 524), he was philosopher, politician and minister at
the court of Theoderich the Great

Boiorix, leader of the Cimbri and friend of Teutobod (the leader of the
Teutones)

Bonifatius – 1 – (about 675 – 754), he was an Anglo-Saxon monk and
missionary in Friesland, Hesse and Thuringia

Bonifatius – 2 – , he was Roman governor in Africa till 429, then he was
defeated by the Vandals (Geiserich)

Caesar, Julius (100BC – 44 BC), first emperor of a Roman Empire

Cassiodor, Flavius Magnus (about 485 – 580), East-Gothic scholar, he
wrote the "Historia Gothorum"

Childerich, king of a tribe of the Salian Franks in the years 457 – 482 and
father of Chlodwig

Chlodwig (466 – 511), he was the founder of the Franconian Empire

Chlothar I (498 – 561), son of Chlodwig and after his death king of
Franconia

Fritigern; he as opponent of Athanarich and fought against him; he died
after Athanarich

Galla Placidia, in 414 she became wife of Athaulf and was half-sister of
the Roman emperor Honorius

Gelimer, in 534 he was the last king of the Vandals and was captured by
Belisar in 534 in Africa

Geiserich (389 – 477), king of the Vandals 428 – 477, in 429 he founded a
Germanic empireon African ground, capital
Carthage

Gildo, a Moorish man and Roman governor in Africa (about 400 in
Carthage)

Gundikar, king of the Burgundi; he was defeated by the Huns in 436 and
is also known as Gunther in the German legend

Jordanes, he lived in the 6th century and was a Gothic historian, his
famous works: "De origine actibusque Getarum"
(till 551) and "De umma temporum vel origine
actibusque gentis Romanorum"

Karl (Charles) Martell, the Hammer, (about 688 – 741), he was
Franconian house-meier and son of house-
meier Pippin II , in 732 he defeated the Arabs
near Tours and 737 near Narbonne (France)

Karl (Charles) the Great (747 – 814), he was the son of the Franconian
house-meier Pippin III who became king in 751

Leo I, pope   440 – 461

Leo II, pope   682 – 683

Leo III, pope   795 – 816

Ludwig (Louis) the Pious (778 – 840), he became co-emperor in 813 and
was son of Charles the Great

Marbod, the first great leader of the Marcomanni, he died in 37

Marius, Gaius (158 BC – 86 BC), Roman general, he defeated the
Teutones and Cimbri 102 BC and 101 BC

Marcellinus, Ammianus, he wrote about the combats against the Goths in
378

Mohammed (about 570 – 632), the great prophet and founder of the Islam

Merowech (about 455), he was king of the Salian Franks (Franconians), father of Childerich I and founder of the dynasty of the Merowingers

Narses (about 480 – 574), general of Byzantium, he destroyed the empire of the Eastgoths in 553

Odoaker (about 430 – 493), Odovakar, he was a Germanic man and Roman officer, in 476 he became ruler over Italy after the deposition of the last (West-)Roman emperor, Romulus Augustus

Orestes, opponent of Odoaker, he was killed in action during the Battle of Pavia in 476

Pippin I, 623 – 640 Franconian house-meier

Pippin II (635 – 714), Franconian house-meier, father of Karl Martell

Pippin III (about 715 – 768), at first house-meier, then 751 King of Franconia

Prokop (Procopius of Caesarea), he lived 490 – 562 and was a writer of history in Byzantium

Pulcheria - P. Aelia Augusta - (399 – 453), Roman empress in Byzantium, daughter of Emperor Arcadius; she was very religious and was canonized later.

Recimir, Flavius, he was Roman officer but of Suebian-Visigothic extraction, since 456 Magister militum and 457 Patricius; he was the most influential man in West Rome; he died in 472

Roderic, he was the last king of the Visigoths in Spain and was killed in action during the battle against the Arabs in 711

Rufinus, he was opponent of Stilicho in Byzantium, there he was murdered by Gothic captains in 396

Scaurus, Aurelius, Roman general during the fights against the Teutones

Segestes, a prince of the Cheruski and father of Thusnelda

Stephen IV, pope   816 – 817

Stilicho, he was a Vandal but with Roman education; he was diplomat and general and fought against Alarich in 396

Sylvester I, pope   314 – 335

Tacitus, Publius Cornelius (about 55 – 120), he was Roman historian, his works: Histories, Annals and Germania

Tassilo III (741 – 794), duke of the Bavarians, in 788 he was sentenced to death but then pardoned by Charles the Great

Teja, he was the last king of the Eastgoths, killed during the Battle of
Vesuvius

Theoderich the Great (about 454 – 526), he became king of the Eastgoths
in 473; in 488 he began the conquest of Italy by
order of Zenon, emperor of Byzantium

Teutobod, he was the famous leader of the Teutones, Battle of Aquae
Sextiae in 102 BC and capture by the Romans

Theodora, empress of Byzantium (527 – 548), she was the daughter of a
circus' director and wife of Justinian I of Byzantium

Thorismund, king of the Visigoths, he was murdered by his brother Eurich
in 466

Thusnelda, she was the wife of Arminius (Hermann the Cherusker)

Totila, he was the last king of the Eastgoths before Teja, killed in action
during the Battle of Tadinae

Varus, Publius Quintilius (about 46 BC – 9 after Christ), Roman general,
he was killed in action during a battle in the deep
forests of West Germany

Veleda, she was a Germanic fortune-teller during the time of the Batavian
rebellion (about 69/70)

Wulfila/Ulfila (about 311 – 383), he was a Visigothic bishop, his dogma
was the Arianism, he created the first Gothic
alphabet, he also translated he Bible from Greek into
Gothic

BIBLIOGRAPHY

Weltgeschichte in Romanen, 2 Das Mittelalter, Paul Frischauer, 1961

Deutsche Geschichte, Band 1-5, Heinrich Pleticha, 1981

Daten der Weltgeschichte, Lexikon-Institut Bertelsmann, 1975

Auf den Spuren der Goten, Hermann Schreiber, 1977

Die Hunnen, Hermann Schreiber, 1976

Die ersten Deutschen, S.Fischer - Fabian, 1975

Karl der Große, Thomas R. Mielke, 1992

Meyers Lexikon, 1924

Die große Bertelsmann Lexikothek (15 Volumes), 1988

Bildatlas der deutschen Geschichte, Wilhelm J. Wagner, 1999

Die Römer am Rhein, Dr. Peter La Baume, 1985

Museum, Rheinisches Landesmuseum Bonn, 3/77 Mai

Führer zu vor- und frühgeschichtlichen Denkmälern, Linker Niederrhein: Krefeld, Xanten, Kleve, 1978

Geschichte des Abendlandes, von der germanischen Frühzeit bis 1648, Krüger, 1950

Atlas zur Weltgeschichte, K. Leonhardt, 1935

Die Sarazanen, Weltreich aus Glaube und Schwert, Rolf Palm, 1978

Die Wikinger, Peter Sawyer (Hrsg.), 1997

Das Nibelungen Lied von Gotthard Oswald, Marbach, 2006

Mohammed, Allahs Prophet und Feldherr, Gerhard Konzelmann 1981

Der Harz, Merian (Das Monatsheft der Städte und Landschaften), 1962

Mit dem Fahrstuhl in die Römerzeit, Rudolf Pörtner, 1962

Information material of the cities Trier, Speyer, Worms, Cologne, Düsseldorf and Xanten

Illustrations by E. Harings

I thank my stepson and my former daughter-in-law in Australia for the inspiration to write about German history, which in general has always been my hobby.

www.ingramcontent.com/pod-product-compliance
Lightning Source LLC
Chambersburg PA
CBHW020605270326
41927CB00005B/184